IBN TAYMIYYAH'S ETHICS

AAR

American Academy of Religion
Academy Series

Edited by
H. Ganse Little, Jr.

Number 34

IBN TAYMIYYAH'S ETHICS
The Social Factor

Victor E. Makari

Victor E. Makari

IBN TAYMIYYAH'S ETHICS
The Social Factor

Scholars Press
Chico, California

IBN TAYMIYYAH'S ETHICS
The Social Factor

Victor E. Makari

Library of Congress Cataloging in Publication Data

Makari, Victor E.
Ibn Taymiyyah's ethics.

(Academy series / American Academy of Religion) (ISSN 0277-1071)
Bibliography: p.
1. Ibn Taymīyah, Ahmad ibn 'Abd al-Halīm, 1263-1328. 2. Sociology, Islamic. I. Title. II. Series: Dissertation series (American Academy of Religion)
BP80.I29M34 170 81-1019
ISBN 0-89130-476-2 AACR2

Printed in the United States of America

ACKNOWLEDGMENTS

Throughout the entire undertaking of my program of study at Temple University, I have become greatly indebted to a large number of persons. The very inspiration to embark upon this ambitious venture, which I now realize could only increase its challenges and demands, came from Dr. Elwyn Smith who at that time was on the faculty of the Department of Religion.

From the time of that suggestion, the support of my wife, and, the innocent acceptance of an increasingly absent father by two young sons who were born to us during the course of this program, have continued to be my major, steady source of encouragement.

My advisor, Professor Ismā'īl R. al-Farūqī, Ph.D., has provided me, like his many other students, not only with a model of academic excellence, but also with the necessary intellectual nurture and challenge to seek after the same excellence. His refreshing honesty, his uncompromising faithfulness to his own very high standards, to his field, to the students, to his colleagues and to the requirements of the Department and the University, together with his marvellous ability to motivate his students with gentleness, have continued to renew my own commitment to the worthiness of the pursuit. The stimulation offered by my other professors and by serious students made that commitment stronger.

The understanding of the congregation of the Wayne Presbyterian Church in Wayne, Pennsylvania, in allowing me released time one day a week for the four years of my course work was a great help; but without the personal support of my senior colleague during those four years, Dr. John T. Galloway, then pastor of the church, I simply could not have performed well my academic work in addition to my full-time responsibilities in the church. Moreover, I have appreciated the considerable scholarship aid extended by the Wayne Church. The dissertation was written after we had moved to Columbus, Ohio, to serve the congregation of the Overbrook Presbyterian Church, which also allowed me a major portion of the released time needed for writing it. I am grateful for this, and for the continued encouragement of Dr. John C. Laske, senior pastor of Overbrook. Dr. Elton Trueblood, a friend from Richmond, Indiana, took a keen interest in my project and gave generous financial aid and personal encouragement. The example of his own style of personal discipline as an author gave me a tool immensely helpful in writing this thesis.

There are other friends, too many to name, whose interest, encouragement, and assistance will not be forgotten: some who bought rare books and shipped them to me from various bookstores in the Middle East; some who wrote notes inquiring about my progress; and others who simply by their friendship were a supportive influence.

In particular, I wish to thank Mrs. Virginia Hake, who labored faithfully to type-write this manuscript, in spite of its peculiarity because of the seemingly endless transliterated Arabic words and titles.

Finally, I would like humbly and lovingly to dedicate this piece of work to our sons, Peter, now seven, and John, four, with the full confidence that the contributions of their own experiences will be exceedingly great indeed.

Columbus, Ohio
Fall 1975

TABLE OF CONTENTS

Acknowledgments v

INTRODUCTION 1

The Problem 1
The General Significance of the Problem 1
The Focus of the Problem 2
Works Available 3
A Note on Method 4

PART ONE: THE FRAMEWORK

CHAPTER I: THE SETTING OF IBN TAYMIYYAH'S LIFE AND WORK 7

Political and Social Life 7
The State of Theology, Social Ideology and Ethics 14
Ṣūfism 18
Shī'ism 18
Determinism and Rationalism 19

CHAPTER II: IBN TAYMIYYAH--A BIOGRAPHICAL ACCOUNT.... 21

His Early Years, His Education and His Intellectual Achievements 21

His Participation in the Affairs of the Muslim *Ummah* 27

PART TWO: THE DOCTRINAL CONTEXT FOR A SYSTEM OF ETHICS: DIVINE REVELATION AND HUMAN RESPONSE

CHAPTER III: GOD--HIS NATURE, HIS WILL AND HIS ACTIONS 33

The Nature and Character of God 34
God's Will and Actions 42

CHAPTER IV: GOD'S REVELATION--ITS MEDIA AND IMPLICATIONS 47

The Prophet 47
The Qur'ān 52
The Response to Revelation 56

CHAPTER V: THE FRAMEWORK OF HUMAN RESPONSE 65

The Origins of the Problem of Determinism/ Free Will 65
The Development of the Problem 67

The Moral and Religious Function of the State 141
The Basis of the *Imāmah* 144
The Investiture of the *Imām* 146
The Qualifications of the Head of State As Politico-Social Values of the Community 147
The Structure of the Islamic State 151
The Political Apparatus 151
The Obligations of the Citizens 154

CHAPTER IX: IBN TAYMIYYAH'S POLITICO-ECONOMIC ETHIC.. 159

The "*Ḥisbah*" 159
Labor--A Socialist View 165
Commerce and State Control 166

PART FOUR: SUMMARY AND CONCLUSION

CHAPTER X: THE ENDURING CONTRIBUTION OF IBN TAYMIYYAH 177

His Contribution and Its Social Worth 180
The Influence of Ibn Taymiyyah on the Future 189

NOTES 195

A SELECTED BIBLIOGRAPHY 227

VICTOR MAKARI, a native of Egypt, completed his undergraduate work in theology in Cairo. He then studied at Princeton Theological Seminary, Columbia Theological Seminary, McCormick Theological Seminary, and Northwestern University. At Temple University he earned a Ph.D. in Islamic Studies under the supervision of Professor Isma'il R. al-Faruqi.

INTRODUCTION

The Problem

It is widely believed that Islamic reformative movements began in consequence of the Napoleonic invasions. More intensive study in the area of reform and modernism in Islam, however, reveals that the roots of such movements must run deeper into history than the 1880's. The question becomes: how deep? Upon investigation, one becomes aware that much of what is recognized as "reformative" today is almost always certain to find some of its origins in the spirit, if not in the thought, of the thirteenth century Ḥanbalī Muslim jurist, Taqiyy al-Dīn Aḥmad Ibn Taymiyyah, who was born in Ḥarrān, in Syria, in 661 A.H./1263 A.D. and died in Damascus in 726 A.H./1328 A.D. His life-pilgrimage had taken him through military involvements against the Mongol Turks (or *Tatar*), and engaged him in the philosophical, theological, ethical, legal, political and social thought and practice of the Muslim Community. Subsequently, his influence has left its mark on it in all these areas, but most prominently in jurisprudence (*fiqh*).

The General Significance of the Problem

Several factors constitute the general significance of an investigation of this problem:

First, the man's work consistently reveals an unrelenting intellectual conviction with which he criticized and often rejected many of the interpretations of Islamic doctrines which inevitably precipitated practices that he regarded as unacceptable according to the standards of the Qur'ānic revelation and Muḥammadan Tradition.

Many of his legal decisions or interpretations (*fatāwā*), i.e., pronouncements that set legal precedents, which I have examined suggest a change in the generally accepted practice connected with the situation in question. Almost every work which he produced[1] is a critique, a refutation or an apology concerning a certain issue. Invariabley, too, Ibn Taymiyyah's opinions and arguments show substantial evidence of Qur'ānic support based on his keen, creative interpretation (*ijtihād*) of the Scripture, an exercise the ʿ*ulamāʾ* had banned in order to maintain the *status quo* in doctrine and practice. In all events, he took care that the legal opinions and the doctrines he articulated were, without personal or partisan prejudice, founded on Qurʾānic revelation and traditional utterance and example.

Secondly, Ibn Taymiyyah may well be considered the watershed that marks the division between the Middle Ages of Islam and its modern era. For that, he should be considered worthy of in-depth study.

Thirdly, the circumstances surrounding his work suggest that a study of it would be significant. His was the era which followed the Crusades, and one in which Ṣūfism had run its full course. Also, the influence of Muʿtazilah and Bāṭinī thought, as well as the impact of Shīʿī heretical views, had tended to pull the community away from what its tradition had understood as normative for its faith and action.

Ibn Taymiyyah's intellectual counter-activity has continued to influence Islamic thought immensely.

Finally, that Ibn Taymiyyah's enormous intellectual productivity in the areas of theology and law as well as Qurʾānic exegesis has ironically received little attention from students of Islamic thought, sufficiently warrants this study.

The Focus of the Problem

Ibn Taymiyyah's legacy may well be said to have been a challenge to his fellow Muslims to show forth their faith in the context of their social relationships and interaction. Society, for him, was the arena for the practice of individual religion.

There was decay in all aspects of life; the impact of the Crusades on the Muslim *ummah* was crushing; and the final blow was dealt by the Tatar. Ibn Taymiyyah keenly diagnosed the malady of the Islamic Community, and provided not only a theoretical foundation for its recovery but also an active leadership. Politically and militarily he went forward to the front lines of battle against the Tatar. He endured prison and exile for his insistence on sound application of the Qurʾānic and traditional principles in individual conduct and social life.

His was a voice speaking out against a prevalent individualistic religion in his day. Man, in his most devotional mood as in his ethical concerns, thought Ibn Taymiyyah, was self-inverted. He sought only the salvation of himself. When he took care to live out his religion in his social relationships, his ultimate motive was to settle his own accounts with God. There was little concern on the part of the individual about national life or government or about international relationships. The interpretation of Scripture and of doctrine, the practice of rituals, the entire direction of *fiqh*, the conceptualization of justice, the exercise of rights and duties--all of these were narrowly construed to accommodate self interests. The works of Ibn Taymiyyah show his general spirit of reform which was deeply concerned with the social application of true Islamic doctrine.

His treatises on Divorce, Common Pleas, the Islamic State, Public Law, Illegal Contracts, Principles of Jurisprudence and others explicitly call the Muslim Community to return to the practices of the normative revelation of the Qur'ān and the example of early traditional Islam.

Works Available

In spite of the magnitude as well as the multitude of Ibn Taymiyyah's works, only few scholars concentrated with any degree of depth on his career as a Muslim theologian and jurist. These include his student, Ibn Qayyim al-Jawziyyah, his follower in the eighteenth century, Muḥammad Ibn ʿAbd al-Wahhāb, and other more recent or contemporary scholars such as Henri Laoust and Muḥammad Abū Zahrah.

A selected bibliography is attached, and contains the most significant resources related to the subject which are available in accessible libraries. Among the books listed, these secondary resources are particularly noteworthy: Ibn ʿAbd al-Hādī's *Al-ʿUqūd al-Durriyyah's*; Laoust's *Essai, Contribution, Une Etude De La Methodologie Canonique*, and *Le Traité*; and Abū Zahrah's *Ibn Taymiyyah*. Laoust's two latter books comprise annotated translations (into French) of Ibn Taymiyyah's *Maʿārij al-Wuṣūl* and *Al-Qiyās fī-al-Sharʿ al-Islāmī*, and *Al-Siyāsah al-Sharʿiyyah*.

The bulk of my own study depends largely on available primary sources.

A Note on Method

The method utilized in the present exploration of Ibn Taymiyyah's contribution to Islamic theology and jurisprudence will follow two main categories, namely, the historical and the ideational.

Historically, I want to trace more clearly the influences that motivated Ibn Taymiyyah's life-work, to examine the role of the special events in his own life-history that directed him toward the respective aspects of his intellectual engagement, and to survey briefly the Islamic developments after Ibn Taymiyyah in order to ascertain his significance to reformist movements of more recent times.

Ideationally, I propose to select some of the more relevant works of Ibn Taymiyyah and analyze them. In addition, it will be necessary to investigate other realms of ideas of his time to sort out which were cuases and which were consequences of his activity in the fields of politics, theology and jurisprudence. Then, it will be of certain importance and interest to discuss the relation of his central ideas to whatever subsequent repercussions they may have had.

This study, therefore, following primarily a historical methodology, begins with the conditions of the Muslim Community in the time of Ibn Taymiyyah and proceeds with a biographical introduction of him which leads to the investigation of his doctrinal ideas. These ideas then become the framework of his ethical views as he applies them to the life of the Muslim individual and his society.

A considerable number of Qur'ānic quotations appear in the text. In order to be faithful to Ibn Taymiyyah's own principle that the Qur'ān should not be translated, the verses quoted appear in Arabic, the reference and the translation being given in corresponding footnotes. The translations used are from ʿA. Yūsuf ʿAlī, *The Holy Qur'ān: Text, Translation, Commentary*, Lahore: 1938.

PART ONE: THE FRAMEWORK

CHAPTER I

THE SETTING OF IBN TAYMIYYAH'S LIFE AND WORK

In order to appreciate more fully the significance of Ibn Taymiyyah for his own time, and the value of his contribution to the succeeding developments in Islamic theology and ethics, a brief review of the conditions of the Muslim community in the period immediately preceding his activity, as well as during his time, is necessary. For it is through the perception of that history that Ibn Taymiyyah's work gains particular relevance, on the one hand; and it is through the verification of that work against the normative sources of Islam, i.e., the Qur'ān and the *Sunnah*, that it gains universality and permanence.

Concerning the general period of Ibn Taymiyyah, that is the seventh and eighth centuries after the *Hijrah*, the historians tell us it was in a shambles. Detailed evidence of this chaotic state reveals at least these main characteristics:

1. Political and Social devastation
2. Theological and Ideological and Ethical degeneration

I. *Political and Social Life:*

The political life of the Muslim Community was terribly disarrayed by three obvious, major enemies. Those were: the internal fragmentation of the Islamic world itself, the invasion of the Tatar from the East and the aggression of the Crusaders from the West.

A. The Muslim world had maintained a political unity throughout its eastern and western territories under the leadership of the Rāshidūn Caliphs in Madīnah and under Umawī rule in Damascus. Under the ʿAbbāsīs a division took place. While they held rule in the east, transferring the seat of government to Baghdad, the Umawīs ruled Andalusia and portions of western Africa. Even though the ʿAbbāsī state had obviously become the more prestigious, having much power and stature in every respect, conflict still arose between the caliphs, signalling the beginning of far reaching disharmony and allowing greater fragmentation to occur through the rise of small independent emirates. Such fragmentation not only suggested different focal points of political leadership, but even more seriously weakened the authority of the caliphs. The result was a sort of cyclical change which continued to allow for further disunity and, ultimately, for foreign invasion. For it was toward the end of the ʿAbbāsī rule, i.e., 334-590 A.H./956-1212 A.D., that the Daylamīs and the Saljūq Turks took over, and that other clan-type states, such as the Fāṭimīs of Egypt, the Ḥamadānīs of Jazīrah, the Sāmānīs, the Buwayhīs and the Khawārizmīs in Mesopotamia, sprang up. Such divisions made ripe the conditions for the invasion of the Tatar and the Crusaders.

Even during Ibn Taymiyyah's era, after the Tatar were halted primarily due to the support of the military strength of Egypt, still it is to be remembered that in spite of such strength, the political climate was dominated by the influence of its Mamlūk rulers. It was characterized by the dictatorship of the ruler, the monopoly of government by the ruling family, the insecurity of the throne as a result of the rivalry between the ruling family and other aspirants, and the constant conflict and frequent violence among the rivals themselves. Moreover, rulers sought to reinforce their positions with religious authority by obtaining the support of the titular caliph, who, by the very weakness of his own position, had no other choice than to extend such support.[1] Under such conditions, the state to which the Muslim world looked for leadership, i.e., Egypt, was a military state, or a police state in the modern sense, where there was neither a constitution nor a consultative style of government--such as a parliament or congress. And though there was a judicial branch of sorts, where the four Muslim Schools of law were represented, political expediency was the predominent principle of government. Cases where the counsel of the scholars *(ʿulamāʾ)* of Islamic law was utilized, were often cases of necessity in which the authority of the *ʿulamāʾ* itself was the only way a certain political objective could be achieved by the rulers. One can imagine that, with few exceptions, the *ʿulamāʾ* must have been subjected to much pressure, and often coerced into handing down rulings against their best judgment, or even against their conscience. It was only occasionally when a certain ruling Mamlūk would show respect for religious law, and genuinely seek the counsel of the *ʿulamāʾ*. Such exceptions included al-Sulṭan Al-Ẓāhir Baybars and his successor Al-Nāṣir, the latter being Ibn Taymiyyah's contemporary who regularly sought his opinions. True, the scholars were considered to be a special class, but they commanded obeissance only insofar as they did not go against the authority of the sultan or interfere with his tax policies. Thus, it was evident that the rulers cared the most about wealth, and they accumulated it by whatever means they saw fit. Baybars, for example, was remembered for heavy taxation and for the usurpation of land from its owners. Regardless of their special status, however, the *ʿulamāʾ*'s esteem in the community must have been reduced for their lust for a share of the state's wealth which was generally satisfied in order to keep them in the sultan's favor.

As for the common citizens, other than those who managed through large trade to enter into the ranks of the elite, they were mostly peasants, laborers or small merchants. The farmers tilled lands owned largely by the wealthy, and the profits of the merchants were swallowed up into tax obligations.

It was in this context that Ibn Taymiyyah exercised his understanding of the Qurʾān and the *Sunnah*. With an unquestionable concern for all classes, his style was uniquely developed with a view toward influencing the elite in order to bring about a comprehensive reform, as well as working for the common people. And so as he had succeeded in winning the favor of al-Nāṣir and secured his military aid against the Tatar, he marshalled his reformative forces into giving the ruling class a more honorable self-understanding of their political positions, and the *ʿulamāʾ* a new sense of dignity in the nature of their vocation to overcome their psychological dependence, through greed, on wealth or status. Likewise, for the sake of the citizenry, he worked to evaluate their social and economic status, by ruling, in 697 A.H./1319 A.D. to divide the land among farmers with greater equity in order to offer them sufficient incentive and a sense of self-reliance. Eighteen years later, he saw wise that some of the land taken earlier from the wealthy should be returned to them in order to gain their co-operation in his reformative effort. It is easy to see, however, how he was envied primarily by his fellow *'ulamā'* as he had gained the respect and support of all social classes, and how many of them must have preferred the most dependent, less risky, life style to one of greater moral responsibility and, without a doubt, greater honor. In the presence of such general corruption, however, it is easy to understand the apathetic mood of the community as reflected in the passivity of the people toward government. Indeed, it was even worse than to be so mildly described. For there was rather a general withdrawal on the part of the citizens from the political affairs of their state. They knew, or at least they thought that there was nothing they could do to change the prevailing patterns, so, assisted by the current religious notions of Ṣūfī non-involvement, and, at least in an equal measure, nurturing these same notions by the evidence of public corruption, they were pushed into personal inwardness, thus completing a vicious circle.

B. These internal political conditions made the external invasions by Western Christians and by Eastern barbarians more readily possible and their impact more deeply penetrating. And it seems rather ironic that the very expansion of Muslim territory had so carried with it the seeds of its division, caused by the warring rivalries and the evident lust for power and control. Ibn al-Athīr thus summarizes the conditions of the Muslim world in its early middle centuries:

> Islam and Muslims have during that period been afflicted by such disasters that no other nation had experienced. One such affliction was the invasion by the Tatar. They came from the East and inflicted overwhelming damages. Another was the onset of the Frankish people (God's curse be upon them) from the West to Mesopotamia and Egypt, and the occupation of its port, that is Damietta, which nearly subjected all of Egypt to their rule, had it not been for God's mercy and victory over them. But another affliction was that the Muslims themselves had been divided, and their swords lifted up against their fellows.

The vulnerability of the Muslim world was, doubtless, the occasion for those enemies to strike.

The Crusades, by the time of Ibn Taymiyyah, had wrought extensive damages, although they were, despite internal divisions, impressively countered. In fairness, it should be stated that the Islamic ideological durability had not been lost with other, material, losses. And though Islam had not always shown adequate military preparedness in the face of the Crusades, it was now at a point where its devoted thinkers could reflect meaningfully, in ideological terms, on what stance should be appropriate for the development of a world-view which could maintain a counter-crusade attitude, and more positively, express that ideological durability which is possessed but which had been overshadowed for a period by military inadequacies.

Taqiyy al-Dīn Ibn Taymiyyah was primarily a jurist. He was a historical contemporary of, but geographically removed from the Seventh and Eighth Crusades of Louis IX. In spite of his geographical indirectness, it is important to consider two historical facts which may be counted as significant: one, the impact of and the reaction against the preceding Crusades were already present in Iby Taymiyyah's formative processes; and, two, the Mongols' (or Tatar's) atrocities were an existential reality for him--a reality which may not be overlooked as unrelated to the Crusades.

In the context of military attack, Ibn Taymiyyah's theory of *Jihād*, or "holy war", is clearly a reaction against both those who forcefully stop the preaching of Islam, and those who cause the internal division of its *ummah*. For him, the entire goal of *Jihād* is that "all religion be God's religion, and that the Word of God be uppermost." "أن يكون الدينُ كلّه لله ، وأن تكون كلمةُ الله هي العليا" Whosoever interferes with the accomplishment of this objective was to be fought, according to the consensus of the *ummah*.

Ibn Taymiyyah sought to mobilize the then divided and frightened Muslims into the recognition that Holy War was indeed a divine imperative for them. Furthermore, he asserted, its virtues were more than could be enumerated. Therefore, it was by consensus, he said, the highest "voluntary obligation," i.e., the most dutiful choice, for the Muslim. By testimony of the Qur'ān and the Ḥadīth, he said, it was more worthy than pilgrimage or prayer, and more honorable than fasting.

Who was to be the object of *Jihād*? According to Ibn Taymiyyah he whose evil ravages the land (المفسد فى الأرض); the ungodly (الكافر), the enemy of God and of His Prophet. He who impedes the preaching of the Prophet through violence, or seeks to disrupt the unity of the Muslim Community was to be fought "in order that there may be no disunity, and that religion be wholely God's."

The implications of this theory of Holy War, as will be seen in greater detail in a later chapter, arose with Ibn Taymiyyah out of a concrete theology of unity that shows itself in his conception of the Islamic Community.

Against the background of Islamic fragmentation, Ibn Taymiyyah calls for a Community, or an *ummah*, whose principal characteristic is solidarity. No doubt he is aware of the achievements of Nūr Al-Dīn and Ṣalāḥ al-Dīn who capitalized entirely on an idea of unity without which the earlier Crusades could not have been successfully encountered. Here, building not only on the examples of history, but more importantly and fundamentally on Qur'ānic directives, Ibn Taymiyyah summons the Muslims to stand up together in the firmness of their faith against their enemies.

Likewise, the Tatar were able to penetrate, and nearly completely devastate the Muslim territory because, at the time, Baghdad, their point of entry, had been victimized by weak ʿAbbāsī rule which tolerated a strand of Shīʿism in government. And so history records that al-ʿAlqamī, the Shīʿī vizir of al-Mustaʿṣim, the last ʿAbbāsī to rule Baghdad prior to its fall, was the Tatar's contact in the great capital. He subverted its ruler, reduced its military forces, and betrayed its political and military secrets to the enemy. The city was thus handed over to them who then ravaged it under the vicious leadership of Hulagu. Al-Athīr attributes this betrayal to the general principle held by the Shīʿah that other Muslims who do not embrace their doctrines are heretics and that as such they are less worthy of the political leadership of their people than even their enemies. Whatever the motive of the Shīʿī vizir, the Tatar were the victor; they destroyed Baghdad and infiltrated Westward into Aleppo in Syria and then into Damascus. Ibn al-Athīr's descriptive record of their ungodliness and destruction is truly vivid; he said

> "I have for several years restrained myself from mentioning the Tatar event, the remembrance of which causes me to shudder. Even now I hesitate to recall it, for who can write an epitaph for Islam and the Muslims? Who can find it possible to recount the tragedy? Oh, that my mother had not given me birth, or that I had died before this moment; Yet, I have been urged by a group of friends to outline a record of the event, and find that to decline their request would benefit me nothing. . . It was such a great catastrophe the like of which the days and the nights are too sterile to produce. It swept all of mankind, but particularly the Muslims. If it is said that since Creation there has been nothing like it the saying would be true. Histories have never seen its likeness; and may Future never bring about anything approximating it until the Final Destruction of the world by Gog and Magog [Armagiddon] . . . They [the Tatar] spared no one: they killed men, women, and children. They cut open the wombs of those with child. They destroyed unborn babies . . . They killed and robbed and vandalized. Even Alexander who, by the consensus of historians, ruled the world, did not invade it as rapidly and as rampantly as these. It took him twenty years, but for them the ravage took less than a year. He did not kill or terrorize, he only subjected the world to his obedience. They ravaged and destroyed. Neither they nor their animals had a sense of discrimination or discernment of what they ate. They knew neither marriage nor fatherhood."[2]

Against such atrocities, Ibn Taymiyyah played an important role in military and ideological leadership. Having persuaded Egypt to send support troops as it had once before to fight against this monstrous enemy, he led the battle successfully against the Tatar. Using the gifts of tongue and pen, he not only bolstered the morale of his fellow Muslims but also took that opportunity to re-align their conceptions of unity and community, their understanding of *īmān* and *islām*, their view of God as well as their religious and social self-awareness.

With respect to the social condition of the Muslim world, it is readily clear that it was influenced greatly by the coming together of various races into it. With the encounter between the eastern, western and barbaric cultures, mores, traditions, customs, ideologies and religions, Muslim society experienced, within the framework of hostility and violence, a confusion of values. Moreover, within Islam itself, the inter-mixture of its varied ethnic traditions, as a result of the flight from one region to another to escape the terrors of the enemies, precipitated a troubled social order. Yet even more serious than the problem of natural assimilation was the very paradoxical Mamālīk's engagement of foreign prisoners of war in the political and social matters of state. The paradox, however, may be more easily understood when it is remembered that the Turkish Mamlūk rulers of Egypt, had themselves been in the near past the slave class, having been purchased and brought there by the Ayyūbīs. They accorded the prisoners of war a privileged status, not so much out of confraternal empathy as from a former slave to another, but rather as from a foreigner to another. Al-Maqrīzī records that Tatar war prisoners were put in charge of naval operations as well as positions of strategic social importance. And though, after a time, many of them professed Islam, accepting the legal authority of Muslim supreme jurists in matters of religious law, they nevertheless applied the Code of Ghingis Khan in their daily interactions, which at many points was in distinct contradiction to the revealed scripture. For such interactions they appointed an arbitrator (*ḥājib*) whose responsibility was to enforce the Code.

II. *The State of Theology, Social Ideology and Ethics:*

In spite of the availability of intellectual wealth resulting from limitless productivity in all areas of pursuit in that period, there was, paradoxically, a climate of inherent stagnation that was counter-productive. Thus, the cumulative intellectual heritage which had been the legacy of the scientific expansion that marked the ʿAbbāsī period, was examined academically, but not invested creatively. There was such a jealousy to preserve its purity, so to speak, that no intellectual interaction with it was allowed. Thus, it became idealized and sealed up, as if in a showcase of a museum, in such a way that no improvement could be made upon it. Such idealization served only to stifle any possibility of building upon it new and original thought. Thus, all areas of intellectual activity suffered, especially theology and ethics. Ibn Khaldūn comments on the placidity of jurisprudence of the age and identifies its source:

> The study of *Ḥadīth* was limited in all regions to the *taqlīd* (i.e., indiscriminate imitation) of the Four Schools. The jurists investigated no further, but closed the door to further investigation by others . . . to the extent that no options were left other than merely copying (*naql*) what had been done before . . . There was, therefore, no new *fiqh*: and he who claimed an ability toward *ijtihād* (creative interpretation) was excluded and discriminated against. All of (the jurisprudence of) Islam now consisted of these Four.[3]

In theology, too, the majority of scholars had accepted the *Ash'arī* system of doctrine as an evolutionary position, developing from the *Salaf*, or early, fundamental, doctrine, in the presence of the Mu'tazilah doctrine. This was, in fact, a compromise between the beliefs of the early Muslims as formulated from the perspective of a revelation-centered theolgoy, on the one hand, and, on the other, a rationalist thought-system that had been the effect of philosophy upon theology. The historian al-Maqrīzī reports that the Ash'arī views were upheld and strongly supported even by the leaders of government Ṣalāḥ al-Dīn al-Ayyūbī and his successors who would be Ibn Taymiyyah's contemporaries. The account continues with a review of some of Abū Ḥasan al-Ash'arī's doctrines, and concludes, "and these are but some of the doctrines that are adopted now by the majority of the Muslim regions, and he who publicly professes different views is executed (أريق دمه)."[4]

There was clearly a strong opposition to philosophy, and consequently, to any intellectual activity that might have the potential of threatening, or even raising questions about, the accepted doctrines. One factor which contributed to such opposition was indeed Al-Ghazālī's campaign against the rational philosophers; although it should be remembered that his campaign as waged against them was carried out following their very methodology. Distaste for philosophy and the philosophers was so emotionally charged that the theologians of the Ayyūbī period obtained a Sultan's order to execute Shihāb al-Dīn al-Suhrawardī, a theologian of note, who because of his rationalist views was charged with heresy.[5] Likewise, a fatwa of al-Shahrazūrī, a theologian-jurist known as Ibn al-Ṣalāḥ (d. 643 A.H./ 1245 A.D.), gained fame on account of hereticating anyone who would study the works of Ibn Sinā. Two centuries later, this antagonism still was expressed, as in the world of al-Imam al-Dhahabī who declared that, "Religious philosophy must be avoided by him who seeks to be worthy and successful (in matters of belief), for this science goes in one direction while that which was revealed through the Prophets goes in another direction. The best treatment (دواء) for these sciences and their scholars, whether they be students or teachers of them, is burning and eliminating them from existence, since religion had been perfect (كامل) until the Arabization of these books and their study by the Muslims. If they were eliminated, it would be an indisputable triumph."[6] Even Ibn Taymiyyah himself was, to an extent, influenced by these views of opposition toward philosophy, as is evident in his works, although his contest with the philosophers was obviously not always for the sake of rejecting philosophy as a science, but rather a refutation of their conclusions and an invalidation of the methods with which they arrived at those conclusions. At any rate, being the fair and objective thinker that he was, he upon occasion, as will be shown, would side with the rationalists against the fundamentalists if the views of the former, as he could see them, were closer to the Qur'ān and the *Sunnah*.

Thus, the intellectual climate of the time of Ibn Taymiyyah was such that very few, with innate capabilities, could exercise originality. For though education was popular as each sect and denomination sought to promote its own doctrines by establishing numerous schools, the teaching was in most cases extremely biased. Each school of thought had its shining leadership figure whom adherents devoutly followed, and other than whose opinions they adamantly rejected. The roots of that current prejudice may be traced to the controversies of the fourth Muslim century between the Shāfi'īs and the Ḥanafīs, the Mu'tazilah, the Ash'arīs and the Māturīdīs, and between the philosophers and the Ṣūfīs. Ibn Taymiyyah sharply criticized the phenomenon of following a certain doctrine for the name of its proponent rather than for its valid arguments, and the methods with which those arguments were advanced. Abu Zahrah insightfully states that the sixth, seventh, and eighth centuries of the *Hijrah* were "known for much [cognitive] knowledge but for little [original] thought." Data were abundantly available, and their consumption was nearly everyone's occupation; yet the investigation of their sources, their vehicles and their objectives were disproportionately small. Yet, there is no doubt that those few had left their mark on the mind of Taqiyy al-Dīn: for it was due to the examples of al-Nawawī and Ibn-Daqīq as well as his own father that he could develop his keen originality of thought and the courage to express it, thus making his own outstanding contribution.

Generally, however, this intellectual stagnation, combined with theological and practical attitudes and thought patterns of Ṣūfism, which had by now been in full force, made for what appeared for that time to be an irreversible decline. This decline revealed itself not only in theology and in ethics, but also in the areas of the natural sciences, education and the humanities in general. In the realm of the religious sciences, however, the deterioration was not keenly manifest. Its chaos was accentuated, on the one hand, by the popularlity of Bāṭinī excessivism and Shī'ī and Ismāīlī falsification in doctrine, but was greatly atrributed, on the other hand, to the effects of Ṣufism. Al-Ghazālī's counsel to look only to the Sharī'āh for salvation, a theme that he explicated in his work *Ayyuhā al-Walad* ("O, Son"), was universally adopted, and greatly diluted, by the Muslims of the succeeding generations. His exhortation was aimed at making the fulfillment of divine law uppermost among the concerns of the Muslim. For the ordinary Ṣūfī, this was an urging toward inwardness, a directive that was fully within the intent of Al-Ghazālī himself, who by that time in his spiritual maturity had come full circle to Ṣufism, becoming its spokesman par excellence.

To the common man, the ideas of Ṣufism meant total disengagement from political involvement, and an internalism that moved him away completely from participation in public life in almost any form. The implications of this involved a change in the concept of knowledge, a change in the concept of God, a change in the concept of the individual, and a change in the concept of society. This attitude of total passivity that characterized the Muslim Community perpetuated itself through the vicious circle of personal and social apathy which led to political corruption, which in turn led to military weakness which led to foreign exploitation resulting in further corruption and compounding apathy. Even where there was a semblance of social organizations, as was the case of economic fraternities and guilds, their purpose was more "spiritual" than economic. Guild members utilized their meeting time for the practice of *dhikr* even in the market-place, rather than for their business affairs.

Ibn Taymiyyah's energy was expended largely in calling the Muslims away from every philosophy, doctrine or practice that stifled their thought, will or action to be the *ummah*, or the community, of the Qur'ān and the *Sunnah*. As will be seen in the following chapters, Ibn Taymiyyah's thought was extensively and vigorously expressed in opposition to the following, popular ideas and practices:

A. *Ṣūfism:*

The fiercest of Ibn Taymiyyah's doctrinal contention, was with the Ṣūfīs. He unequivocally resisted at least three of their major, land-mark ideas: namely, pantheism, gnosticism, and a deterministic view of total religious resignation. Because of their numerous misconceptions, but even more actively because of the devastating implications of their misconceptions, Ibn Taymiyyah considered the Ṣūfīs the major practical enemy within the Muslim Community. And it was to the refutation of much of their doctrine as will be noted in greater detail, that he devoted unrelenting intellectual energies.

B. *Shī'ism:*

On this front, he fought religio-political extremism. The major point of contention with the Shī'ah and their subdivisions was the age-old issue of succession in the caliphate, which was responsible for their original break from the traditional Community of Islam. Within the Shī'ī camp itself, there was considerable disagreement which had resulted in cessation by certain groups, identified as the *Zaydiyyah*, the *Kīsāniyyah*, the *Ithnā-Ashariyyah*, the *Naṣīriyyah* and the *Ismā'īliyyah*.[7] Ibn Taymiyyah had much to say about *Shī'ī* doctrine, as well as their political activity which, in part, facilitated the Tatar invasion. Moreover, he not only denounced the *Shī'ah* as a general sect, but he addressed himself to the specific fallacies in the doctrines of the *Ismā'īlīs* and the *Naṣīrīs*, for example, which clashed with traditional understanding.

C. *Determinism and Rationalism:*

Another battlefront in which Ibn Taymiyyah was engaged was against the *Jahmiyyah* (or *Jabriyyah*), i.e., the Determinists, as well as the *Mu'tazilah* (or *Qadariyyah*), i.e., the Rationalists who held human free will as the basis of human action. As is discussed in more detail in a following chapter, the problems debated by Ibn Taymiyyah were those of the createdness/uncreatedness of the Qur'ān, human free will/determinism, the divine attributes, capital sin, etc. Yet on another side stood the followers of Abū al-Ḥasan al-Ash'arī with whom Ibn Taymiyyah did doctrinal battle. Here, as will be seen, the major issues concerned determinism/free will, the divine attributes, the beatific vision, and others.

It is in the context of these circumstances of political, social, and intellectual upheaval that Ibn Taymiyyah appeared and, as it were, lifted up a new ideal by calling the *ummah* back to the solid and resourceful foundation of Islam. He gave himself fully and relentlessly, as is evident in all his available writings, to pointing the way to the knowledge that

> The Prophet has shown the fundamentals and applications of religion, its intent as well as its expression, its [intellectual] knowledge and its action. This [fact] is the foundation of all fundamental knowledge and belief; and he who most adheres to this foundation is most worthy of the truth--both to know and to do it.[8]

CHAPTER II

IBN TAYMIYYAH--A BIOGRAPHICAL ACCOUNT

I. *His Early Years, His Education and His Intellectual Achievements:*

Taqiyy al-Dīn Ibn Taymiyyah[1] was born on the tenth day of Rabīʿ al-Awwal, 661 A.H./1263 A.D. in Ḥarrān, located in Northern Syria near the present Turkish border, and known for its strategic commercial significance as a link between Iraq and Mesopotamia as well as for being a philosophic center for the ancient Sabaeans.[2] It was also known in the Muslim world as a center of activity for the Ḥanbalīs.

He had lived there until he was seven when Northern Mesopotamia was invaded by the Mongols, sometimes known as the Tatar, whereupon his family fled to Damascus, where his father, whose erudition in the study of *Ḥadīth* became readily known, was offered the post of head *shaykh* at the Ḥanbalite institute of tradition, Dar al-Ḥadīth al-Sukkariyyah, in the Qassāʿīn quarter of the city.

Taqiyy al-Din enjoyed an illustrious family background. His father, Abū Muḥammed Abū al-Maḥāsin ʿAbd al-Ḥalīm Ibn ʿAbd al-Salām al Ḥarrānī,[3] who was known as ʿAbd al-Ḥalīm Ibn Taymiyyah (627-682 A.H./1229-1284 A.D.) had earned the position which he inherited from his own father as the *shaykh* and the *khaṭīb* of Ḥarrān. He also came to be known as an authority of the rights of succession in Islamic government.

Majd al-Dīn (ca. 570-625 A.H./1172-1207 A.D.) father of ʿAbd al-Ḥalīm and grandfather of Taqiyy al-Dīn, had first studied the science of *Ḥadīth* under his uncle, Fakhr al-Dīn who himself had had celebrated achievements,[4] and then headed for Baghdad where he stayed for at least six years. It was at Baghdad that his scholarship developed; and his vast Islamic erudition, now released, was bound to make him one of the most respected authorities of Ḥanbalism in his time. He had studied theology, law, the Qurʾān, the doctrines of various sects, and philology. According to biographers, Majd al-Dīn studied the sciences of the Qurʾān and law under Ibn al-Ḥalawī and al-Fakhr Ismāʿīl, philology and the laws of *khilāfah* (succession of caliphs) under Abū al-Baqā al-'Ukbarī. Acclaimed as a "notorious traditionist," he taught tradition in Ḥijāz, Iraq and in Syria. Henri Laoust notes that Majd al-Dīn was "perhaps the only learned person in the family who was systematically devoted also to the publication of collections of *ḥadīths*. Hence his principal work which his biographies cite: *al-Muntaqā* and an important commentary on *al-Hidāyah* by Abū al-Khaṭṭāb; also *Muntahā al-Ghāyah fī Sharḥ al-Hidāyah* of which only a part remains. In addition, Majd al-Dīn wrote the renouned treatise on legal methodology, *al-Muswaddah fī Uṣūl al-Fiqh*; which remained unfinished but was published by his grandson. His writings on law are recognized as "the most important part of his juridical activity; his *al-Aḥkām al-Kubrā* and his *al-Muḥarrar fī al-Fiqh* have to be unanimously appreciated and utilized internally by the Ḥanbalī school."[5] Majd al-Dīn, who died at Ḥarrān in 625 A.H./1227 A.D. ranked among the highest authorities of his school, whereupon "he was often referred to (by his colleagues and students, presumably) as Al-Majd (the glory of Islam, or of Ḥanbalism), and was often associated with the celebrated Muwaffaq al-Dīn Ibn Qudāmah[6] under the title of 'The Two Shaykhs'".[7] Ḥanbalism in Egypt could be traced back to Majd al-Dīn, through Najm al-Dīn Ibn Ḥamdān (603-695 A.H./1205-1297 A.D.) who studied under him at Ḥarrān, Aleppo and Jerusalem. Majd al-Dīn who himself wrote important treatises on dogmatics, and legal methodology, was the jurisconsult in Cairo where he had an illustrious career also as a teacher.

It is this kind of background that Taqiyy al-Dīn inherited, and it is to this quality of heritage that he himself was faithful in his own study and personal self-discipline. In Damascus, to which his family emigrated by night before the pursuing vicious Mongols, with a minimum of belongings, most important of which was his father's valuable library, that Taqiyy al-Dīn developed his keen knowledge of the sciences of his religion. The combination of Ibn Taymiyyah's innate and environmental gifts and the opportunities for personal, cultural and scholarly development could hardly be improved upon.

The young lad was known for an unusual alertness of mind, quickness of perception, and sharpness of memory. He became not only the envy of his peers, but often the object of interest for Syrian scholars.

A story is told[8] that a learned shaykh from Aleppo came to Damascus and asked to meet young Taqiyy al-Dīn. Inquiring where he might find him, the shaykh waited at a tailor shop for the boy's school to be dismissed. When a group of youngsters passed by, Ibn Taymiyyah was pointed out as the boy with a writing slate tablet. The shaykh called him and dictated a dozen traditions which Ibn Taymiyyah was able to read back perfectly. He asked him to erase them for another dictation. This time, the shaykh gave him the attributions of several traditions, and the boy read them back most intelligently. The Aleppo leader remarked, "If this boy live, he will surely have a position of esteem," and that he had never witnessed the life of his ability.

Abū Zahrah[9] observes that while this apparently is an unexaggerated report of the incident, "by contrast to tales about Mālik," the time of Ibn Taymiyyah's early education was not such that it depended greatly on memorized learning as had been the case in Mālik's; rather it was the time of committing everything to writing which had the effect of liberating the mental energies to concentrating on the meaning inherent in the content.

Ibn Taymiyyah, however, had both a keen memory and a penetrating perception. Memory, apparently, had been a family trait. His father's fourteen years' teaching the Ḥadīth at the Great Mosque of Damascus, was distinguished among that of his colleagues by his independence from a written manuscript. The son's logical pursuit followed the direction of his family. It was natural for him to be absorbed solely in learning, whereas for another, such as Abū Ḥanīfah whose father was a merchant, to follow first in that or another direction.

Early in Ibn Taymiyyah's development, he took up the memorization of the Qur'ān, then the Ḥadīth and its sources from the masters of Ḥadīth. He would also listen to eloquent preaching and to the great *dawāwīn* (complete poems). Regularly he would hear readings from the *Musnad* of Aḥmad Ibn Ḥanbal, the *Ṣaḥīḥ* of al-Bukhārī, the Jāmiʿ of al-Tirmidhī, and other sources of Ḥadīth science. The author of الكواكب الدرية records that the first book of *Ḥadīth* he mastered was al-Ḥamīdī's *Al-Jamʿ bayn al-Ṣaḥīḥayn* ("Reconciliation of the Two Authentic Collections of True Traditions"[10]). He is reported to have sat at the feet of more than two-hundred *Ḥadīth* scholars, and heard the *Musnad* of Ibn Ḥanbal numerous times.

Nor was Ibn Taymiyyah's education restricted to his father's specialty, namely, the *Ḥadīth*. Indeed he showed superior and diversified interest and ability in mathematics, but even more particularly in the Arabic disciplines: philology, grammar, history and literature, both poetry and prose. His studies in each of these disciplines possessed the intensity of specialization and the competence of criticality. With his foundation and background, Ibn Taymiyyah, however, favored Islamic law, especially of the Ḥanbalī School, in conjunction, of course, with Qur'ānic hermeneutics. His father's authoritative conversance with these subjects was not only an inspiration for him, but a great support.

This quality of personal and intellectual development could be expected in Damascus at that time. The most significant city in Syria, it was an "uncontested cultural metropolis." Since the Ayyūbī rule, it had continued to flourish as a major capital in the eastern Mediterranean. Politically, it was the second capital of the Mamlūk Empire as Baybars would visit it as frequently as he would Cairo. As the place of residence for the governor of the Syrian state (*mamlakah*), it also was a military center with its citadel serving as one of the bastions of the *salṭanah* of Cairo against internal conspiracies as well as against the external invasions of the Mongols. Economically, the city was populous and abundant with wealth as could be expected in a city of its political significance. Industries, particularly of war equipment, had flourished, as did the educational enterprise. The city's economy was enhanced by the cultural rhythm of the royal presence. Even funeral industries thrived as the community was sensitive to the commemoration of its cultured and pious dead. The city's intellectual development did not operate in a vacuum. Baghdad to the east, which Laoust contends "was not immediately buried after the Mongol conquest,"[11] was still pulsating intellectually, and scholarly exchange still flowed between the intellectual leaders of the community. Cairo to the west was the residence of both the Caliph and the Sultan, and was always a "magnetic pole" for the learned community, and as such was beginning "to assume the intellectual leadership of Arabic Islam which it preserved until the present."[12] Midway between those two great cities lay Damascus which combined their cultural and intellectual wealth. In addition, and in the particular interest of Ibn Taymiyyah, it housed a very strong Ḥanbalī school near the Great Mosque but far less conservative, and more influenced by extraneous elements than that of Ḥarrān.

It was here, where Ḥanbalism had already a fair climate for over a century,[13] that Ibn Taymiyyah received his early formal training. And it was there that his name was later to be associated with that of al-Shaykh Ibn Qudāmah[14] of whom Ibn Taymiyyah himself said, "No jurist with greater knowledge than Muwaffaq al-Dīn had entered Syria since al-Awzaʿī." This association is not be to taken lightly, for the works of Muwaffaq al-Dīn, of which the most important are now available in print,[15] are considered among the most valuable that exist in Ḥanbalī thought. According to Laoust, it was from his treatises that his contemporaries derived their knowledge of the law. In the course of establishing the background for Ibn Taymiyyah's academic preparation in the Ḥanbalī tradition, Henri Laoust describes how Ibn Qudāmah's thought was so comprehensively and thoroughly critical by giving this example:

> En théodicée, Muwaffak ad-Dīn n'a laissée que quelques traités d'un intérêt secondaire. On cite de lui une ʿaḳida dans le style ordinaire des professions de foi hanbalites, une dissertation sur le sens allégorique du Coran, une autre sur la prédestination, une lettre enfin a Fakhrad-Dīn b. Taimiya sur l'éternité des peines qui frappent les hérétiques en enfer.[16]

In addition to his most celebrated work in methodology, *Rawḍat al-Nāẓir*, Ibn Qudāmah's graduated series of manuals was a necessary tool for any serious scholar of the Ḥanbalī School, as was indeed Taqiyy al-Dīn Ibn Taymiyyah. The series contained in ascending order, *al-Umdah*, a basic definition of Ḥanbalī opinions held by the author which later moved Ibn Taymiyyah to write *al-Muqniʿ*,[17] an intermediate expository sourcebook of law entirely sufficient for the making of a jurisconsult who, nevertheless would be a follower of the pre-set legal opinions ("*muqallid*") but not a creative interpreter ("*mujtahid*"), and, finally *al-Kāfī*, comprehensive application manual of the law.

The crown of Ibn Qudāmah's works is *al-Mughnī* in which the author, with habitual clarity, placed the Ḥanbalite law within the total context of Islamic law and proceeded to provide a critical study of *uṣūl*, or sources of law. Laoust makes the point that a reader influenced by the convincing arguments of *al-Mughnī* would feel an unrestricted freedom to exercise absolute *ijtihād*.[18] It was this kind of scholarship that made its imprint upon Ibn Taymiyyah's consciousness, and gave him the impetus and the courage to exercise his intellect constructively.

Ibn Taymiyyah's career followed a turbulent series of events because of his liberated and original expressions of his understanding of the dynamism of Islamic faith and life as revealed and exemplified in the *Qur'ān* and the *Sunnah*. At a young age, he achieved a position of great respect because of his scholarship. Lengthy praise is bestowed upon him by his contemporaries and biographers such as Ibn al-Wardī in his encyclopedic work on history, Al-Ḥāfiẓ Shams al-Dīn al-Dhahabī in several of his works, Ibn al-Alūsī in his work *Jalā' al-ʿAynayn*, Ibn Rajab in his *Ṭabaqāt*, Ṣalāḥ al-Dīn Ibn Shākir al-Kutubī in his *Fawāt al-Wafiyyāt*, and others.[19] It is common to find critiques of lavish acclaim such as this: "With respect to *Ḥadīth* (i.e., The science of Tradition), his word has final authority concerning attribution; it may truly be said that whatever *ḥadīth* (i.e., saying of the Prophet) is not known to Ibn Taymiyyah is not a *ḥadīth* . . .;" or "With regard to the comprehensiveness of his knowledge, Ibn Taymiyyah holds in his memory the sum of all sciences and is thus able to recall [from that reservoir] whatever he chooses . . ." If such claims might be suspected of exaggeration or bias because they are made by his friends, a word from one of his contemporary intellectual adversaries, the chief of the Shāfiʿī School in Syria eloquently attests to Ibn Taymiyyah's genius:

> If he were asked a question in any of the sciences, it would appear as though he knew that science masterfully, to the exclusion of other sciences; and it would be judged that no one knows it as well as he. The jurists of all Schools would benefit from his knowledge in their own schools, and would learn about them what they would not have known before . . . It is not known that any scholar could win a debate against him . . . He was

> master at interpretation, expression, organization, categorization and clarification . . .[20]

His erudition, and its subsequent recognition by his Ḥanbalī School as well as others, won him the greatly honored post of head of the Ḥadīth School in Damascus, following the death of his father.

II. *His Participation in the Affairs of the Muslim* Ummah:

Ibn Taymiyyah demonstrated in his own life work that Islam is a religion of faith and action, and without the one the other is not complete. For him, doctrine was inseparable from life, the latter being shaped by the former and receiving concrete direction from it. Belief in God and the desire to accomplish His will left no doubt that the enemies of the faith who sought to oppress it by their irreverent and violent abuse of the faithful and their land should be crushed. Such was the meaning for Ibn Taymiyyah of faith and of "striving in the way of God" (i.e., *jihād,* which came to mean "holy war" in its technical use). To strive in the divine way was for him to stand up and to take action in the name of God in whom one believes. It was also to spend and to be spent in doing God's will, thereby pleasing him in whom one affirms one's faith.

Thus we find Ibn Taymiyyah in the midst of the battles with the Tatar where he fearlessly approached their king, in 699 A.H./1200 A.D. and averted an attack that was designed to annex Egypt to the already spreading Mongol empire. In the face of another potential confrontation between the frightened armies of Syria and the savage Tatar, Ibn Taymiyyah's leadership in drawing a military strategy for his nation's army was illustrative of his unusual practical genius, even though he was primarily an academician and a legislator. He began with raising the morale of the Syrian soldiers by assuring them of the sovereignty and might of God in whom they trust; then he drew upon the military power of Egypt which by then, having been jolted into the realization of the ferocity of the Tatar's danger, had attained impressive sophistication and considerable preparedness. His challenge to the Egyptian rulers, under whose control Syria also was, bespeaks his courage, his prowess as well as his persuasiveness. He said, "If you turn your back on Syria, and refrain from protecting her, we shall have to raise up a ruler of our own who can offer us security, protection and leadership now and in time of peace." He continued, "Even if you were not the rulers of Syria also, but Syria came to call on you for help, to win a victory for her, it behooves you to achieve that victory. How much more then when you are her rulers and her people your subjects. They are your responsibility." And, having issued this compelling challenge, he offered them encouragement in the assurance that with the help of Almighty God, they were bound to win the battle for the Syrians and, consequently, for themselves.

In a third round with the Tatar, in 702 A.H./1304 A.D., Ibn Taymiyyah was himself in the very front lines of the battle. It was the battle of Shaqḥab where he marched side by side with the Sulṭan, according to the record of Ibn Kathīr, and where a remarkable defeat was inflicted upon the enemy by the Syrian troops.

The authenticity of Ibn Taymiyyah's action was also known in the internal affairs of the life of the Muslim *ummah*. Biographies abound with incidents reflecting his courage and boldness for the truth.[21] One such incident shows him in the presence of an unjust landlord exposing his oppression. When the tyrant mocked him by suggesting that he himself ought to have come to Ibn Taymiyyah, the latter being "a religious man worthy of reverence," Ibn Taymiyyah replied harshly, "Moses, was a much holier man than you, yet he went to the Pharoah, who was more evil than you, three times every day to offer him the opportunity to repent and to believe."

His stance against drinking and the liquor trade was also widely known as he often would take a band of friends and raid the local bars, smashing up the bottles and scattering away the clients.

Likewise, he headed campaigns to destroy shrines that Muslims had made it their custom to visit, always pointing out unequivocally that God is one and nothing is to be associated with him in worship.

By the same token that he was admired for his courage, Ibn Taymiyyah, however, made some enemies, especially among Ṣūfīs whose practices he abhorred and publicly fought. Many of their leaders resisted him; and those among them who had sufficient influence used it against him with the ruling authorities. As a result, he was once exiled in Alexandria, and three times imprisoned. His writings were banned; and in his last imprisonment, he was forbidden to read, write or communicate with family or friends. For him, imprisonment for truth constituted ultimate freedom. He had, in fact, welcomed prison as an opportunity to think and to write, but when his books were taken away and he was no longer permitted to commit to writing what he believed, this was the severest punishment. That was the beginning of the end for him, for in less than six months he died in his cell in Damascus.

Yet when he had died in 728 A.H./1328 A.D. innumerable citizens came to pay him their last respects. Ibn Kathīr records that even though his body had been prepared at dawn he was not buried until mid-afternoon because of all the crowds that gathered to honor him in his death, and that at the funeral procession thousands of women who had come from all over the countryside lined the streets and covered the roof tops. The men, Ibn Kathīr estimated, approached sixty- to a hundred-thousand in number, or even perhaps two-hundred thousand. He was so honored and remembered for the demonstration of his faith in action, a faith that had enabled him to say: "In this life is a paradise which must be entered before that of the life to come can be enjoyed: What could my enemies have done to me? My heaven and my paradise is in my breast; wherever I go it accompanies me. My imprisonment is only an opportunity to be alone; my murder is only a testimony; my exile from my country is a holiday!" It was the same faith that, in his last imprisonment, inspired him to pray, "Almighty God, assist me to remember Thy goodness, to thank Thee and genuinely to worship Thee, according to Thy will."

PART TWO: THE DOCTRINAL CONTEXT FOR A SYSTEM OF ETHICS: DIVINE REVELATION AND HUMAN RESPONSE

CHAPTER III

GOD--HIS NATURE, HIS WILL AND HIS ACTIONS

The most prominent doctrine in Ibn Taymiyyah's theological formulations is the doctrine of divine unity. It is the singlemost conception which undergirds his entire system of doctrine. Moreover, in Ibn Taymiyyah's juristic thought and work where we know him best, the unity of God appears to be the fundamental principle. In theology as well as in jurisprudence, his consistent, characteristic method is established on the textual revelation of the Qur'ān and the verified traditions of the Prophet. Thus the formula he so often repeats in his discourses of the doctrine of God is: that God be characterized as He characterizes Himself and as His Prophet characterized Him, without distortion or neutralization (allegorical interpretation of His attributes), without anthropomorphism or figurization (بلا تعطيل او تشبيه).[1]

That God should be described only in the terms of His own self-description through the Qur'ān explains the reason for Ibn Taymiyyah's exegetical method most notably recognized in his *Commentary on the Ikhlāṣ Sūrah*, but also conspicuous in his numerous treatises relating to his conception of God.

Nor does Ibn Taymiyyah's primary concern with regard to the doctrine of God appear to be expressed to provide proofs for the existence of God directly, although he necessarily addresses himself to the problem both exegetically and rationally. For him, the existence of God is a given, based on the universal instinctive recognition of His being (*al-fiṭrah*),[2] and on the divine evidences, or signs, in the world (*al-āyāt*).[3] On the other hand, he vigorously opposes the logic of Ibn Sinā's argument which makes a distinction between the essence (*māhiyyah*) and the existence (*wujūd*) of God. Ibn Taymiyyah, in consonance with his insistence on the unity and uniqueness of God, maintains that divine essence-existence is abstract and wholly other and therefore "may not pass from the subjective realm to the objective realm."[4] Likewise, God's attributes and His will and actions, inextricably related to His essence, are to be understood in terms of His unity and transcendence.

It is fitting that we examine now Ibn Taymiyyah's understanding of the unity of God, and the relation between this doctrine and other divine attributes and action.

I. *The Nature and Character of God:*

In elucidating the doctrine of God, Ibn Taymiyyah takes as his point of departure the verses of the Qur'ānic *sūrah*, "Al-Ikhlāṣ," or "purity (of faith)," which in spite of its brevity, he takes to equal "one-third of the Qur'ān":[5]

"قل هو الله أحد ، الله الصمد ، لم يلد
ولم يولد ، ولم يكن له كفوا أحد ."[6]

Herein is found the fundamental doctrine of Islam, namely the doctrine of the unity of God (*al-tawḥīd*). For it proclaims the absolute incomparability of God, which it places above any proof or positive determination.

Ibn Taymiyyah's doctrine of God, which projects itself through and through in his construct of social justice, begins by being abstractive as it repeatedly affirms that "nothing is like unto Him, whether in His essence, his attributes or His actions" (ليس كمثله شيء ، لا في ذاته ، ولا في صفاته ، ولا في أفعاله) This initial position is within the Ḥanbalite tradition, and, at least in its *prima facie* significance conforms to the scriptural understanding, by the earlier faithful (*al-salaf*), of the nonfigurization (*bilā kayfa*) of God. In its underlying significance, however, Ibn Taymiyyah's idea is more philosophical and profound than simplistic. It is at once an affirmation of the absolute uniqueness of God, and a refutation of the arguments and methodologies of the philosophers whose method of dealing with the problem of divine transcendence amounted to an affirmation of the general coupled with the negation of the particular. Ibn Taymiyyah's method, on the contrary, was to base the concept of divine incomparability on "the affirmation of the particular and negation of the general" (الإثبات المفصّل والنفي المُجْمَل). Thus, "nothing is like unto Him," meant for Ibn Taymiyyah the affirmation, in the fullest detail, of all that is revealed of the Divine Being, i.e., the divine names and the divine attributes given in the Qur'ān and reiterated in the

Tradition, rather than the opposite approach "of the Jahmiyyah, Qarāmiṭah, Bāṭinah and other heretics" who characterize God by identifying in detail what He is not, and generally acknowledge "an absolute but meaningless existence...a type of existence formulated only in their minds but is not substantiated in reality."[7] With similar vigor, Ibn Taymiyyah reacts against both the intellectual anthropomorphism of the philosophers for whom God is an idea, and the existential monism of the Ṣūfīs, particularly of the School of Ibn ʿArabī.[8] Ibn Taymiyyah seems to emphasize the point that any knowledge about the nature of God comes only from what God Himself has revealed about himself, and that at any rate nothing is like unto Him. Thus the concept of the absolute incomparability of God implies not only that He is unique in His essence and in His attributes, but also that complete knowledge of Him is not possible to man, since the question of "how" can never find an answer.[9] He says:

> To speak of the attributes is to speak of the essence; for there is nothing like unto God in His essence, in His attributes or in His actions. For as God has an essence which is not to be likened to other essences, so also His attributes may not be likened in their manner to the attributes of other beings.[10]

Thus to inquire of "how" God is seated on His throne (with reference to the Qur'ānic verse ("والرحمن على العرش..."), for example, is heretical. What is known so as to be believed is that God is enthroned, though the "how" of his enthronement is not only unknown but also unknowable. Not only is the human answer to the "how": *ignoramus*, but it must always remain: *ignorabimus*.

The incompleteness of the human knowledge of God, predicated upon His incomparability, suggests however a relative knowledge, a positive notion which Ibn Taymiyyah has developed and extended to the different domains of his doctrines.

There is no division among Muslims on the principle of the unity of God, Ibn Taymiyyah acknowledges. The division, he explains, has resulted from the semantic disagreements of the scholars and the spokesmen of the various sects with regard to such terms as "*tanzīh*," "*tashbīh*" and "*tajsīm*," all having to do with the anthropomorphization or the deanthropomorphization of God. What some mean by one term does not conform to what others suggest it means. To affirm *tawḥīd* and *tanzīh*, the Mu'tazilah, for example, reject all divine attributes. Theologians of other sects, he continues, reject all or some of the "descriptive attributes" (الصفات الخبرية), such as the designations "living," "knowing" and the like, with reference to God. Others yet suggest that the only valid designations are such "negative" ones as "ancient" (i.e., "eternal"), or such "active" or "compound" ones as "Creator of the Universe," "Lord of Creation," etc. Ṣūfī pantheists attach yet a different element to the meaning of the unity of God, namely, that God is the Absolute Existence, i.e., that God is Himself Existence, or Being, and is thus revealed in all manner of other existences. Exposing the various interpretations of the sects, Ibn Taymiyyah insists that the doctrine itself must nevertheless remain unaltered: God is one; there is none like unto Him. And though he clearly takes a distinctly different view concerning the divine attributes, he does not hereticate either the Mu'tazilah or the Ash'arīs for their distorted interpretations, as he recognizes that neither had denied or rejected the revelation of the Qur'ān. Rather, he pronounces them "deviant" ("أهل الزّيغ"). The Mu'tazilah, like the philosophers, were guilty of affirming the "negative" attributes and rejecting those which had positive and affirmative import. They explained away the Qur'ānic designations of the Godhead as "appellations of the transcendent essence" ("اسماء الذات العليّة"), signifying the actions of God in His creation. The philosophers contented themselves with such "negative" attributes which indicated God's transcendence such as eternity ("القدم"), total otherness than created beings ("المخالفة للحوادث"), and sovereignty over creation ("انه ربّ العالمين وخالق الأكوان"). The pantheists, or al-Ittiḥādiyyah (communionists) who were the followers of Ibn 'Arabī, contended that "the Transcendent Essence is itself Absolute Existence, and manifests itself in finite beings." The esotericists, or Baṭinīs which include the Qarāmiṭah, believed that God's existence may be conceived by reason and may not be seen or visualized ("يدرك فى الاذهان ولا . . . يحقق فى العيان") consequently rejecting the attributes, thus, in effect "neutralizing" them, and subsequently "negating" the divine essence, according to Ibn Taymiyyah. Finally, the Ash'arīs were charged by him of being selective of the attributes they affirmed, thus neglecting, or perhaps implicitly rejecting, other attributes of equal standing in Qur'ānic revelation to those they chose to affirm.

Ibn Taymiyyah unequivocally rejects altogether the views of the philosophers, the esotericists and the pantheists, but he disagreed only in part with the views of the Muʿtazilah and the Ashʿarīs: Both of the latter groups would validate his view, the difference being one of methodology, namely, that while they extensively interpret, he accepts the textual revelation willingly and without a sense of necessity for subjecting them to the human categories which he considers to be the inevitable risk of the interpretation ("تأويل"), of the attributes.[11]

Ibn Taymiyyah is content to present as his own view of the nature and the character of God what was specifically revealed in the Qur'ān, and accepted by the earlier generations of the faithful ("السلف"), beginning, of course, with Muḥammad. The attributes in their totality, largely affirmatively revealed in the Qur'ān were a sufficient *textus receptus* for his theological creed:

الله لا إله الا هو الحى القيّوم. . .قل هو الله أحد الله الصمد
لم يلِد ولم يولَد ولم يكن له كفوا أحد . .وهو العليم الحكيم. وهو
السميع البصير. وهو العليم القدير. وهو العزيز الحكيم. وهو الغفور
الرحيم وهو الغفور الودود . ذو العرش المجيد . فعّال لما يريد ،وهو
الأول والآخر والظاهر والباطن ، وهو بكل شىء عليم. هو الذى خلق
السموات والارض فى ستة أيّام ثم استوى على العرش ، يعلم ما يلج فى
الأرض وما يخرج منها وما ينزل من السماء وما يعرج فيها . وهو معكم
أينما كنتم ، والله بما تعلمون بصير. فسوف يأتى الله بقوم يحبهم
ويحبونه أذلّة على المؤمنين وأعزّة على الكافرين . . . رضى الله عنهم
ورضوا عنه ذلك لمن يخشى ربه . . . ومن يقتل مؤمنا متعمّدا فجزاؤه
جهنم خالدا فيها ، وغضب الله عليه ولعنه." "وكلّم الله موسى تكليما."
"وناديناه من جانب الطور الأيمن وقرّبناه نجيّا." "ويوم
يناديهم فيقول أينَ شُركائى الذين كنتم تزعمون؟"
"انّما أمره اذا أراد شيئا أن يقول له كُنْ فيكون."
" هو الله الذى لا إلٰه الآ هو الملك القدّوس السلام. . ."[12]

Such texts, as well as any authentic traditions which refer to the transcendent essence of God Ibn Taymiyyah affirms are valid and sufficiently suggestive of the nature and character of God, and as such they require belief as an act of receiving the Qur'ānic and prophetic revelation, which belief at face value neither conflicts with the principle of deanthropomorphization nor departs nor digresses from assent to divine unity. Nor should such belief suggest a sanctioning of the anthropomorphization of God or the drawing of parallels between the Creator and created beings. Ibn Taymiyyah contends that likeness of appellation does not necessarily mean likeness of description ("اتحاد الاسم لا يستلزم التشابه فى الوصف"): For example, "If we necessarily suppose the existence of an eternal Being which is in Himself necessarily existent, and (also) the existence of a created (object) which may or may not be caused to exist, we must grant that the former and the latter both exist. However, the existence of the one is not of necessity to be assumed to be identical to that of the other. One existence may be an entirely different category from the other existence though they both bear the appellation of "existent."[13]

Rather than expend his energy interpreting the meaning of a revelation that already seems sufficiently clear, Ibn Taymiyyah defends a methodological and, at the same time, theological principle, namely that God must be taken at His word which is given in the Qur'ān and through the Prophet: i.e., if He has chosen to disclose that He is omniscient, the response to His revelation can be none other than complete belief, without the question of "how," since it is also already revealed that "there is none like unto him." Suffice it to say for Ibn Taymiyyah that the genus of divine knowledge is different from that of human knowledge; but rather it is such that it is worthy of Himself. Likewise, that He is a living God should not be confused with the conception of the life discernible to humans. He is a living God, yet he also creates the living out of the dead, and returns the living to the dead. The two levels of "living," i.e., that pertaining to God and that describing His creatures are not only separate, but mutually exclusive, yet the level of created life is necessarily dependent upon the necessarily existent.

In so doing, Ibn Taymiyyah not only proffers a convincing rational argument for the doctrine of God's unity and incomparability without falling into the trap of unnecessary and ultimately distorting interpretation; he also underscores the validity of a hermeneutical principle that was largely and conspicuously unutilized by the so-called scholars of his day, namely, that the chief sources for the Muslim are the Qur'ān and the Sunnah, not philosophy or even theology. Nor was his resistance to indulge in interpretation with regard to the doctrine of God in any way incongruent with his brilliant exercises of "creative interpretation" in the case of *fiqh*, i.e., jurisprudence. There were important differences: (1) The kind of interpretation he rejected was indulgent philosophical-theological interpretation, under the aegis of *ta'wīl* (exegesis, eigesis), which practice he considered at best to be inferior to *tafsīr* (explanation, clarification);[14] (2) He resisted the exercise of interpretation of whatever kind when it was unnecessary, as he deemed in this case where there were ample, complementary texts given with ample clarity; (3) The science of *fiqh* demanded the exercise of prudent, creative interpretation (this is known as *ijtihād*, as will be discussed in later chapters), because jurisprudence dealt with the specifics of human conduct in the Muslim society for which the Qur'ān and the Sunnah were a general constitutional framework; (4) In his *ijtihād*, Ibn Taymiyyah's conclusions were not only based on Qur'ānic revelation but also were at length in the same spirit of the Qur'ān whereas in the case of *ta'wīl* by the philosophers' and the theologians' conclusions invariably veered off quite a great extent from the intentions of texts.

Ibn Taymiyyah sums up his methodological defense by offering a statement of principle and advice:

> ...God may be characterized by how He characterizes Himself and by how His Prophet characterized Him. The course to be followed [in understanding this doctrine] is that of the *salaf*, the people of faith and knowledge, and of the meanings understood from the Book and the Sunnah. Response [to revelation] ought not to confuse it for such would be a distortion, a disbelief, an abandonment of the Book...[15]

While Ibn Taymiyyah's position may, therefore, be placed as a median between those who reject the attributes (*nufāh*) and the anthropomorphists (*mushabbihah*), it seems at the same time to rise above both extremes. He says, "The position of the salaf (that is also his own) is between *ta'ṭīl* and *tashbīh*.

They do not liken God's attributes of His creatures as they do not liken His essence to the essences of His creatures. Nor do they reject what He Himself had revealed to characterize Himself, or the Prophet's descriptions of Him, for that would be a neutralization of His "fair appellations" (i.e., the 99 attributes) and His transcendent attributes, a distortion of the revealed texts and a disbelief in God's nature and miracles.[16] The position is developed even more fully into an affirmation of the transcendence (تنزيه) of God:

> The Qur'ān from beginning to end, the Tradition from beginning to end, then the whole of the utterances of the Companion and their followers, and of the faithful leaders contain in abundance either direct texts or unmistakable indication that God transcends everything (literally "is beyond everything"): He is beyond (i.e., upon) the throne; He is beyond the heavens... Neither is it said in any of these sources that God is not upon His throne, that He is not in the heavens, that He is not everywhere that all places are alike to Him, that He is not in the world or outside it. For one may not point to Him as though to a perceptible, palpable, empirical direction.[17]

To believe, therefore, in the realities of God's throne, His descent to receive the supplications of men, as the *ḥadīth* says, in the beatific vision in the world to come by those who believe, is indeed a duty, but to investigate its manner, Ibn Taymiyyah says, is a dangerous pursuit.

Laoust views Ibn Taymiyyah's position as one which gives harmony to the relation between the essence and the attributes. This, transposed to the domain of theodicy, is a harmonization between the principle of unity and the notion of multiplicity in the doctrine of God. For Muslim theology and philosophy have always held "an arithmetical conception of unity," Laoust remarks; they have considered "plurality as a secondary manifestation, diverted from genuine [revelation]."[18] For al-Ash'arī, God in Himself is one: in Him there is no multiplicity except as may be revealed by His activity toward men. Hence the distinction between the attributes of essence and the attributes of action. Diversity according to al-Ash'arī, is the subjective human recognition of things, since the reality of [the essence of] God is not knowable in itself. Philosophy, on the other hand, sought to safeguard the principle of the fundamental unity of God, thus limiting the attributes of God. The Ṣūfīs, in the process of guarding the doctrine of unconditional divine unity, but also in an attempt to explain their pantheistic position which at best suggests an element of diversity, invented the theory of emanations adopted of the ancient Gnostics and, the ten intelligences which serve as a series of intermediaries between God and the created world. Although Ibn Taymiyyah does not accept the conclusions of either the philosophers or the Ṣūfīs, he nonetheless capitalizes on the method of reconciling unity with diversity. By insisting on the inseparability between essence and attributes, he substitutes the mathematical conception of unity with an organic one. His formula: " الذات كالصفات " suggests that there can be no speaking of the essence without the attributes; for " الكلام فى الصفات نوع من الكلام فى الذات i.e., to speak of the attributes is to speak of the essence,[19] as has been pointed out. The concept of God, therefore, combines the ideas of unity and comprehensiveness at the same time.[20] Laoust through rather awkward and even offensive diction, attempts to put this idea forward:

> Cette conception de la totalité impliquant simultanement l'unité et la multiplicité, et dont la conscience donne la première notion, est capitale dans la doctrine d'ibn Taimiya: nous la retrouverons dans sa prophétologie, sa méthodologie, sa sociologie politique et, à plus forte raison, dans son éthique.[21]

The attributes of God which are inseparably bound to His essence are likewise inseparably bound to His attributes of action. This notion of inseparability as maintained by Ibn Taymiyyah, explains his apparent "hierarchization"[22] of attributes in terms of "the diversity of the participation of all the attributes in the harmony of the whole, rather than in terms of a diversity in the nature or the character of God." Thus he introduces the notion of the active functions of the divine attributes in his reception of them as a revelation of His character.[23]

II. *God's Will and Actions:*

Closely related to the indicative, descriptive attributes (الصفات الخبرية) of God are His consequential or actional, attributes (الصفات الفعلية). Yet these categories are perceived only from the vantage point of human conceptualization. Because God is one, though He may reveal Himself through a multiplicity and a diversity of ways, the Muslim doctrine of the Divine Being renders any notion of divisibility or categorization inadmissible. The distinction, therefore, may be said to be revelatory rather than essential in God's nature.

With this fundamental principle in mind, Ibn Taymiyyah successfully and with admirable finesse addresses the divine attributes of action in a manner of continuity of, rather than transition from, the attributes of character and nature.

God's will as Creator becomes pivotal in Ibn Taymiyyah's thought-system. Here, though summarily, he reasserts the orthodox doctrine of Islam against the speculations of the philosophers, improving upon it in the emphasis on the centrality of the will of God to all His acts of Creation.

Ibn Taymiyyah notes that thought not spelled out, God's will (*irādah*) and His speech (*kalām*) are veritable attributes. Indeed, he suggests, the reason they are not specifically revealed in the Qur'ān is that they are necessarily implied in, and underlie all of the divine actions: "The texts have given the appellations of omniscient (العليم), almighty (القدير), all-hearing (السميع), all-seeing (البصير), whereas they have not explicitly given the names 'willing' (المريد), or 'speaking' (المتكلّم) which only points to the absolute will (مطلق الارادة) and the absoluteness of speech (مطلق الكلام) [of God], but have instead given evidences of His praiseworthy speech and His praiseworthy will, not by an appellation which may include both whatsoever is praiseworthy and whatsoever is blameworthy. Will and speech as may pertain to the Lord and refer to Him are not separate from Him..."[24]

That God's will is not separate from His essence, i.e., not incidental to Him as had been suggested by the Mu'tazilah and the Jahmiyyah, affirms its transcendence and implies that His act of creation was an act of divine freedom and not of logical necessity deriving from a classification of proportionate or contingent attributes. This assertion clearly contradicts the philosophers' theory that God's act of creation is uniquely the consequence of His knowledge: God "thinks up" the world, so to speak; and it is created. Ibn Taymiyyah, following in the manner of al-Ghazālī, attacks the philosophers indignantly for their assertion that God's act of creation is such that reflects only an attitude of general interest in the universe on His part. Ibn Taymiyyah criticizes them severely for their subsequent conclusions that God's creativity is reduced to being capable of deduction by human knowledge, that matter is coeternal with God and that a doctrine of evolution, through the transmutation of substances is therefore also possible.[25] Ibn Taymiyyah's was a God of absolute freedom--a freedom to exercise a sovereign and eternal will, a freedom governed neither by an external coexistence of matter, nor by God's very foreknowledge, a freedom which is therefore essentially immeasurable and unpredictable.

Ibn Taymiyyah also reacted to the gnosticism of the theory of the existence of ten intelligences which served as a device for reconciling the unity of God with the multiplicity of His attributes, as well as the existence of that which is praiseworthy with the existence of that which is blameworthy ("المحمود والمذموم"), i.e., the divine and the profane. Ibn Taymiyyah's reply again carried through along the lines of al-Ghazālī's thought, consisted in confronting his intellectual adversaries with the argument that a notion of intermediary multiplicity which is suggested by the theory of emanations and intelligences serves only to complicate and obscure the conception of God, and certainly does not at all support the principle of His unity upon which its philosophy claims to be based. Ibn Taymiyyah, however, does not offer a detailed, positive substitute proposal for the scheme. He only suggests that the doctrine of God be constructed from a notion of the totality of revealed attributes in the one, incomparable Being.[26]

As for the notion of the eternity of matter which was held by the Muslim philosophers and refuted by al-Ghazālī in a large portion of his major work *The Incoherence of the Philosophers (Tahāfut al-Falāsifah)*, Ibn Taymiyyah reacts in unequivocal rejection. In his *Minhāj* as well as the *Commentary* on al-Ikhlāṣ *sūrah* he argues that the philosophers, e.g., Ibn Sīnā, al-Farābī and Ibn Rushd, in their apparent attempt to harmonize the Qur'ānic revelation of God with Aristotelian assertions, they do harm to both the Qur'ān and Aristotelianism. He declares that the philosophers' attempt toward conciliation strips the God of the Qur'ān of liberty, and makes of the Aristotelian God a mere efficient final cause ("علّة غائيّة"), a prime immovable mover, a goal toward which the spheres tend, drawn by its desire for ideal perfection.[27] Ibn Taymiyyah's critique subscribes to the assertion, clearly delineated by al-Ghazālī, that the necessary and the possible are mutually exclusive, and advances to pose the question: If the notion of eternity of matter were to be accepted), does it not make God necessarily non-existent (" ممتنع الوجود "), and establish matter as the sole veritable necessarily existent reality?[28]

Thus, against the theory that God had created from existing atoms all energy which was to become autonomous, which theory was held by Muslim philosophers and agreed with the mechanical world view of Ash'arī occasionalism, Ibn Taymiyyah summarized the anti-atomistic arguments of his predecessors, al-Naẓẓām, Abū Ḥātim, al-Ghazālī, Fakhr al-Dīn al-Rāzī, al Shahristānī, al-Nasafī, al-Taftazānī and al-Ījī, and influenced the thought of succeeding generations of scholarship as represented most directly by Ibn al-Qayyim al-Jawziyyah. In effect, he says that a notion of pre-existent homogeneous and identical atoms (" جواهر الفرد ") is a "pure invention of the intellect; it is an idea incapable of being imagined or conceived (*taṣawwur*) by the spirit, a hypothesis that cannot be supported by sensory experience, and, above all is not necessary for rendering intelligible the continuity and the change of the physical or moral world." Returning to the argument on the divine unity, he marshals the evidence of innate conscience ("الفطرة") and of common sense, reaffirming an eternal will not only eternally free from the influence of other existences, but also a good and just will perennially involved in the world God created.

The justice and goodness of God's will are revealed in His giving of a law, i.e., "*sharī'ah*" which governs the physical and moral worlds. This law is always consistent (" حكم واحد "),

and calls for an infinite number of graces ("محاسن"), an unparalleled wisdom ("حكمة"), an infinite mercy ("رحمة"), and an unequalled justice ("عدل"). For Ibn Taymiyyah, three particular characteristics of God's law, or *Sharī'ah*, appear to demand strong emphasis. They are: the divine law is total in its dimension; it is rational in its conception; and, it is beneficial in its application.[29]

The comprehensive nature of the divine law is attested to by its coverage of every domain of individual and social life, material or spiritual. It offers a complete disclosure of divine prescriptions in their general principles as well as in their particular applications ("الأصول والفروع"), in their most profound significance and in their explicit and literal stipulations ("الباطن والظاهر"). The Law is furthermore rational, i.e., it relates the authentic texts ("النقل الصحيح") to sound reason ("العقل الصريح"), and itself indicates that both are two manifestations of the same reality. Issuing from the divine will, the Law possesses not only ultimate authority but ultimate wisdom. It is neither capricious nor ulterior of motive.[30] The Law is, finally, beneficial in its application, i.e., issuing in المصلحة: it aims at the well-being of creation. God has given it out of His eternal liberty and infinite liberality, and not out of any obligatory kindness ("لطف واجب") whatso ever, as suggested by al-Ṭūsī and al-Ḥillī. Because of God's very integrity ("صدق"), He would not issue for His creatures a commandment that is impossible to meet. Because of God's beneficence, His Law aims at the welfare of His creatures in all the circumstances of their lives. Laoust observes that it is at this point that Ibn Taymiyyah departs from the normative formalistic definition of *Sharī'ah* propounded by the jurists of his day and arrives at an empirical understanding of its expediency.[31]

Ibn Taymiyyah's doctrine of God thus appears to aim at offering a basis for his ethics and its application in the social and juridical realms. For him to know God is neither to speak of Him academically nor to unite with Him existentially. It is, on the basis of the revelation of the Qur'ān, to witness His actions of power, love and justice, and to respond in the way that His will commands. Such response is indicated, in these revelations, for example, " وما خلقتُ الإنسَ والجنّ إلّا ليعبدونِ",[32] and " لا إلٰهَ إلّا أنا فاعبدونِ . . . " This required total servitude ("العبادة") is indispensable for the understanding of the doctrine of God in Ibn Taymiyyah's theological and ethical construct. It is offered as the premise for his treatise *Al-Ḥisbah* and prevails throughout his treatise on public law, *Al-Siyāsah Al-Shar'iyyah*.[33]

CHAPTER IV

GOD'S REVELATION: ITS MEDIA AND IMPLICATIONS

The wisdom and the mercy of God, as attested in the Sacred Scripture of Islam and reiterated by its scholastics, have, as a matter of consequence, culminated in the disclosure of His character and His will. Indeed, some have asserted that divine wisdom as well as mercy, have necessitated His revelation.[1] Ibn Taymiyyah's view, though free from the necessity of encumbering God with an obligation (*wujūb*, or *iqtiḍā'*) toward revelation, presupposes revelation as an inseparable aspect of the creative and communicative God, i.e., the God among whose very attributes are *khalq* and *kalām*, in whom he believes. The divine revelation, exercised through a variety of modes such as creation (*khalq*, or *khalīqah*), innate human consciousness, or conscience (*fiṭrah*) and deductive knowledge, i.e., reason (*'aql*), is consummated through and, as such, inseparable from, the Prophet and the Qur'ān. Furthermore, having been made, revelation confronts its recipients with the necessity of a response which response is itself guided by it.

I. *The Prophet:*

It is important to note at the outset that Ibn Taymiyyah's works on prophethood and the Prophet[2] primarily reflect a critique of some of the Shī'ite conceptions, as expressed by al-Ṭūsī and al-Ḥillī, and to an extent, of other notions of the Ṣūfism of Ibn al-'Arabī. It is equally important to realize that Ibn Taymiyyah's interest in the subject, besides being first an expression of his religious loyalty, more obviously resides in his socio-ethical concern than it arises out of a preoccupation with mere scholarship or even dogma. The concept of prophethood (*nubuwwah*) in the thought of Ibn Taymiyyah is developed with a view to its theological-juristic function. Thus, it should be understood in terms of its consequences in the social and political life of the community, which are nevertheless a manifestation of its religious belief.

Methodologically speaking, Ibn Taymiyyah's conclusions regarding prophethood and the Prophet, as is the case with respect to other doctrines, are drawn directly from the Qur'ān and the tradition, which, he insists, are the primary and fundamental sources of faith and practice in Islam.

Ibn Taymiyyah takes as his point of departure the Qur'ānic doctrine of divine unity and absolute incomparability which, of necessity, implies God's freedom to choose and to commission prophets. This initial supposition is posited in direct contradiction of the notion of rational necessity being responsible for God's commissioning of the prophets--a notion advanced by al-Ṭūsī and Al-Ḥillī. According to Ibn Taymiyyah, and on the basis of the Qur'ān, God communicates His message with humankind in these ways: by direct speech, as with Muḥammad on the night of his ascension (*mi'rāj*); through His angels who are His servants and messengers; and through inspiration by a vision or a dream.[3] The philosophy of al-Farābī and, to an extent, that of Ibn Sīnā, later tinted by mysticism, had asserted the plausibility of a union of the human intellect and an intermediary intelligence, epitomized by the archangel Gabriel. Such a union would mean "a simple communication between the soul and the intelligible world, and not a full identification between man and God." Revelation and inspiration being identical in their nature, are different only in the means whereby they are received: for whereas the mystic achieves union through his meditation, the prophet receives revelation through the exercise of a particular power of imagination (*takhayyul*).[4] Ibn Taymiyyah sought, through the use of Qur'ānic evidence, to show that the Prophet had been singularly assigned to deliver a certain revelation which neither had been given before, nor is achievable through meditation, concentration, imagination or rationalization.[5] In the Shī'ī doctrinal system of al-Ṭūsī and al-Ḥillī, on the other hand, a prophet's chief function was to serve as a mediator (*wāsiṭah*) between God and man. He himself is "a man who communicates with God without mediation."[6] Revelation as transmitted by the prophets is given to offer men certitude in matters of belief, to assure them against their doubts, to compensate for the inadequacies of the mind which by its nature is given to incomprehensiveness and to forgetfulness, and to be the fundamental source of the individual's happiness and the guarantee of his future salvation, as well as the fountainhead of social justice and its chief discipline. On this point, there is evidently a rare agreement in principle, between the Shī'īs and Ibn Taymiyyah. Their disagreement, however, consists, on one hand, in al-Ḥillī's affirmation that revelation is predicated upon a constrained grace (*luṭf wājib*) on God's part, whereas for Ibn Taymiyyah, it is a free act of benevolence and mercy (*raḥmah*).[7] Another difference, which on the surface appears to be a semantic difference, is the relationship between *imamah* and *nubuwwah* in prophethood. Clearly Ibn Taymiyyah subscribes to the affirmation that the Prophet is not only an instrument of communication between God and man, he is also the chief spiritual guide of the community, and, indeed, the world. In addition to the Shī'ī assertion that Muḥammad was sent exclusively to a select group, al-Ḥillī defines the *imām* as a prophet, who without revelation, does not communicate directly with God. Ibn Taymiyyah, however, inverts this definition and proposes that the prophet is an *imām*, i.e., a leader of the community, who, moreover, possesses the privilege of serving as a mediator between God and man. The difference is capital: al-Ḥillī's argument seeks to assign to the *imām* a role like that of the Prophet. Ibn Taymiyyah shows that the Prophet, rightfully, has all the prerogatives of spiritual, political and social leadership in addition to his chief function as a medium of divine revelation. Here again, the ethical and social element in Ibn Taymiyyah's thought emerges to the forefront of his system of doctrine. He calls the Prophet the absolute(ly) (perfect) *imām* (*al-imām al-muṭlaq*) i.e., the ideal *imām*. He is *par excellence* the first among believers--both in matters of belief and religious practice, on one hand, and in the material and temporal affairs of the community. He is the model of human conduct and its ideal exemplar. He is the perfect "saint" (*waliyy*) in whom are concentrated all the virtues of probity (*amānah*) and of irreproachable aptitude (*qudrah*): the Prophet has brought to the world the revelation of perfect justice. He is the chief guide (*murshid*) of the individual's and the community's conscience, and is the highest judicial interpreter (*mujtahid*) in decisions of law (*fatāwā*). As the one receiving final revelation (*mahdī*) Muḥammad historically has set the example of the ideal community. As indicated by the Qur'ān and the tradition, the Prophet has made clear for the *ummah*, i.e., community, the divine will, in terms related specifically to its daily living, as he fulfilled his mission of being God's law giver (*wāḍi' al-nawāmīs*) in it.[8] On the Day of Judgment and Resurrection, the Prophet Muḥammad will serve as intercessor (*shafī'*) for the Muslims. He will ask God to show mercy toward those whose destiny is uncertain (*ahl al-mawqūf*), when the intercessions of Adam, Noah, Abraham, Moses and Jesus would all be in vain. Muḥammad will also ask God to hasten the reward of the believers (*ahl al-jannah*) as they await their turn to walk the straight and narrow path (*ṣirāṭ*) onto paradise. Lastly, Muḥammad's intercession will be made in behalf of those who deserve the punishment of fire and those who have already been tossed in hell. Muḥammad's intercession is valid only to the extent that the Prophet is capable of presenting an individual before God with at least a minimum of faith and virtue, which, after all, must remain the basis of potential justification. At any rate, since there can be no conflict between the will of God and the requests of the Prophet on the day of Final Judgment, such intercession can take place only with the permission of God. Beyond this definitive statement of intercession by the Qur'ān as reiterated by Ibn Taymiyyah, he rejects any other claims, such as will be seen with respect to the prevalent superstitious practices of visiting the graves of the dead and of saints to request their intercession on their behalf.

In Ibn Taymiyyah's system of doctrine, the condition of infallibility of the prophets is affirmed. Although this conception is not made explicit in the Qur'ān (indeed, it is indicated rather that Muḥammad is a man among men, and as such is exposed to human error), the assertion of the Prophet's infallibility is in consonance with the unqestionability of his mission and the finality and inerrance of his message.

This doctrine is adopted by Ibn Taymiyyah. Fakhr al-Dīn al-Rāzī, in his *Al-Muḥaṣṣal* and *Ma'ālim Uṣūl Al-Dīn* as well as in *Dalā'il Al-Nubuwwah*[9] had already made infallibility the precondition of the prophets' miraculous actions (*mu'jizāt*). Al-Ṭūsī and al-Ḥillī proceeded in al-Rāzī's footsteps. It is noteworthy, but not surprising, because Ibn Taymiyyah was known for his fairness and scholarly integrity, that for the most part his view coincides with those who, with respect to other doctrines, are considered his intellectual adversaries. Laoust indirectly explained this phenomenon; he said that those whom Ibn Taymiyyah had vigorously and repeatedly attacked "have, subsequently, had the greatest influence on the formation of his doctrine."[10] This influence, exerted positively, resulted in the adoption of a doctrinal construct most elaborately designed by al-Ṭūsī and subsequently adapted by al-Ḥillī. With only a few modifications, Ibn Taymiyyah, in his *Minhaj al-Sunnah*, has reproduced the formula which is founded in the Qur'ān itself, that a prophet, in order to be trusted with a message of truth, must be true to himself and free from sin (*ma'ṣiyah*), otherwise he cannot effectively impart the commandments and the prohibitions of the divine law. Similarly, if the prophet's example is to be worthy of following, or his traditions and sayings worthy of transmission (*naql*) he must demonstrate an ideal conduct, otherwise the incongruity of his words and his actions would mark an absurdity. Ibn Taymiyyah, intensely concerned with the socio-ethical dimension of doctrine finds in this segment of Shī'ī theology a worthy affirmation. In so concurring with them, far from wavering between their camp and his own Sunnī camp, and far from an approach of expedient utilization of their doctrine, Ibn Taymiyyah seems to demonstrate his own intellectual honesty, and his characteristic conciliatory method wherever he found it possible to do so. On the other hand, he could not sincerely share the extreme Ṣūfī view of infallibility, where Muḥammad seems to have been stripped entirely of his human contamination. Ibn Taymiyyah protested that to do so is to impoverish the Prophet. He charges the mystics with the same error the philosophers committed in dealing with the divine attributes, namely, النفي المفصّل والإثبات المُجْمَل

Thus Ibn Taymiyyah concludes with a positive description of the Prophet, attributing to him the most perfect of virtues (*jāmi' kamālāt al-faḍā'il*). It behooves men, therefore, to accord him their utter obedience inasmuch as their ultimate aim is to render unto God full service (*'ibādah*). For in God's service and the Prophet's obedience is the completion of religion which must manifest itself outwardly in the life of the individual within the community, as well as in the internal and external affairs of community life.

The person and the character of any prophet matter only because of his mission. Muḥammad's mission was to deliver God's message to his people. God had commanded him: "يا أيّها الرسول بلّغ ما أنزل اليك من ربك."[11] Clearly, that was his obligation, "وما على الرسول الاّ البلاغ المبين."[12]

The message communicated through Muḥammad is no less than "the eternal word of God," i.e., the Qur'ān itself.

II. *The Qur'ān*:

The question of the eternity of the Qur'ān had been the subject of controversy ever since the first known Muslim rationalists, al-Jahm Ibn Ṣafwān and his cohort al-Ja'd Ibn Dirham (ca. 125 A.H.), proposed that God's speech was not a divine attribute, but an incident taking place in time, and therefore His word was also an act of creation. The Mu'tazilah advanced the notion set forth by their intellectual benefactors to the point that by the early third century after the *hijrah*, during the rule of the Caliph al-Ma'mūn, the doctrine became state-imposed and enforced. Among traditionalist thinkers who resisted the state's coercion to acknowledge the createdness of the Qur'ān, Aḥmad Ibn Ḥanbal, the founder of the School of Tradition which was later named after him, was a champion. Ibn Taymiyyah, more than three centuries later, defended his School's, i.e., the Ḥanbalī, position that the Qur'ān was indeed the uncreated word of God. He asserted that Ibn Ḥanbal had only restated the position of pure, pristine Islam (*al-salaf al-ṣāliḥ*). That position precisely consisted in that the Qur'ān was the speech, i.e., word (*kalām*) of God, and as such, an eternal attribute. It was synonymous with His will, or commandment (*amr*), and with his knowledge (*'ilm*). God's *kalām*, *amr*, and *'ilm* were not created, the Ḥanbalī School asserted.

In elaborating his School's position, Ibn Taymiyyah explained, on the basis of the internal evidence of the Qur'ān, that the word of God itself is not created, though its communication, or revelation, was historic. Its "recitation" (*qirā'ah*) by the Prophet, a term implying its very pre-existence, and its subsequent hearing by men, are not identical with the Qur'ān itself. The utterance (*nutq*) of the words, and the voice of the reader are the created instruments whereby the eternal word is communicated. Likewise, the ink with which the words are written is not identical with the words themselves; as it is said in the Qur'ān, "قل لو كان البحر مدادًا لكلمات ربّي لنفد البحرُ قبل أن تنفدَ كلماتُ ربّي ، ولو جئنا بمثله مددا"[13]

Ibn Taymiyyah sought carefully to interpret the doctrine of the non-createdness of the Qur'ān, without declaring positively, at least in one of his major discourses on the subject,[14] that the Qur'ān in its form, i.e., the letters in their order and the sounds of syllables, is "eternal." He states that Ibn Ḥanbal did not go beyond saying that the Qur'ān was not created, and that non-createdness and eternity are not necessarily synonymous, since "not all that is related to the transcendent Being (ما يقوم بالذات العليّة) is co-eternal with Him." For example, he says, created beings are incidents, i.e., historic beings (*ḥawādith*), but the creativity of God is not incidental. He also says that to suppose that non-createdness is identically synonymous with eternity is only the product of the speculative reason of the philosophers. An example of Ibn Taymiyyah's defense is illustrated by this excerpt from his argument:

> The *salaf* agreed that the word of God was sent down (*munazzal*), not created...so it was deduced by some that they had meant it was itself eternal (*qadim al-'ayn*). Others said that it [the word] is uniform in meaning (*man'nā wāḥid*), i.e., [consistent] in its commandments, proscriptions and disclosures, and that if God expressed it in Arabic, it was the Qur'ān, in Hebrew, the Torah, or in Syriac, the Gospel. This is contradictory to revelation.[15]

Ibn Taymiyyah elucidated only little in this context on the diversity of revelation, and its language. He maintained the finality and the unalterable totality and universality of the revelation of the Qur'ān; he affirmed the uniformity of the word of God without diversification or fragmentation (*bilā tanawwu' aw taba''uḍ*), although he also defends the liberty of God, in accordance with His unity, in declaring His will and power in whatever form or sequence. Although this time using the term *qadīm*, i.e., ancient, eternal, with regard to God's Speech, not the Qur'ān, per se, Ibn Taymiyyah said,

> Therefore, [God's] speech is eternal, and gives expression to His will and power. So, if it is said that he calls (*yunādī*) and speaks with a voice, the eternity of a certain voice is not necessarily to be inferred from that. And if He had spoken by the Qur'ān, the Torah and the Gospel, it is not impossible (*lam yamtani'*) that he speaks with the letter "b" before the letter "s" (i.e., in the order intelligible by the recipients of revelation) ...[16]

From the extensive discourses of Ibn Taymiyyah's arguments, which, it must be remembered, are available to us in the form of collected works, it appears that he, in adhering to his Ḥanbalī tradition, attempted to raise the conception of the word of God to a higher level of appreciation than the controversy over the letters and the sounds of contemporary language. By insisting that the Qur'ān is not created, and by suggesting that he does not exactly claim eternity for it, he vindicates Ibn Ḥanbal, and avoids the possible challenges of both sides of the issue. At any rate, his own arguments, it appears, are not completely free from ambiguity, so that an interpretation of the Ḥanbalī position was later offered by the nineteenth-century Egyptian thinker and reformer, Muḥammad 'Abduh. 'Abduh thus attempting to clarify Ibn Taymiyyah's defense of the Ḥanbalī position, said, in part,

> There is no debate that the words expressing God's (attribute of) speech are themselves created, and chosen to deliver what He wished delivered to His creatures. Nor (is there any controversy) that they issue forth from His power, in their explicit and implicit meaning, in such a way that no other (words) could in any way be substituted for them.... To say that the Qur'ān as it is recited is eternal is the ultimate in heresey and absurdity which the Qur'ān itself condemns.... Nor does it dishonor the Qur'ān to acknowledge that God caused the Qur'ān to exist (*awjad*) without the intervention of man's participation in its existence....[17]

Throughout his arguments, however, Ibn Taymiyyah makes clear that there should be neither doubt nor controversy that the Qur'ān is indeed the word of God, sent down directly and in its every utterance upon the Prophet Muḥammad as an expression of His most holy and gracious will. It is complete, and amply clear (*mubīn*). And, should there be any want for clarification, resulting from the human imperfections of those who hear it and not from any deficiency in revelation or its instrument, the Prophet is given all authority and wisdom necessary and sufficient for furnishing such clarification (*bayān*).

That it was "sent down," Ibn Taymiyyah explains in a separate treatise,[18] clearly suggests, first, that it was sent from God,[19] second, that it was sent from heaven above,[20] i.e., from an unsearchable height; and third, that it is not created, since the verb is not used in connection with any of the created things.

That further clarification might become necessary, indicates the realism of the Qur'ān. It recognizes the insufficiency of the finite minds of the creatures to comprehend the full revelation of God.

Ibn Taymiyyah sets forth the principles which should underlie understanding the Qur'ān in his treatise *Introduction to the Fundamentals of Interpretation*. As reflected in that book, his hermeneutical theory largely conforms to the traditional theory of the *salaf*.

Asserting that the Prophet had made clear to his companions not only the meanings of the Qur'ān but its vocabulary also, and, subsequently, that among the Companions themselves there was virtually no disagreement with respect to the words or the teachings of the Qur'ān, Ibn Taymiyyah describes the differences in the interpretations of the *salaf* in terms of diversity (*tanawwu'*) but not contradiction (*taḍādd*), adding that to know the occasion, or occasions in the case of repetition, of a revelation is important in interpreting the Qur'ān, and that where there is a variation of interpretation, there is normally a variation of the cause of that particular revelation.[21] He attributes the wide variations of interpretation that followed in later Islam to affiliation with the various sects, to the unreliability of many incidents reporting the traditions of Muḥammad, and finally to the prevalent method of interpretation by opinion (*al-tafsīr bi al-ra'y*).

Ibn Taymiyyah criticizes this method harshly, for several reasons. First, it is not necessary, since the Prophet had indeed fulfilled his mission of interpreting the Qur'ān completely and in all the necessary detail. Any need for clarification should be referred to the Prophet's interpretive traditions. Second, it most often indicates the interpreter's prejudice to which the Qur'ān is subjected; and the Qur'ān is nobler and more honorable than to be bent to any human bias. Third, it often leads to interposing a double meaning in the Qur'ān. Finally, it presents a temptation to interpret the Qur'ān to those who either have not the tools or have inadequate tools.[22]

Ibn Taymiyyah's position on *al-tafsīr bi al-ra'y* does not meet with what might be expected from an otherwise giant of *ijtihād* as will be seen in relation to his legislative theory. Indeed, it almost appears incoherent that he should arrow such a criticism when he has also called for the reawakening of Qur'ānic scholarship as a primary source of social responsibility. Yet, our own criticism of his position should not itself be so harsh if we realize that it was produced in reaction to the rampant allegorism of his day.[23] Moreover, there are instances of his own interpretation by opinion,[24] which leads us to think that in the process of his own intellectual maturity, he may well have revised his view.

Finally, Ibn Taymiyyah offers his formula for interpreting the Qur'ān.[25] His first and foremost hermeneutical principle is the interpretation of scripture by scripture, utilizing the occasion(s) of revelation and the textual context. Then, the tradition, i.e., the sayings and illustrations, of the Prophet should be sought, but only on the basis of their reliably reported sources. The interpretations of the Companions rank next. And, finally, in the absence of these others the interpretations of those of later generations, and, here, only where they are concurrent and unanimous, for "the community cannot concur upon a deviation."

III. *The Response to Revelation:*

It is an act of mercy that God has revealed His word through the Prophet, in the Qur'ān. As it is written: "لقد منّ الله على المؤمنين اذ بعث فيهم رسولاً يتلو عليهم آياته"[26] and,

as it is also written: [27] " تنزيله رحمة من الرحمن الرحيم. "
It is, similarly, an act of grace that God has shown man in this revelation how he may respond to it.

For Ibn Taymiyyah, the sum of all religion is *īmān* and *islām*, i.e., conviction and submission through affirmative action. A third kind of response, namely *iḥsān*, i.e., doing good, benevolence, is added, actually as part of *islām*, for re-emphasis. In a separate, substantial work titled *Al-Īmān*, as well as in other, less formidable treatises and references, Ibn Taymiyyah sought to elucidate the meaning of faith. In it, he makes the distinction between *īmān* and *islām*. He adopts the Muḥammadan definition which states that "*īmān* is belief in God, His angels, His Scriptures, His prophets, the Last Day, and in *qadar*, both its good and its evil; *Islām* is the (public) testimony that there is no God but God, and that Muḥammad is the Apostle of God, and the fulfillment of prayer, the payment of alms, the fasting of Ramaḍān, and the pilgrimage if it is at all feasible."[28] Both *īmān* and *islām* are indispensable elements in the human religious response, for it is otherwise possible to be a Muslim, i.e., one who has yielded in *islām*, without being a believer, as it is possible to be a believer without being necessarily a Muslim.[29]

It is clear, however, that such definitions of *īmān* and *islām* are not mutually exclusive, for there are assertions throughout the Tradition that *īmān* must include both inward assent as well as the public manifestation of it in acts of obeisance to God and the Prophet. Thus *īmān* in the One God is defined in the *Ḥadīth* as the declaration of the creed *and* the practice of prayer, and charity. Ibn Taymiyyah notes that it is "known that this requirement of works cannot be made without the prior assumption that belief of heart is also required."

That *īmān* is the response of the inmost being of man is attested to by several *ḥadīths* from which Ibn Taymiyyah deduces that its resultant response is *islām*. He says, in effect, if the inner man (*al-qalb*) is made righteous by *īmān*, the outer man (*al-jasad*) is made Godly by doing God's will (*islām*), which itself is of *īmān*. The opposite, however, is not true, according to Ibn Taymiyyah; for "he who may achieve outward *islām* and at the same time may believe in his heart but does not

fulfill what inner faith requires may be subject to punishment."[30]
The reference here is to acts of righteousness (*a'māl al-birr*).
Personal piety, the individual's mode of conduct as well as
other-directed acts of charity are part of *īmān*, especially
when the term is used without reference to *islām*. Such actions
include, for example, love for, and obedience to, the Prophet
as well as social responsibility stemming from love for one's
fellows. *Īmān* also requires working for the right, and combatting evil. To believe in what God has revealed, to fulfill
the religious obligations of the faith, and to urge others to
do good and refrain from evil, is to fulfill the divine commandment (*al-waṣiyyah*), to reverence God: " لقد وصّينا الذين أوتوا الكتاب
[31] من قبلِكم وإيّاكم أن اتّقوا اللّـه . " The Prophet's exhortation
to a certain Mu'ādh, upon commissioning him to go to Yaman, was,
likewise, to "Reverence God wherever you may be; Return good
for evil, thus you will eliminate it; and treat men with nobler
character." The exhortation is clear: one's obligation is
twofold, to fear and love God, and to do good toward men, even
when one is met with evil. Indeed, Ibn Taymiyyah affirms with
a constant view toward the implications of revelation in the
social context, that to do good and to refrain from evil is a
tangible and concrete way of showing godliness. To be godly
is "to do all that God commanded out of a sense of obligation
and out of a willing desire (*ījaban*), and to refrain from what
He had prohibited precisely because He had proscribed them,
but also because of the resultant purity (*taḥrīman wa tanzīhan*).
In this is the requirement fulfilled, both toward God and men."[32]
To heed what God said above all else is to acknowledge His
absolute unity. Herein lies the all-inclusive concept of
'ibādah, or servitude, which for Ibn Taymiyyah is the utmost of
faith and surrender.

In his treatise *Al-'Ubūdiyyah*, Ibn Taymiyyah advances a
comprehensive view of man's response to the revelation of the
One God. In reiterating the call to servitude as issued by God
Himself, " يا أهلَ الكتاب تعالوا إلى كلمة اللّـه سواءٌ بيننا وبينكم ألّا نعبد
إلّا اللّـه ولا نُشرك به شيئا، ولا يتّخذ بعضاً أرباباً من دون اللّـه،،فإن تولّوا
[33] فقولوا اشهدوا بأنّا مسلمون ", he reaffirms that all men, good
and evil are God's servants (*'ibād*), because God Himself is the
Lord of all and is sovereign over all. The difference between

those who respond in faith and those who choose the way of *kufr*[34] is that the former acknowledge God and believe in Him as Lord.[35] The treatment of the doctrine of servitude by Ibn Taymiyyah reveals also his perception of the nature of man in that, if a man thinks himself higher than to serve God, he inevitably serves another. For every man possesses an urgent motivation (*humām*), i.e., will, and he whose motivating will does not tend ultimately toward God, but rather supposes himself higher than to worship Him, will necessarily be obsessed by another desired and loved object (*murād wa maḥbūb*) which enslaves him and debases him...be that wealth, fame, image or other gods such as the sun, the moon, the stars, idols, the graves of prophets or saints, the angels, the prophets, the saints, etc."[36]

In God's servitude there is freedom; there is freedom from any form of slavery whether it be conscious or unconscious, wanted or unwanted. "Man is in need of a means of subsistence (*rizq*), and will therefore seek it. If he seeks it from God, he becomes His servant, poor unto Him, and dependent upon Him. But if he depends on creatures he will become their captive (*asīr*). Freedom is the liberty of the heart; servitude is the servitude of the heart."[37] Likewise, in the realm of political affairs, those who seek power and elevation are enslaved to those who help them achieve them; and though they appear externally to be commanding the obedience of their people, they in fact heed them and are controlled by them: they endow them generously and pardon their offenses. Where this is the case, both those who rule and those that are ruled are, in fact, enslaved to one another, and both abandon their dutiful servitude to God.[38] Ethically, too, if servitude to God is placed in the highest priority, then mutual service is not only desirable but productive.[39]

In God's service, there is ultimate happiness and dignity; for in it there is the assurance of His aid. Thus servitude becomes the "ultimate cause" (*al-'illah al-ghā'iyyah*) as well as the "effective cause" (*al-'illah al-fā'ilah*) of man's action, as it is stated in the very first *sūrah*: "إيّاك نعبد وإيّاك نستعين".[40] Such totality of motivation, Ibn Taymiyyah suggests, is the effect as well as the implication of the Muslim credal affirmation in the unity of God, i.e., "لا إله إلّا الله"[41].

The unity of God, which compellingly demands that He singularly be the object of man's worship and service, rules out as contradictory certain prevalent conceptions and practices of Ṣufism, which conceptions and practices Ibn Taymiyyah opposed vigorously and criticized in works written specifically against them. These notions were the mediation of saints, the intercession of, and supplication to, the dead, and the enshrinement of, and the seeking of omens from, the dead, including visitation to the Prophet's grave.[42]

Ibn Taymiyyah begins his argument by acknowledging that God endows certain faithful and godly men with extraordinary gifts of power and sensitivity that they are able to perform miracles (*karāmāt*). Such powers may reside in their hearing, or in their vision that they could hear or see or know what others could not by their ordinary capacities or faculties. These miracles are usually the fortune of prophets, and in their case they are called *muʿjizāt* because they "defy" the challenges of opponents, thus proving the authenticity of the prophet's message. For other than prophets, however, "extraordinary actions (*khāriq*) according to Ibn Taymiyyah, may be wrought for a spiritual benefit if they are good and commendable, for a temporal benefit, or a certain grace, which God permits and for which He should receive due gratitude; or, they may be wrought as a punishment, if they are not acts that are otherwise proscribed. The working of miracles, however, does not attach additional virtue or credit to those who perform them, since they are only instruments used by God to bring about an action. For that reason, supplications should be addressed to God alone.

Moreover, it is possible that a man who is not necessarily obedient to God possesses such extraordinary abilities as to perform unusual acts. He also could well miss on occasion, Ibn Taymiyyah adds, as could a person exercising *ijtihād*. Therefore, such men, as well as those who may put their trust in them, ought rather to place their confidence in the Scripture and the Tradition.[43]

Ibn Taymiyyah thus attacks the *karāmāt* only as they are understood by the Ṣūfīs in the case of *karāmāt al-awliyāʾ*, but not such *karāmāt* as can be done by God. Hence all prayers to God alone.

Likewise, to seek the intercession of godly men before God is impermissible and unacceptable by God. God is the only source and giver of grace, mercy, pardon, and temporal aid. God, Ibn Taymiyyah states, forbade Muḥammad against interceding for forgiveness for those who associate any person or object with God, to wit: "ما كان للنبى وللذين آمنوا أن يستغفروا للمشركين ولو كانوا أولى قربى من بعد ما تبيّن لهم أنهم أصحاب الجحيم" [44] The Prophet is quoted as saying to his nearest kinsmen that he is no more favored by God than they.[45] The Prophet, however, receives answers to his intercessions for the believers, not as a mediator without whom requests would not be granted, but as one who had the privilege of communication with God. In the Last Day, he will also intercede, by the permission of God.[46] At any rate, the Prophet's intercession is valid only as he lived, and as he will live on the Day of Judgment.

In no event should appeal for help be sought (*istighāthah*) from anyone other than God,[47] whether they be men, living or dead, angels, prophets, or others. Similarly, victory against an enemy, rain for the fields, or guidance of the heart, is to be asked of God alone. Moses called unto God, "اللهم لك الحمد وإليك المشتكى وإليك المستعان وبك المستغاث وعليك التكلان ولا حول ولا قدرة إلا بك" [48]. Seeking from men aid that only God can give is likened to "a drowning man seeking another to rescue him," or "a prisoner seeking another to release him."[49]

The Ṣūfī practice of visiting the graves of the dead to summon their aid, thereby to gain God's favor, was considered by Ibn Taymiyyah particularly abhorrent. He reacted to it by reaffirming that the only allowable part that could be played by believers and pious men when they have died is the example of their godliness while they were living, which should be remembered, followed and emulated. To do otherwise is to associate other objects with God. Ibn Taymiyyah states emphaticallY;

> We ought not to expect anything from prophets or believers after their death, even if they were alive in their graves, or capable of praying on behalf of the living; or even if it were reported [that it is permissible], let no man seek the dead. It was not done by the earlier generations (*salaf*), for it would have been a pretext of (or a step away from) *dharī'ah* associationism, and

> of worshipping other than God. To ask the living to pray for one is a different matter, and would not precipitate association [with God].[50]

In his anti-Ṣūfī social order, Ibn Taymiyyah relates to this practice that of pledging material contributions of any kind to the graves of the dead, which he ruled is evil, and is deserving of the punishment of death since it indicates association and paganism. Not only would it be of no avail, as Ibn Taymiyyah sees it, but, thinking uniformly in terms of social value, he suggests the alternative of "spending [the pledged money or oil] on lighting the mosques and for the welfare of the poor of the community.[51]

Most controversial of all of Ibn Taymiyyah's related assertions, however, was that pertaining to the visitation to the grave of the Prophet Muḥammad, which cost our jurist severe harassment and ultimately his last imprisonment in 726 A.H., which lasted for five months until his death.

He acknowledged that to visit the graves is permissible in the *Sharī'ah* only for offering a prayer for the deceased if the latter were among the believers, for reminding oneself of the ephemeral nature of human life and for heeding the revelations regarding the world to come.[52] He forbade the visitation of the Prophet's grave, however, and that against the doctrines upheld by such prominent Muslims as al-Ghazālī and even Ibn Qudāmah. Ibn Taymiyyah's premises for this argument were his protest against the pagan practices of Ṣūfism, his insistence on the sole lordship of God and at the same time His approachability by every believer, and the admonitions of the Prophet himself against such a potential practice. The Prophet, on his death bed, reportedly said, "God cursed the Jews and the Christians because they turned their prophets' graves into shrines," and requested, against current custom, to be buried at home, in the chamber of 'Ā'ishah. Ibn Taymiyyah explains that the Prophet's request was aimed precisely against the possible building of a mosque or a shrine on the site of his burial. Until the eighth century, A.H., the burial site remained separately located from the mosque where the Prophet worshipped, and inaccessible to the public. Ibn Taymiyyah argues further that at prayer the earlier generations always faced to the

Qiblah in the east and not to the direction of Muḥammad's grave. The Prophet's own prayer, "O God, make not my grave an idol to be worshipped..." is the foundation, Ibn Taymiyyah contends, for the concurrence of many traditionalists against supplication at the Prophet's graveside, touching his tombstone, or the like. All such argumentation understandably conveys Ibn Taymiyyah's staunch defense of the doctrine of divine unity: thus, if visitation to the graves of godly men was prohibited as a caution against possible association, far more importantly visitation to the grave of "the Prophet of unity" need be eschewed.

Opponents of Ibn Taymiyyah protest that the very visitation to the burial site of the Prophet of unity is a most positive affirmation of divine singularity, for why else would the Prophet be revered in death? Contemporary opponents[53] argue that even till the present time the practice which has continued has not produced the associationism feared by Ibn Taymiyyah, for God "has forever safeguarded His unity; as Muḥammad himself declared, Satan has despaired of being worshipped on Arab soil."[54] They also argue that early Muslims had visited the grave of Muḥammad, prayed for him and sought his blessing.[55]

Ibn Taymiyyah had warned against touching or kissing the Prophet's grave and considered such act to be a violation against Muḥammad's implicit admonition against the turning of his grave into a shrine.[56] He also attacked his opponent's use of such *ḥadīths* they had used as unreliable and false.[57]

It is to be kept in mind that Ibn Taymiyyah's doctrinal system was framed, in large measure, in reaction against the cumulative, debilitating theories and practices of Ṣūfī theology and ethics. He aimed primarily at directing the life of the Muslim community (*ummah*), corporately, as well as its individual component parts, toward the service of God, out of love and submission, not out of fear or oppressive subordination.

He thus calls on Muslims to express their *īmān* in an attitude of love for God and the Prophet, as may be reflected in a life of personal piety and of mutual concern. Such love, stripped of all the impurities of mystic overtones, is active and strong. It is the most intense of human emotion, and when released, is most far-reaching. It disciplines the intellect, and stimulates the conscience; it inspires hope and instills assurance and peace. Its highest aim is striving (*al-jihād*) in the way of God and in the way of the Prophet, the sum of which striving is the fulfillment of God's commandment and the refraining from committing that which He had proscribed, in piety (*taqwā*) and in diligence (*ṣabr*). To have one without the other constitutes inadequate, incomplete religion, indeed, a kind of irreligion. To have the one, or the other, only when it is convenient, feasible or expedient is utter evil.

It is clear that Ibn Taymiyyah's choice of these virtues, i.e., piety and diligence, as well as his subsequent argument,[58] is aimed at the Ṣūfī "misconception that faith and disbelief, good and evil are alike."[59]

The life of *īmān* and *islām*, as characterized by service to God, must, therefore, comprise consistently both godliness and perseverance. Both *ṣabr* and *taqwā* require, and manifest themselves in, acts of mercy (*raḥmah*). Translated into the context of personal and community living, *raḥmah*, like *iḥsān*, is other-directed: aiding the poor, lifting the down-trodden, feeding the hungry, supporting the weak, and "working in concert"[60] for good, as a means of realizing the will of God, faithfully, upon the earth.[61]

CHAPTER V

THE FRAMEWORK OF HUMAN RESPONSE

The meaning of *īmān* and *islām*, and the value of the manifestations of human response in the profession of faith, prayer, fasting, charity, the pilgrimage and the holy warfare, would be elusive unless they are placed in their proper context. This context, namely a proper and an effective understanding of the ancient, thorny question of determinism/free will, provides the only possible link between revelation and ethical responsibility. And since, from the beginning, we have proposed that Ibn Taymiyyah's world view seeks a consummation in the realm of responsibility toward God and man, it is indispensable that we understand how he regarded the issue of determinism/free will. To understand Ibn Taymiyyah's response, however, we need to review the development of the issue, examining its origin briefly, then the setting against which Ibn Taymiyyah's view was expressed, i.e., the predominant positions of the major sects and of the traditional Schools, and finally his own answer.

I. *The Origins of the Problem of Determinism/Free Will:*

No one seems able to assert with certainty where the question began to be discussed formally, or who was the first person to identify it as an object of human concern or disciplined study. One scholar[1] suggests, though not in exactly these terms, that the question is as ancient as the creation of man himself. It began with his self-consciousness and with his consciousness of the order of creation, and has been present in all other questions pertaining to those levels of consciousness and the relationship between them. Then the question began to appear in one form or other in relation to the collective self-consciousness which manifests itself in the religions of the world since their known beginnings. Illustrations are given of the ancient Indians' spirit-god Karma, the Zoroastrian warring gods Ormazd (lord of good) and Ahriman (lord of evil), and the Greek Goddess Nemesis, who have irresistible controlling powers affecting the actions of men. Also, the same author notes the ancient Babylonian's attribution of the very lives and actions of individuals to the constellations of their respective stars. The Egyptians of the ancient world believed in a balance between a determinative power and the power of human free will, and established a religio-ethical construct wherein they assigned to heavenly courts the judgment of the merits and demerits of each individual.[2] Judaism, Christianity and Islam, too, have since their respective beginnings addressed themselves to the perennial dilemma of whether human actions are wrought completely independently, or according to an inescapable design from beyond the boundaries of their control; and is there a possible reconciliation between the two poles?

The questions of being, such as who am I, whence came I, whither go I, heightened by unchosen birth or death, but answered in part by purposefulness and productivity, have been confounding to man. Moreover, on the level of investigation of revealed religion, no easy or simple help is available. For our purpose, the Qur'ān gives several manifestations the possible interpretations of which, if not their *prima facie* texts, indicate contradiction.[3] Such apparent contradictions in the texts have been used by academicians, who are not always unbiased, to point to doctrinal inconsistency, or even to inauthenticity. One such instance is Goldziher's direct attribution of theological controversy to the conflicting texts of the Qur'ān.[4] Indeed, the fierce controversy had reached such proportions that a contemporary of Ibn Taymiyyah named Aḥmad Ibn al-Mukhtār al-Rāzī compiled a volume which he titled *Hujaj Al-Qur'ān* ("The Evidences of the Qur'ān") in which he listed the details of each argument and cited Qur'ānic verses to support it.[5] Ibn Taymiyyah reports, according to documentary sources, that the Prophet came upon some of his Companions who were debating determinism and free will. Some said, "Did not God say...?" Others, of the opposite view, said, "But did not God say...?" The Prophet's response was one of dismay at their use of the Scripture which was given not to reveal self-contradiction but coherence, and it was their obligation to heed its commandments and refrain from those things which it had prohibited.[6]

II. *The Development of the Problem:*

Implicitly, thus, the Prophet indicated that though there appear to be conflicting texts, there is a greater unity of revelation the wisdom of which is not readily or fully comprehended by men. This trust in the unity of Scripture, now mysterious as regards this dilemma, was the basis for some to go only so far with reason, i.e., as far as reason was in consonance with the revealed truth, but acquiesce in awe before that which they were not able to explain rationally. For them reason was simply not enough. These were orthodox Muslims, and came to be known, in a positive sense, as the "textualists" (*naṣṣiyyūn*) or "legationists" (*mufawwiḍūn*), a type of affirmative agnostics, because they acknowledged the supremacy of a divinely revealed text over the human rational power, but at the same time yielded, or deferred in understanding it rationally to the divine wisdom not yet realized in its revelation. Of course, some of those "adherents" to the text did not live up to the positive connotation of their label, according to Ibn Taymiyyah, but tended toward a kind of literalism that attempted to explain away the ambiguous and the contradictory texts, for which the prophet later proffered clarification, by saying that "the meanings of these texts were not explicated by the Prophet, or that the Prophet did not know their meanings; or that the Prophet knew the meanings but did not elucidate them..."[7] To those, Ibn Taymiyyah replied:

> ...How [can you say it], while the Prophet is the most knowledgeable of the truth among all men, the most capable of clarifying it, and the most heedful in following it? He was commissioned to relate it, and was given the Book so that he might show men what was revealed to them. Undoubtedly his preaching and teaching and interpretations are most thorough, and complete. How, in spite of this, [can you say] that he did not clarify the truth?[8]

Other textualists, however, adopted the view of relegating the matter of unexplained or inexplicable texts to God, and sought to conform to the requirements of the clearer texts of command or prohibition. An example is that of ʿUmar who, failing to understand the meaning of the word "أبّ" "fodder" in the Qurʾānic verse "وفاكهة وأبا" (LXXX. 31), reprimanded himself even for wondering what it had meant, and said, "'Umar, this is presumptuous. Why do you need to know what 'fodder' is? Seek what has been made clear of this Book and do it, and what you do not know revert unto its Lord." Although quite different in his approach, as will be seen, Ibn Taymiyyah rightly belonged to the textualists, since he was an uncompromising advocate of the supremacy of divine revelation, and since he possessed, in addition to a keen intellect which he applied to this problem, an unwavering personal piety as well.

The issue of determinism/free will generally divided the Muslims into at least two main camps, however, with the possibility of a third. Logically, some held to determinism (*qaḍā'* , *jabr*, and, sometimes, *qadar*);[9] others to human free will (*ikhtiyar*, *qudrah*, or, frequently *qadar*).[10] Others yet, uncertain of the validity of either extreme tried to assert a reconciled view, or at least a reasonable moderation combining the extremes.

The determinists are assumed to be the followers of Ja'd Ibn Dirham, and al-Jahm Ibn Ṣafwān,[11] and the volitionists the followers of Ma'bad al-Juhanī and Ghaylān al-Dimashqī.[12] These pioneers of both extreme camps, according to al-Shahrustānī, were contemporaries of some of the Companions of the Prophet, e.g., Ibn 'Amr, Ibn 'Abbās, Jābir, and Abū Hurayrah. Some[13] suppose that determinism was at least fortified by the Umawīs, beginning with Mu'āwiyah's rule, who did all they could to advance among the people the idea of his divine appointment over them, and subsequently attributed all their actions to divine determinism. In this light, the activities of Ma'bad and other volitionists were viewed as a reaction to Umawī oppression; and this view is supported by the fact that al-Hajjāj, an Umawī, murdered Ma'bad, and Hishām Ibn 'Abd al-Malik killed Ghaylān.[14] This view is discredited by evidence of the fact that the Umawīs had also murdered both al-Ja'd and al-Jahm, the acknowledged heralds of determinism.[15] The author of the latter theory suggests that this doctrinal controversy had little to do with the murders, but attributes them to an inherited temperament, characteristic of the Umawīs. The fact remains that division did not cease with the death of their protagonists, but continued to occupy the thoughts of Muslims in all generations, affecting their entire system of doctrine and influencing the style of social and individual life as well. One contemporary doctrinal commentator,[16] attributes the wide disparity to an ill-conceived methodology which tended to "forget that oftentimes an inquirer into doctrine inappropriately applies human considerations [here the reference is to reason] to divine matters, and that Islam came to purge doctrine from the fallacies sustained by the fiction of approximating the creature to the creator," in direct contrariety to the Qur'ān's admonition "فلا تضربوا لِلّٰهِ الأمثالَ" and, "ليس كمثله شيء إنّه السميعُ البصير."[17] "إنّ اللّٰه يعلم وأنتم لا تعلمون"[18]. The greatest sin, however, states 'Abduh,[19] is the subjection of the Qur'ān to the various interpretations by their adherents, rather than consulting the overall wisdom of the Scripture for the sake of the truth. Hence the chasm between reason and revelation, which Ibn Taymiyyah treated in a celebrated treatise called *Dar' Ta'āruḍ Al- 'Aql wa Al-Naql.*[20]

III. *The Views of the Theologians:*

A. *The Determinists:*

This school comprises the followers of Jahm after whom the determinists (*jabriyyah*) came to be known as the *Jahmiyyah*. Although al-Jahm is reputed to have followed al-Ja'd in issues of doctrine related to responsibilities, he was credited with the leadership of *jabriyyah* because the determinist view had so influenced his thought that he elaborated all the other doctrines of belief within a deterministic bias.

The basic motivation of the determinist doctrine is its defense against the suggestion that an incident may occur, or is caused by an act of other than God. If He is the Creator of all things and sovereign Lord over them, then nothing may be caused by a will other than His own. Indeed there is no other will than His. Ibn Jahm is quoted as saying,

> Man is not capable of anything, and may not be characterized by ability. On the contrary, he is determined (*majbūr*) in all his actions, without power, will or choice. It is God who creates actions through him, in the same manner that He creates through the inanimate world. Actions are attributed to him [man] allegorically (*majāzan*) as they are in the case of inanimate objects; as it may be said, "the tree bore

> fruit," "the water ran"..."the sun rose or set"..."it rained"...Likewise, reward and punishment are determined (*jabr*) as actions are determined.... And since determination is [thus] proven, so is the commandment [or capacity] (*taklīf*).[21]

In explaining the determinists' doctrine, Ibn Ḥazm said, "They attempted to validate their argument by suggesting that 'since God is the only Creator the like of whom does not exist among His creatures, it necessarily follows that there is no other creator.' They also said, 'To attribute an act to man is only analogous to saying: a man died, when in fact God caused him to die: or saying: the building rose, when in fact God erected it.'"[22] This is not to say that human capability is totally denied by the Jahmis, suggests one author, but it simply means that the existence of human capability is as effective as its inexistence.[23] Their theory is thus reported by al-Ash'arī: "No action takes place in reality except it be by God, for He alone is Creator. Actions are attributed to men as the movement of the stars in their courses is attributed to them.... The difference is that God created in man the capacity to act; the will and the choice are also created, as a man's height and complexion are also created."[24] If a man, therefore, wills and chooses an action, his choice and his will are both determined by God.

The *Jabriyyah* base their argument on Qur'ānic as well as on rational evidence. They cite several verses that clearly appear to support their theory;[25] and, on the basis of the verses related to the singular, creative power of God, say, "if we suppose that man is the author of his action, it follows that there exist some such actions that are not wrought after the divine will and choice. From that it follows that there is another creator besides God. But Muslims of all times and of all places agree that there is no creator other than He whose alone is the power. Unless man is the instrument of such actions, he would still have to be determined to do them."[26] There is no difference with Jabriyyah, therefore, between what happens to man and what occurs through, or by, him; for each is created and enacted by God, and man serves only as a platform for divine action.

B. *The Volitionists:*

In the opposite camp stood a class of theologians who asserted the freedom of man to choose his course of action, on the basis of his ability both to judge and to do. Man is singled out in all creation with the power to reason and to put into effect a moral decision. Called *al-Qadariyyah* because they attach to man the "capability" of decision-making and of action, the extremists among them argue according to al-Ashʿarī that... God knows all things before they occur, except the actions of men, which he knows when they occur."[27] It was Ghaylān of Damascus who championed the *Qadariyyah* movement especially after the assassination of Maʿbad in 80 A.H./681 A.D. This Ghaylān is identified by al-Shahrustānī as a disciple of a Christian convert.[28] Abū Zahrah, on that basis, suggests that the doctrine of free will was "introduced to Islam from without, and became popular in an environment where the presence of a foreign element was felt."[29] And though the context of a similar suggestion by Goldziher and Horton was somewhat different, this conclusion appears to be the same.[30] ʿAbduh suggests, however, that if it is true that the doctrine was in any way affected by non-Muslim influence, the effect would have to be on its formulation, but not on its formation, since it is necessarily co-existent with the determinist view.[31]

In any event, the doctrinal mainstream of the *Qadariyyah* who later included the Muʿtazilah consisted in their assertion that man is the author of his actions, both good and evil, and deserves for them his due reward or punishment; and that God transcends the attribution of evil, oppression or any act of unbelief or transgression, for if He were the creator of oppression He would be an oppressor, indeed as He is just, being the Creator of justice."[32] This view is based also on Qur'ānic and rational evidence. From the verses cited by the volitionists,[33] they conclude that "man is capable of sensing, knowing, and subsequently differentiating between, freedom and coercion; that the moral law and its subsequent reward or punishment hinge on free will and capability; and that if the actions of men were wrought by the power of God, they would necessarily be attributed to Him, and He in turn would necessarily be judged by them." Then one must ask, "how is this to be understood in the presence of a clearly defined moral law and an attendant promise of reward or punishment?[34] For their latitudinarianism, the Qadarīs were called "the *Majūs* (i.e., Zoroastrians) of the *ummah*," meaning doctrinal outcasts, who made man the god of evil.

C. *An Attempt at an Intermediary Position:*

As each side of the controversy fiercely opposed the other, the logical outcome was that each group became even more fervent in its belief. The wide rift between the two camps had caused the school of the textual legationists to flourish further. Their conception that God is sovereign Lord over all creation, omnipotent and supreme over all his work, and at the same time that man is given the freedom to choose and to act, upon which choice and action he is to be rewarded or punished, tended to attract not only those who acknowledged no competence for theological argumentation, but also who could not honestly and fully accept the position of either extreme. Thus, while the conflict intensified between the extremists it was inevitable that some would reflect intellectually on the problem with less excitability and more perspicacy. One such vigilant was Abū al-Ḥasan al-Ash'arī al-Ḥanbalī who had been a Mu'tazilī but became so disenchanted with their libertine views that, after a debate with his master al-Jubba'ī, he appeared in the mosque and announced: "O people,...I used to proclaim that the Qur'ān was created, and that I am the author of my evil actions; but now I repent and desist. I recant. I will expose and resist the Mu'tazilah." Upon his reappearance, al-Ash'arī wrote his celebrated treatise Al-Ibānah[35] in which he attacked both the extremists and the Mu'tazilah calling the latter the Zoroastrians of Islam. In the book he stated that he would not favor one group over the other but would reject both, and asserted that his doctrine is founded on an unwavering adherence to the Qur'ān and the Sunnah, the reports of the Companions and the views of the *imāms* of *ḥadīth*, i.e., the scientists of the Tradition, identifying himself with Ibn Ḥanbal and avoiding those who disagree with him.[36]

It appears from al-Ash'arī's statement that, upon carefully weighing all the evidences of the opposing view, which he found "in equal balance" (*takāfa'a*), he had arrived at no new result and gave assent to the position of the textualists but without conspicuous emphasis on acquiescence or "legation" (*tafwīḍ*), and without apparently any reference to the theory of "acquisition" (*kasb*) as we shall see. His distinction is inherent in an articulation which these textualists were obviously ready to adopt; and, thus, learning from them he became their leader. In elaboration, the outline of his doctrine contained the affirmation that God is the sole sovereign Lord, that He is the author and the capacitor of human action,[37] that man is incapable of creation [of his own actions] since he himself is created,[38] that God has guided the believers into His obedience, but has led the unbelievers astray, yet if He had mercy on them they would become righteous,[39] etc. He concludes his creed with the statement: "We believe in God's decree, its good and its evil, its bitter and its sweet; and acknowledge that whatever is ordained to befall us shall not miss us, and what passes by us cannot possibly have been supposed to befall us."[40]

From this review of al-Ash'arī's theological statements, no reference is made to the theory of acquisition (*kasb*), ordinarily attributed to him, i.e., the notion that man acquires an action willed and wrought by God as his own will corresponds to and coincides with the divine will and action. Although absent from his writings, the idea of acquisition is attributed to him by some interpreters, such as Ibn 'Asākir who said that al-Ash'arī's conception perceives both the human capacity for action and the actual occurrence of an action are both permitted by God the Creator. Such was also the position of al-Juwaynī, who added, for clarification, that the will, the capacity and the occurrence of human action constitute the realization of the divine Creation and will.[41] And it appears that al-Juwaynī's elucidation was, in some measure, helpful for Ibn Taymiyyah's formulation. There were others, however, such as Fakhr al-Dīn Rāzī and Abū Bakr al-Baqillānī who, attempting to interpret the "acquisition of al-Ash'arī," projected their own ideas, the former suggesting that acquisition is man's carrying out the evil possibility in the divine will, whereas the occurrence of the good is the direct action of God,[42] and the latter, in essence, asserting that divine capability, will and action would constitute the cause, and the human will and action constitute its [inevitable] effect.[43] Al-Shahrustānī offers the following interpretation of the Ash'arī theory of *kasb*, which interpretation, if it is proven valid,"would also coincide with al-Maturīdī's perception of acquisition":

> [What al-Ash'ari meant is that] capability in itself has no effect on actions....Yet God established His law in such a way that an action occurs in consequence of generative ability or in subsequence of it, if man wills it and applies himself to it. This is called acquisition: the creative originality is God's, the execution man's, acquired by the latter and conditioned by his ability.[44]

It seems that, whatever its origin or interpretation, the Ash'arī device of *kasb* was intended and defended in order to place the divine Creator above any possibility of association, although it has been attacked, rather appealingly, on this very count.[45]

Yet it should be noted that both the determinists' and the volitionists' intentions and arguments, too, were aimed at the same result, i.e., that God remain above any suggestion of association.

It is likely, as one scholar suggests,[46] that the real reason behind the Ash'arites' and Maturidites' origination and defense of the concept of acquisition lies in their expostulation with the determinists, and their consequent rejection of their view, and at the same time in their inability to accept completely the views of the rationalists especially in the presence of contrary Qur'ānic evidence. Yet they desired confrontation with neither of the extremes. Hence their assertion with the determinists that God is the Creator of man and his actions, yet their apparent departure by adding that the latter acquired those actions. And, within the Ash'arī-Māturīdī camp, the former attached acquisition to action without genuine consequence of the human role in that action, while the latter chose to attach acquisition to action when the human will asserted itself and directed the course of an acquired action. Both, however, sought an intermediary position between the extremes of determinism and volitionism (*manzilah bayn al-manzilatayn*).

D. *Ibn Taymiyyah's Interpretation:*

Against this background of conflicting ideas, and against the social conditions of the *Ṣūfīs'* total resignation to determinism, on one hand, and extreme rationalist secularism which defied man, his power and will, on the other, Ibn Taymiyyah in the manner of the four traditional schools severely criticized the "emptiness of the philosophers," but with unique ability utilized their own terminology to refute them. Likewise, he vehemently attacked the determinists to whom he attributed the social evils of his age. He thus offered a combination of unquestioned piety and unrivaled intellectual persuasiveness with regard to the question of human responsibility.

His method, therefore, combined the use of both text and reason for his argument. The thesis of his book *Dar' Ta'āruḍ al-'Aql wa al Naql*, is summed up in these words: "Any evidence established on the basis of the exposition of the intent of the Prophet which may be in contradiction to the [definitive] evidence of reason, is false. Such evidence would instead be insulting to the Prophet, and to those who look to his words for evidence."[47] In the same vein, he states,

> ...But to address the rhetoricists (*aṣḥāb al-iṣṭilāḥ*) in their own *terminum technicum* and in their own idiom is not undesirable, when it is necessary, and when the terms are used in their proper meanings....Therefore, when the terms, verified by the Scripture and the Tradition, are utilized with those who understand them for distinguishing between their proper and improper usages, the benefit is significant....To do so requires knowledge of the concepts [rhetoric] (*ma'ānī*) of the Scripture and the Tradition, knowledge of the terms of those concepts, and then the careful comparison of the uses of those terms by the texts, and by the theologians....[48]

From this methodological note, we cannot help but surmise and be impressed by the implicit suggestion that the texts of the Qur'ān and the Sunnah though unclear, at certain points, to the orators, i.e., the theologians, of the different camps are consistent and coherent. Their improper applications and interpretations, however, are the culprit in the resulting contradictions and conflicts. Ibn Taymiyyah then rises to answer "those who systematically set out to falsify the Prophet and to promote a contraposition between the rationally sound and the authenticated texts, and in the process built up a large following..."[49] He clearly and amply reveals that "the premises [or principles] of the theologians [of the divided camps] are not the principles of religion."[50] He proceeds to assert that rational evidence may not be considered equiponderous with revealed evidence; rather it may only be part of it, since revealed evidence may mean that it is accessible to reason, but is nevertheless indicated by a text. Whether an evidence becomes available through rational investigation or not, but is revealed through a text, it is authentic and valid. Yet, on the basis of the principle of non-contradiction, no valid and conclusive (*qaṭʿiyy*) rational evidence may be found in contravention of the authentic texts.[51] It is only when a rational evidence is speculative (*ẓannī*) that the possibility of textual contradiction exists. In the case of speculative evidence, it is futile to try to establish a veritable doctrine, because "speculation does not promote certitude."[52]

As for the content of Ibn Taymiyyah's view of human responsibility, it should be noted that his thought had apparently been influenced by that of ʿAbd al-Mālik al-Juwaynī (419-478 A.H./ 1020-1078 A.D.) and that of Abū al-Walīd Ibn Rushd (520-595 A.H./ 1120-1195 A.D.). Al-Juwaynī, in his *al-ʿAqīdah al-Niẓāmiyyah*,[53] departed from his otherwise Ashʿarī theology in stating that the affirmation of a human capability which has no effective power is no less objectionable than the negation of human capability altogether. Therefore, it is necessary to attribute man's action to his capacity not in the sense of creation or origination--as if from nothing--but in terms of its contingency upon another cause. Attributing capacity to a prior cause is analogous to attributing human action to human capacity. Thus a chain of regressive causation is established that reaches back to the Prime Mover, i.e., the First Cause, the Creator, who is absolutely independent. Interpreting his theory into terms of moral responsibility, al-Juwaynī adds that human capacity is created and is itself effective. Human action is man's responsibility and may be attributed to the Creator only in relation to the chain of causality in which it must be understood that the capacity which produced it had itself been created. This capacity is "the property of the Creator," i.e., is attached to man as a trust and the freedom to act upon it is given to him, with God's foreknowledge of human actions. Man is responsible for the use of his capacity.[54] Al-Juwaynī's view for the most part resembles the Muʿtazilī position, and is distinguished from it by his attribution of the "createdness" of human capacity to God.

Ibn Rushd, whose thought in this issue also influenced Ibn Taymiyyah's significantly, echoes the theory of al-Juwaynī with the added clarification that the human will and capacity depends on the dictates of natural law which is in perfect harmony with moral law.[55]

Now Ibn Taymiyyah's response to the question of human responsibility consisted first in his strong rejection of determinism as being "worse than the unbelief of the Christians and Jews"; for those do believe at least in a moral law (*amr* and *nahy*), and in reward and punishment even though they distorted and replaced [the truth], and chose to believe certain parts of it and to reject others." If these are called the unbelievers for their having believed only in part "how much more unbelieving are those who rejected all?"[56] Ibn Taymiyyah then proceeds with six rational and textual arguments which hinge on the ethical implications of the issue and which are directed primarily against the *Ṣūfīs* and the *Jahmīs*.[57]

a) If man is predetermined, and his actions are foreordained, then this must be a universal human condition, under which it would be totally unjust to penalize robbers, murderers, and the like. Under this same condition, no man should have the right to be angered by an aggressor, or should complain if his rights are disregarded. The net result would be the sure and speedy destruction of the world.

b) To believe in predetermination implies that the devil (*iblīs*), the people of Noah who had mocked his preaching, the Pharoah of Egypt, whom God has punished with eternal damnation ought to be vindicated.

c) To accept determinism is to eliminate the distinction between belief and disbelief, between good and evil, between light and darkness. The Qurʾān, on the contrary, says, "وما يستوى الأعمى والبصير ولا الظلمات ولا النور ، ولا الظل ولا الحرور ، وما يستوى الأحياء ولا الأموات"[58]

and says, "أم نجعل الذين آمنوا وعملوا الصالحات كالمفسدين فى الأرض. . ."[59] and, "أم حسب الذين اجترحوا السيّئات أن نجعلهم كالذين آمنوا وعملوا الصالحات سواء مَحْياهم ومماتهم . ساءَ ما يحكمون"[60]. It is true that the destiny of all of these had been foreknown by God, but His foreknowledge is not an acceptable excuse for those who do not obey His commandments.

d) Therefore, it is our duty to believe in the omnipotence of God, but not excuse ourselves and our actions by it, even as it may not serve as an excuse for the devil and the transgressors of the law. Determinism is an impediment to engaging in endeavoring in the way of God, and to doing good and refraining from evil.

e) The Prophet, when asked about the issue, replied "There is not one of you but that has been assigned a seat in hell or one in heaven"; but queried further on whether it would be of any avail to work, or it would be just as well that work be set aside in favor of what had been written, he said: "But nay! You must work, for every man is a facilitator (*muyassir*) of what had been apportioned for him."

f) God has appointed the events and the destinies of men as He has also foreknown them (it is important here *not* to base one divine act upon another, since that would imply a progression in the divine Being, based on a time sequence, which is far from Ibn Taymiyyah's thought). In this respect, God has foreknown and foreordained, for example, that a certain man believe and do good and thus enter heaven; or that another reject faith, or transgress God's commandment and thus be eternally punished. Such action is the effect of a man's choice, even though it already is known to God what his action and reward would be. This is likened to a man's choice to plant a certain seed and reap a certain harvest as a consequence, even though it had been foreknown to God what he would plant and what he would reap. Likewise, a man for whom it is foreordained to have a son, must choose first to unite with a woman, even though it had been foreknown to God that he would marry and beget a son. Nor can a man depend on being predetermined to have a son, and thus choose not to unite with a woman; because the effect is contingent upon the cause, and the cause in this case, is a man's free choice.

To transgress God's commandments earns man severe punishment in the same manner that obedience earns him great reward--but both are within the framework of God's natural and moral laws. "What man chooses not to do is necessarily not predetermined by God for it could not be determined but not achieved. Therefore man's capacity and will are both created by God who in His omnipotence is independent and absolute (*mustaqill*), but man's capacity depends on God's will."[61] "The actions of men, therefore, are in potentiality created by God, and in reality accomplished by men. The distinction is thus made between the act of creation and that which is created, on the one hand, and, the actor and the actions, on the other."[62]

In response to the Mu'tazilīs, he justly acknowledges belief in man's independent ability to choose between good and evil, and to recognize reward and punishment as their respective consequences; but he also exposes the error in their estimation of the omnipotent divine decree. He attacks their supposition that to affirm a supreme will (*mashī'ah 'āmmah*) and an all-inclusive power (*qudrah shāmilah*), and a comprehensive creation (*khalqan mutanāwilan kulla shay'*), would be affrontive to the justice and the wisdom of God."[63] To that supposition, he replies,

> The conception of the will of God is twofold: the law-giving, commanding will (*irādat amr wa tashrī'*), and the will to decree and determine (*irādat qaḍā'wa taqdīr*). The former is concerned with obedience, not transgression, whether they occur or not.[64] The latter includes all beings and all incidents....The former is indicative of God's purpose, as well as His love and mercy, [and the latter His] power.[65]

He then adds that "only he who looks upon [human] actions with these two eyes may see and have insight. To look upon them in one light only is to view them with an impaired vision." Yet, on the whole, he is closer to the view of volitionists in that he insists on the freedom of human will, without attributing to man the power to create--as if from nothing. It is significant, however, that he arrives at his conclusions, not purely from the rational point of entry, but by both textual revelation[66] and reason together. As for those who attempted to reach a sound solution through the science of theology alone,

one recalls al-Juwaynī's personal statement, "...I have now learned the word of truth: profess the miraculous religion [i.e., one that defies categorical argumentation]....Therefore unless I am found by the mercy of truth to be professing this religion when I die....Woe is Ibn al-Juwaynī."[67] Ibn Taymiyyah reflects in a similar way on the fate of the great Ṣūfī-Mu'tazilī philosopher al-Ghazālī, saying, "...in spite of his [al-Ghazālī's] excessive intelligence and piety, and in spite of his thorough knowledge of theology and philosophy he reaches, in this matter, a complete halt, and resigns himself in the end to the manner of illumination (*kashf*). He who has any intelligence or cleverness knows that that way will not lead to the desired goal."[68]

The Ash'arīs according to Ibn Taymiyyah rank on the same level as the determinists. He attacks their theory of a human will that is ineffective, for such a will, in effect, is not free and is as good as inexistent. Furthermore, he criticizes their indistinction of the double-aspect of the divine will, namely, the active or positive, desiring will, and the passive, or negative, permissive will (*maḥabbah* vs. *riḍa*).[69] He corrects their erroneous interpretation of the verse[70] " والله خلقكم وما تعملون " which they had lifted out of context and rendered it as "God created you and whatever you do," rather than the meaning implicit in the context of the divine prohibition of worshipping created idols in which case the verse would mean "God created you and what you make."[71]

As for the notion of acquisition," Ibn Taymiyyah declares it among the "most fantastic of human distortions!" He categorically rejects the idea that man's actions are wrought only to coincide with the divine action, as foreign to the Scripture and the *Sunnah*.[72]

In his arguments, Ibn Taymiyyah's clarity renders him inescapably convincing. He expresses a view that is at once lucid and profound--and in harmony with both reason and revelation, just as he had intended. He said,

> Man is, in actuality, the author [of his actions]; his ability (*qudrah*) and his capacity (*istiṭā'ah*) are real. Natural law is also an undeniable reality. Reason is God-given, for by it we discern the winds that cause the clouds,

> the clouds that produce rain, the rains that cause the plants to grow. They [the *Salaf*, himself adopting their view] do not deny the effects of natural forces, but acknowledge them both in word (*lafẓ*) and in meaning (*maʿnā*), and acknowledge that these are the effects of the causes and the forces....The human will is such an effective force, created by God, and bestowed upon man to fulfill the divine will.[73]

Thus Ibn Taymiyyah not only exposes the fallacies and the confusions of the various camps and their subdivisions but also points the way to a unity of purpose inherent in the order of creation, a unity of meaning in the divine commandments, a unity of perfection in the human choice to abide by them, and a perfect harmony between the natural and the moral laws rooted in the unity of God their author, and potentially manifest through their ethical realization by the people whom He graced with His revelation. Herein consists the ground of morality for the Muslim individual and society.

PART THREE: THE SOCIAL ETHIC OF IBN TAYMIYYAH

CHAPTER VI

IBN TAYMIYYAH'S JURISPRUDENCE

I. *His Legal Theory:*

We have seen, in the preceding chapters, that Ibn Taymiyyah's conceptions of the Muslim Community, its State and its economic affairs, are connected through their relation to Islamic Law, which is founded on the Qur'ān and the Tradition. It is fitting now to focus our attention on Ibn Taymiyyah's jurisprudence, the study of which provides us not only with an insight into the style of his career as a jurist, but also with a sense of the totality of his ethical system. For this reason, we find it necessary to examine in greater detail than we could in the preceding chapters, his legal methodology and discuss a certain selection of legal issues that bear his distinctive mark.

A. *Ibn Taymiyyah and the Schools of Jurisprudence:*

We should note, at the outset, that long before the time of Ibn Taymiyyah in the seventh and eighth centuries after the *Hijrah*, the body of Islamic Law according to the four major schools of Abū Ḥanīfah, Mālik, Al-Shāfi'ī, and Ibn Ḥanbal, and according to the other schools of the Shī'ah, Ithnā 'Asharīs, the 'Ibādīs, the Ẓāhirīs, etc., had been collected and written down. Moreover, by his time, they had been so interpreted and reinterpreted, and expanded by the numerous jurists and disciples of each of the various schools that there was hardly a contemporary legal issue that had not been tackled by one school or another. This itself may be the major reason why creative interpretation (*ijtihād*)[1] had become so stagnant by Ibn Taymiyyah's time that there was an instant readiness on the part of the '*ulamā*' to attack him for his interpretive efforts. Be that as it may, the fact remains that large systems of law had been in existence, and were available to anyone interested and equipped to study them.

Such was Ibn Taymiyyah; and his interest and keen capability rendered him most knowledgeable in each system as well as in the dynamic relations between them. He had also become thoroughly steeped in their sources, so that he could achieve the intellectual independence necessary for enlightened selection between the alternatives in question and in some instances, for rising to the level of relating his selection directly to the sources of Islamic Law.

It was in the study of law (*fiqh*) that Ibn Taymiyyah first achieved his intellectual maturity and independence, for as has been seen, this was the profession of his father and grandfather before him. And it was to Islamic law that his intellectual consciousness was first awakened. Born into Ḥanbalism, he naturally studied it first; at length, the responsibility of completing *Muswaddat Al-Uṣūl*, a work on the Ḥanbalī School begun by his grandfather and continued by his father, fell upon him. Yet he simultaneously studied other schools, and became well-versed in comparative Islamic Law, as is evident in his frequent references to the various opinions of the four major jurists. That he studied other developments of *fiqh*, such as those of the Shī'ah, is evident in his detailed refutation of Al-Ḥillī's *Minhāj Al-Karāmah*, as has been seen in the discussion of his political theory.

Besides the motivation of intellectual curiosity which impelled him to study the four schools of law, Ibn Taymiyyah in so doing reflects a sense of religious obligation and an unquestionable appreciation for them. His monograph titled *Raf' Al-Mulām 'An Al-A'immah Al-A'lām* ("In Defense of the Four Imāms"), epitomizes his devotion to them for the unequalled leadership they had given to the Muslims of all generations after them. In his introduction, he wrote:

> ...It is incumbent upon Muslims after showing obeissance to God and his Apostle, to show obeissance (*muwālāh*) to the faithful.... especially to the doctors (*'ulamā'*) who are heirs of the prophets, and whom God gave the status of the stars for guidance in the darkness of land and sea. Muslims are unanimous on their enlightenment and knowledge. For while the teachers of other nations before the advent of Muḥammad were their most iniquitous, the Muslim *'ulamā* are their righteous choice. They are the successors of the Prophet, the resuccitators of what may have been forgotten from his *Sunnah*; and by them the Book is upheld....[2]

He puts forward the thesis that the four *imāms* are in unanimous and sure accord regarding the obligation to follow the Prophet, and that none of them had intentionally offered a deviant opinion. However, in the remainder of his book, Ibn Taymiyyah offers three explanations for any divergence from an authentic tradition (*ḥadīth ṣaḥīḥ*) of Muḥammad. These explanations (*aʿdhār*) are: lack of knowledge of the specific *ḥadīth*, or possibly doubting that the Prophet had said it; his belief that it does not pertain to the issue in question; and, his belief that it had been abrogated.[3] Such reasons, effectively detailed and illustrated from the experiences of the Companions and *Salaf*, by Ibn Taymiyyah, point to the fallibility of the chief jurists of Islam, but do not in any way reduce their inestimable worth for all Muslims. Rather, they are applauded for their initiative and their scholarly enterprise. For to err in *ijtihād*, in spite of one's sincerity and capability, is not unpardonable. If a qualified *mujtahid* ("one who assumes the task of creative interpretation") achieves an opposite opinion, he deserves a double reward: a reward for assuming the task, and a reward for making the mark; if he errs, Ibn Taymiyyah says, he still is entitled to a reward for his initiative and effort. Were a *mujtahid* to be condemned for error he asks rhetorically, who will want to set out to do *ijtihād*? Ibn Taymiyyah stipulates, however, that when divergences must exist they be confined to the applications (*furūʿ*) of texts, and not in the fundamental doctrines (*ʿaqāʾid*). Where the four scholars appeared to hold different doctrinal views, Ibn Taymiyyah explained that such "differences were differences of detail (*ikhtilāfāt juzʾiyyah*), not of essence in doctrine. He adds, the differences are nearly all semantic (*lafẓiyyah*)."[4]

B. *Ibn Taymiyyah's View of Ijtihād:* Ibn Taymiyyah's tolerance of the very differences of the major Islamic legists itself reveals his own attitude toward the sectarianism of his day. More importantly, it discloses a vigorous view of interpretation (*ijtihād*) itself.

In spite of the inclement conservatism that had stifled *ijtihād* in the time of Ibn Taymiyyah, some of which is due perhaps to unwavering partisan loyalty, he was not hindered from following his conviction that the signs of the age were now calling not so much for original systems of law, but for the Scripture and Tradition to throw their light on the existing *fiqh*. For this he saw no urgency for radical *ijtihād*; rather it was necessary to synthesize his own understanding of the Qur'ān and *Sunnah* in light of the work of the legists, especially Ibn Ḥanbal, his mentor, whom he considered the most comprehensive in scope, and the closest among them to the sources of law.

According to the five level scale of *ijtihād* recognized by a number of jurists,[5] Ibn Taymiyyah would fall clearly within the highest level. Although he certainly qualifies as an interpreter of the first degree, i.e., as exercising absolute *ijtihād*, yet he never claimed that honor for himself. For that reason, and for his repeated association of his *ijtihād* to that of Ibn Ḥanbal, he is considered a second-level *mujtahid*, i.e., he practiced "associated," or affiliated (*muntasib*) *ijtihād*. Briefly, the five categories of the scale are:

(1) Independent (Absolute) *Ijtihād*: The Practitioner of this first type is not affiliated with any of the schools of *fiqh*. He is not bound by the principles (*uṣūl*) of another legist (*imām*), and may reach conclusions which are at major or minor variance with those of others. Ibn al-Ṣalaḥ, a cataloguer of *ijtihād*,[6] claimed that this definition of independent *ijtihād* must remain strict, and claimed consequently that no more absolute *ijtihād* is possible, since the doctors had exhausted all the principles (*uṣūl*) of *fiqh*, and had dealt with an abundance of applications (*furū'*).

(2) Associated (Affiliated) *Ijtihād*: This level is in every respect similar to absolute *ijtihād*, except that it strictly follows one of the *imāms* in its methodology. This may be due to the *mujtahid*'s nurture in a particular school; but it may equally be the scholar's independent conclusion that a certain school most nearly matches his own studied opinions. Abū Zahrah indicates that numerous interpreters of Ibn Ḥanbal, Mālik and Shāfi'ī's contemporary disciples belong to this category. Others were claimed as *mujtahidūn* of Ḥanafī affiliation but have been deemed independent, since they departed noticeably from the method and applications of Abū Ḥanīfah.[7] According to Abū Zahrah, this category of *ijtihād* is to be credited with the expansion of a *fiqh* school, since its *mujtahidūn* constantly address themselves

to new events and problems in the spirit and the method of their school, but with the qualifications of original scholarship, illuminated by the activities of their predecessors.

In this connection, a distinction is drawn between independent clarity (*bayān*), which characterizes *ijtihād*, and imitation (*taqlīd*) which ought not to be mistaken for it. Though the opinions of a jurist of this class may differ in their applications from the school with which he is identified, they are nonetheless grouped together. And though the particular opinion in a given case may be at variance with the opinion of the *imām* himself, it remains part of the body of law of that *imām*'s school, enhancing it and expanding its horizons. This juristic tolerance is called *wujūh*.

(3) Restricted *Ijtihād*: Performers of this type of interpretation are for the most part editors, cataloguers and codifiers within a certain school. They collect and categorize the opinions of the school, and extract and generalize their rules. They may occasionally offer an opinion in a new case not previously addressed by their *imām* or his school, but they must always conform to its framework. Whereas in affiliated *ijtihād* an interpreter utilizes the inductive method, in the case of restricted *ijtihād* he is bound by the deductive. His choice of the principles of a particular school is governed by *taqlīd*. Although such an interpreter is expected to be knowledgeable about the sources of the law as well as the procedures of *ijtihād*, he never exercises this prerogative where his *imām* had already given an opinion. He does so only in new situations.

(4) Verification *Ijtihād*: Here the work of the *mujtahid* is narrowly defined ascertaining the veracity of certain opinions as they become needed.[8] He is a degree below the practitioner of restricted *ijtihād* in that he expresses a legal opinion only in case of extreme need, that is, in the absence of a more qualified interpreter. He may not speak for the school with which he is identified, although he may hand down a decision (*fatwā*) according to that school.

(5) Transmission (Recitation) *Ijtihād*: In this category, an individual may hardly be recognized as a *mujtahid*, since his legal opinions are merely reiterations of those of the school. He may not offer explanation of the preambles of recited

opinions or the arguments of their conclusions. He is, however, a *mujtahid* insofar as he accurately learns the body of legal information of his school and is able to retrieve it for application. The basic prerequisite for this type of *ijtihād* is innate aptitude toward *fiqh*, i.e., to be "*faqīh al-nafs*."

Ibn Taymiyyah's jurisprudential activity qualifies him for the category of affiliated *ijtihād*, since he maintained his affiliation with the Ḥanbalī School, and few of his opinions depart from it significantly. He would not belong to any lower category of *ijtihād*; for he was thoroughly versed in the Sunnah and in comparative *fiqh*. His concurrence with Ibn Ḥanbal was based on his own study of the *uṣūl* which brought him independently to the same conclusions; and his agreement with Ibn Ḥanbal on some applications of the law was rooted in specific arguments and evidences which he marshalled for that purpose.

If Ibn al-Ṣalāḥ's opinion that absolute *ijtihād* had been consummated by the fifth century A.H. is to be upheld, Ibn Taymiyyah would have missed his possible recognition as a first degree *mujtahid* by a mere chronological accident. Appropriately enough, therefore, Abū Zahrah reminds us that, "*Ijtihād* is not viewed only from the vantage point of time, but is measured by the scholastic efforts of him who exercises it. Others, such as Ibn al-Humām, who came after him in the Ḥanafī School, for example, were thought to be numbered among the independent (absolute) interpreters. It should not be strange that Ibn Taymiyyah be counted at least as a *muntasib* interpreter. He is to the School of Aḥmad what al-Maznī is to the School of Shāfi'ī. Though he be late in time, his determination and qualifications should in no way be discounted."[9] At any rate, Ibn Taymiyyah was not an imitative (*muqallid*) interpreter. He admonished his colleagues against *taqlīd*, and exhorted them to undertake the task of *ijtihād*. He argued that the qualified jurist should never be satisfied with anything less than all arguments and full evidences for any jurisprudential position. For the unqualified, *ijtihād* remains open so long as it is possible for him to undertake mastery of all the evidence; whereas *taqlīd* remains permissible wherever original *ijtihād* is not feasible.[10]

C. *Ibn Taymiyyah's View of Inter-School Interpretation:* Ibn Taymiyyah's sanctioned interdenominational interpretation and he himself exercised it. This is understandable since he insisted on informed and substantiated originality.

With genuine appreciation for the four leading legists, Ibn Taymiyyah asserts that a creative interpreter is not bound by an opinion of his own school if he discovers the validity of another's. Indeed, he goes further, holding that "It is not fitting to prefer one's own school, with respect to a certain legal matter, to another if the other position is closer to equity." A jurist's goal should always be justice for its own sake. Therefore the seeker of justice, though he identify himself with a certain legal school, should not abide by it when the truth lies with another. Ibn Taymiyyah says, "Man is nurtured into the religion of his father, or of his master or his race, as a child follows the religion of his father....When he is come of age, he is obliged to follow in the obedience of God and His Apostle wherever it leads him....Anyone who deviates from following the Qur'ān and the *Sunnah* from the obedience of God and the Prophet, only to regress to the manner of his father and of his race, belongs to the Age of Ignorance (*Jāhiliyyah*). Likewise, he who, in dealing with a certain issue, comes to know the clear truth with which God had sent His Apostle, and then departs from it for his own wont, is untrustworthy and shall receive [eternal] punishment (*min ahl al-dhamm wa al-'iqāb*)."[11]

In elaboration, Ibn Taymiyyah discusses the conditions under which a seeker of the *Sharī'ah* may cross the boundaries of his school. From his *fatwā*, it appears that it is permissible to do so in either of two cases. First, if a man has acquired the necessary and detailed knowledge of legal argumentation, is skilled in the use of the tools for measuring the more authentic among them, and possesses an indispensible comprehension of the texts, the analogies and the precedents, he is not only permitted, "but is required to seek after the truth in religion." Ibn Taymiyyah takes this affirmation, citing these Qur'ānic verses:

" فلا وربك لا يؤمنون حتى يحكموك فيما شجر بينهم ، ثم لا يجدوا فى أنفسهم حرجا مما
قضيت ويسلموا تسليما "[12] and " وما كان لمؤمن ولا مؤمنة إذا قضى الله ورسوله
أمرا أن يكون لهم الخيرة من أمرهم . . "[13]

Ibn Taymiyyah, in addition, offers a rational explanation,

namely, that the four *imāms* are the interpreters *par excellence* of Islamic Law; yet on a given matter, one of them may possess a keener understanding of the Prophet's utterance in the same matter. Therefore, it is incumbent upon the student of the Law to follow that *imām*'s ruling, even though it differs from that of his own *imām*. Second, a common man who does not have the proficiencies for investigating the truer interpretation through original comparative study "is permitted, indeed obliged, to follow the direction of an *imām* other than his own after the example of a man of that school, who in comparison with another of his own seems more knowledgeable or more righteous."[14] Unless the reader is alert, the *prima facie* connotation of this admission may be misunderstood in view of the fact that Ibn Taymiyyah has so consistently urged first-hand examination of the truth. However, there is no incoherence here; for Ibn Taymiyyah has, without contradicting or compromising his own principle, permitted *taqlīd* for the common man (*ʿāmiyy*). Furthermore, if the Muslim's ultimate aim is the obedience of the revealed divine will which aim he sees being achieved by a man of another *madhhab*, he should do well to follow in his example.[15]

In the same manner also, Ibn Taymiyyah rules that a man shall not be permitted to abandon his school for another for convenience or for an ulterior motive of personal gain, or merely by reason of caprice (*hawā*). This constitutes an irreverent tampering (*ʿabath*) with the schools and with religious law. For a man to believe a certain action is obligatory or forbidden, then to believe it voluntary or permissible for the sake of pleasure, does not conform to the legitimate conditions of trans-denominationalism. A man who claims priority [in the right to acquire a given object] on the principle that he is first neighbor, which is legal in the Ḥanafī School, then refuses to abide by the same principle when he is on the opposite side of the issue, claiming for example that the documentary evidence is uncertain, has likewise violated the sanctity of the schools. Such individuals, says Ibn Taymiyyah, are to be numbered with those who embrace Islam for material gain, or abandon Makkah for Madīnah to marry a wealthy woman or to establish a thriving enterprise. The reference here, of course, is to the Prophet's *ḥadīth* affirming the conformity of consequences to the intentions behind men's actions, which *ḥadīth* occupies an appreciable portion of Ibn Taymiyyah's work.[16]

Among the collected legal opinions (*fatāwā*) of Ibn Taymiyyah, there are many which embark upon an extensive comparative study of the four schools, and the vast majority made repeated references to them. Such detailed comparisons are apparent in opinions including, for example, the *fatwā* on "Warfare,"[17] the *fatwā* on "The Effects of Natural Disasters,"[18] and the *fatwā* on "Contracts and Stipulations."[19]

A segment of his legislation on contractual conditions, for example, shows a reasoned preference, in this particular instance, for interpretations of the School of Mālik. He contends that, in comparison to the rulings of his own Ḥanbalī School, The School of Mālik is rightly closer to the traditional custom of Islam in the case of conditions relating to the marriage contract. Mālik rules that such conditions "are not binding unless they are [legally] authorized (*mā lam takun bi-muqtaḍāh*), or unless they verify the legality of what they dictate (*mu'akkidah li-muqtaḍāh*). For this reason, Mālik concludes, Ibn Rushd stated,[20] that absolute [or, binding] conditions in the marriage contract should be specified and made known by the scholars in order that they may take effect; as it said of Abū Shihāb that he had known judges who acted on the premise of the Prophet's *ḥadīth* requiring the primacy of the conjugal relationship in the marriage contract.[21] The insistence by certain courts on stipulating such a condition expressly in the marriage contract, Mālik suggests is out of order, because, according to the *Madhhab* and to custom (*'urf*), it is more desirable than obligatory. Therefore, it is not admissible in a marriage contract. Another such unnecessary condition is the stipulation by one party that the other does not marry another spouse while married to the one being contracted. The contract is valid, and the condition is unnecessary, and would not be binding, anyway, although to meet it is desirable (*mustaḥabb*). Ibn Taymiyyah concurs with the prohibition of the stipulation of conditions in a marriage contract. Abū Zahrah explained the wisdom of this principle by quoting the author who said he "counseled a judge to admonish the people against marriage by stipulations, and to exhort them to marry for the partner's piety and integrity."[22]

2. *Ibn Taymiyyah--A Ḥanbalī Jurisconsult:*

Although Ibn Taymiyyah occasionally adopted the legal opinions of the other three lawmakers of Islam, and though he sometimes assumed independent legal positions, he considered the School of Ibn Ḥanbal nearer the ideals of Islamic law than the others. He declared his allegiance to it by asserting that

> Aḥmad was more knowledgeable in the contents of the Scripture and the *Sunnah* than others as well as in the opinions of the Companions and their righteous successors. For this reason, there can hardly be found an opinion of his in contravention of a text [of *Ḥadīth*] as is the case with the others. There is not one weak opinion in his school but that it is balanced by an opinion strongly supported. The majority of his unique rulings (*mafarīḍ*), none of which is in contravention [of the texts], are more likely to be valid...such as: his favoring the testimony of free non-Muslims living in Islamic territory over the testimony of Muslims when necessary, the [declaration of a] will before a journey, the prohibition of the marriage of an adultress until she repent, etc.[23]

Ibn Taymiyyah gained knowledge of Ibn Ḥanbal's *fiqh* through his thorough study of the works of Ibn Ḥanbal himself and of the works of his disciples, including his own grandfather Abū al-Barakāt Ibn Taymiyyah, his grandfather's uncle Ibn ʿAbd-Allah, as well as his own father.[24] On the basis of his extensive study, both of Ibn Ḥanbal and of the other *imāms*, Ibn Taymiyyah thus states that when Ibn Ḥanbal took a solitary legal stance, he was more plausibly nearer an accurate reflection of the text on which he based his stance. He further suggests that if Ibn Ḥanbal and Mālik stood unsupported by the others in a decision, it is still to be considered more valid. The reason, as deduced by Abū Zahrah,[25] may be that Aḥmad Ibn Ḥanbal's School contained such a diversity of opinions ("he was an avid collector of the Tradition") that if in one place the argument regarding a given issue is weak, there is certain to be another reference within the *madhhab* that would be stronger. "If it became impossible for [Aḥmad]," says Abū Zahrah, to verify the transmission [of a *ḥadīth*] personally, he depended on the authoritative concurrences with Mālik; [Ibn Ḥanbal] never resorted to analogy except in extreme cases of need."[26]

The variations in the statutes of Ibn Ḥanbal are explained also by Ibn al-Qayyim, a disciple of Ibn Taymiyyah who may have reflected his master's conviction. Ibn al-Qayyim said, "If he [Ibn Ḥanbal] had come upon some variations among the sayings of the Companions, he would select from among them those which were nearer the Book and the Tradition. As for the sayings that would not seem to coincide with the texts, he would merely report them without giving a decisive opinion. If later he were cited with regard to the issue in question, both strands of the report were quoted...hence the attribution of both to him."[27] Abū Zahrah remarks that the variations in the Ḥanbalī tradition, which to some seemed approximating conflict, were "useful and helpful to Ibn Taymiyyah; he viewed nothing irregular about Aḥmad's school simply because of such varying reports, since there can be no less preferable opinion without there being another which is preferred." For Ibn Taymiyyah, this was an advantage that opened his eyes to the riches of Ibn Ḥanbal's *corpus juris*, which led him to the comprehensive study of the Companions and the *Salaf*, and, in the final analysis, liberated him even to prefer the views of others in certain issues. Therefore, Ibn Taymiyyah always acknowledged his allegiance to the school of Ibn Ḥanbal, even in the issues wherein he was distinguished by his own *ijtihād* above all the traditional schools; he so acknowledged his allegiance, not at all simply out of partisan attachment, nor out of provincialism, but in deference to his own overarching conviction of loyalty to the *Salaf*.

Ibn Taymiyyah's work as a Ḥanbalī jurist was produced for the most part during his stay in Egypt, especially following his release from his second imprisonment there in 700-711 A.H./ 1300-1311 A.D., when he was regularly consulted by al-Nāsir Ibn Qalāwūn, its reinstated ruler.[28] It is characterized by the methodological uniformity of accurate *Ḥadīth* research, clear elaboration of the schools' analogous opinions, and systematic consistency of evidences.

His judicial opinion with respect to crimes committed under intoxication[29] is but one of many examples of his Ḥanbalī jurisprudence.

In this legislation, Ibn Taymiyyah's premise reflects Aḥmad's general framework. He says, "The condition of liability, or legal capacity (i.e., responsibility, "*taklīf*"), is cognizance ("*fahm*," i.e., being informed of one's rights or duties). It follows that an insane, or drunken person is not held legally responsible for his actions. For example, divorce pronounced under intoxication is not legally binding; likewise, murder under this condition does not entail the fullest measure of penalty. If it is argued that a man became drunk then committed murder, therefore he is guilty on both counts, it is to be deduced that guilt is imputed on the basis of liability (or capacity), since an incapable person may not be determined guilty. To this, it may be replied in two ways: first, guilt may not be imputed on the charge of murder, but on that of drinking and intoxication. In this case, the accused is treated in the same manner as an insane person in what he says or does, but with liability; or, second, if guilt is established on the basis of murder and drunkenness, a sober murderer who later became drunk and a drunken murderer would be considered alike; and this would be unacceptable; for how could a drunken man, who is obviously not in full mental control, be judged guilty and punished in the same way that a man who, being fully aware of his action and its consequences, commits the crime?"[30] Ibn Taymiyyah goes further with the hypothesis in order to cover all the possibilities. He supposes that a drunken murderer had become drunk for the purpose of committing the act of murder, "to numb his conscience and to extinguish his consciousness, so he may come to the crime without fear or hesitation." "He, in that case," Ibn Taymiyyah rules, "deserves the same penalty of a sober man, and more; that is, if he indeed had, prior to becoming drunk, premeditated the act of murder or that of adultery, but if his crime had not been precontemplated before his drinking, and someone else initiated the aggravation, then his guilt is less than what it would be in the former case."[31]

3. *Ibn Taymiyyah--An Independent Jurist:*

As has previously been indicated, Ibn Taymiyyah, a Ḥanbalī by affiliation and a universalist in character, rightly fulfilled all the requirements of independent *ijtihād*, although he voluntarily did not claim that highest level of legislation. Always seeking the truth first in the sources of jurisprudence, he could not help departing from some of the traditional views, although he never did so in dissent from or in disloyalty to the *Salaf*.

1. *His Theory of the Principles (Sources) of Law:* It would seem appropriate at this juncture to consider Ibn Taymiyyah's conception of the four sources of law:[32]

(1) The Qur'ān and the *Sunnah*: No judicial rules can have binding power unless they are framed within the precepts of an overall body of law which gives such rules constitutionality. The highest source of the Islamic *corpus juris* is the Holy Qur'ān, which is interpreted and exemplified by the *Sunnah*. The *Sunnah*, i.e., the utterances and the life-model of the Prophet Muḥammad, continued in the life-example of his Companions, constitutes the second highest source of legal authority. All Muslim lawmakers agree that the principles, or sources, or jurisprudence are included in a definition by ʻUmar set forth in a letter to Shāriḥ, a justice of the courts. ʻUmar said, "Judge by what is in God's Book; and if you do not find in it [an explicit ruling], then by the *Sunnah* of His Apostle; and if you do not find it there, then by the judgments of the worthy who have preceded you, and by what the people had approved unanimously."[33]

Ibn Taymiyyah acknowledges the Qur'ān as the law's undisputed primary source. "None of the *imāms* disagreed on this," he said.[34] The authentic *Sunnah*, according to Ibn Taymiyyah, is inseparable from the Qur'ān, because it reveals the intent of the divine revelation. Both the Qur'ān and the *Sunnah* in the Ḥanbalī tradition, are referred to as the texts (*nuṣuṣ*), and as such they are held in a uniquely authoritative position, as the authority of the *Sunnah* is an extension of the authority of the Qur'ān itself, by divine witness: " وما أتـاكم الرسول فخذوه ، وما نهاكم عنه فانتهـوا "[35] Ibn Taymiyyah holds this injunction to validate the authentic *Sunnah* whether it directly interprets Qur'ānic *prima facie* expressions (*ẓawāhir*) in which case either it becomes complementary to it, or it introduces a new ruling not theretofore indicated by the Qur'ān, such as the determination of the amount of reparation penalty for theft, or the sentence of punishing an adulterer by stoning, etc.[36] Ibn Taymiyyah is convinced that the *Sunnah* must be held in the highest regard in legislation, because it is the key to understanding the Qur'ān, and because authentic

Sunnah can never contravene the Qur'ān. Ibn Taymiyyah refutes the Khārijīs, for example, for rejecting portions of the valid *Sunnah*. He cites the Prophet's *ḥadīth*, "Will ye not trust me when He who is in heaven trusts me?"[37]

(2) Consensus: Throughout Ibn Taymiyyah's writings that are concerned with the legitimate sources of Islamic law,[38] consensus (*ijmā'*) is deemed significant in its proper place and under certain conditions. He advances the thesis that consensus has never been established since the dispersion of the Companions into the different regions of early Islam, since genuine *ijmā'* can never be known where the scholars of the Islamic *Ummah* are so numerous and so widely separated geographically. By Ibn Taymiyyah's definition, *ijmā'* requires, among other stipulations, the unconditional, unanimous agreement of the scholars in any given age. Where there is exception, there is no *ijmā'*, he says, and explains, "In many issues, some think *ijmā'* has been established, while it is not so....That some consider the agreement of a certain number of the members of the Community, such as the four *imāms* or others, an *ijmā'*, is neither true nor binding. On the contrary, the *imāms* themselves have demonstrably admonished the people against their imitation, and commanded that if they found stronger evidence in the Qur'ān, or in the *Sunnah*, they should prefer it to their own...."[39]

And if *ijmā'* means the agreement of all the *'ulamā'* without exception, as it evidently does for Ibn Taymiyyah, then it is impossible to ascertain. Furthermore, there must exist very little *ijmā'* as a result. Ibn Taymiyyah thus invalidates the assumption that "most of the problems of Islamic law are dealt with through *ijmā'*." He suggests, on the contrary, that

> he among the latter (scholars), who asserts that *ijmā'* is the documentary evidence (*mustanad*) of most of the *Sharī'ah* reveals that, by reason of his deficient knowledge of the Qur'ān and the *Sunnah*, he is in need of *ijma'*....Aḥmad used to say, "there is not a question [of law] but that the Companions have addressed it, or they addressed themselves at least to a similar question:...they most often spoke the Qur'ān and the *Sunnah*, and seldom spoke an [original] opinion."[40]

Another condition for the validity of *ijmā'*, which for Ibn Taymiyyah is of utter importance, is that it should be supported by a text (*naṣṣ*) of an authentic *ḥadīth*, and that the text be known at least to some of the scholars participating in the consensus, if not to all. At any rate, a consensus of opinion should never contravene a text. Nor should a *ḥadīth* be found simply to proof-text an opinion already agreed upon since consensus follows the text, but not the opposite.[41]

Closely related is another condition that requires that *ijmā'* be resorted to after seeking first the Qur'ān and the *Sunnah*. To reverse this order, i.e., to seek consensus before seeking the texts, is like reversing the places of the branch and the root. Ibn Taymiyyah puts forward 'Umar, Ibn Mas'ūd and Ibn 'Abbās, "the Companions most reputable to litigate," whose method consistently followed the formula of "advancing" first the evidence of the *Sunnah* [of Muḥammad], then that of Abū Bakr, then that of 'Umar. He refers to the *ḥadīth*, "Follow ye the example of those that come after me: Abū Bakr, and 'Umar."[42] He subsequently shatters the arguments of those who place *ijmā'* before the texts, giving as their reasons either the supposition that, if indeed a text were known which contravened the consensus, such a text must have been abrogated by another which itself would have been the basis of the consensus, or, the assertion that, in the absence of a text, the consensus itself must have abrogated it. Ibn Taymiyyah charges that such argument is contradictory both to the rules of reason and the rules of understanding the issue of abrogation. His logic indeed confounds theirs: how could anyone be expected to believe that decisive texts should be abandoned, he asks, for the sake of inconclusive opinions? Such a course of action betrays only that he who takes it seeks the easy way. In reply to the first argument on the last page of his treatise, *Ma'ārij al-Wuṣūl* he says: It is unreasonable to say that a consensus is based on an authentic, but unknown, text, while only the text supporting an opposite view exists. This kind of assertion could only mean that the Community has lost the documentary text and kept the abrogated text. Such charge would be too unbecoming an entire and unanimous *ummah*.[43] As to the second argument, he replies: the rules of abrogation demand that the Qur'ān may be abrogated only by the Qur'ān, and the *Sunnah* only by the *Sunnah*; a text that abrogates another must have sufficient weight to remove the one being abrogated. How, then, may the Qur'ān be removed by what is other than Qur'ān; and how may the *Sunnah* be removed by what is other than *Sunnah*? In sum, *ijmā'* has no power over the Qur'ān or the *Sunnah*.[44]

Finally, it may be misconstrued from what has been said that Ibn Taymiyyah does not fully favor consensus as a valid source of the law. Not so. *Ijmā'* is indeed a valid source, but it may serve as a reference only to the extent that it may be the only reference available for litigation, and as such, it must be based on a text, though the text on which it is based may not be known to all the scholars who formed it.

In effect, Ibn Taymiyyah constructs an argument for the possibility of *ijma'*,[45] then constructs a subsequent argument to delimit it. His apparent conclusion is that though it is possible for *ijmā'* to occur, as indeed it had among the Companions, it does not actually occur.[46]

(3) Analogy: Ibn Taymiyyah's circumspection for this important source of Islamic law is evident in his setting apart a special treatise in which he gives his definition of it, and demonstrates the distinction between that definition and the premises of the *madhāhib*, but particularly the Ḥanafī School.[47] The main import of Ibn Taymiyyah's treatise on analogy (*qiyās*) is his assertion that *qiyās* as a method of legislation is an inconclusive term which is capable of admitting both a true (*ṣaḥīḥ*) and a false (*bāṭil*, or, *fāsid*) form of application. Ibn Taymiyyah's distinctiveness in the consideration of this method lies in his insistence on sorting out the two applications, and, consequently, utilizing only true *qiyās* in the practice of jurisprudence. And though he acknowledges that his opponents do not knowingly utilize it improperly, and that they in fact arrive at length at conclusions similar to his own in settling certain cases by applying discretion (*istiḥsān*), he maintains that discrimination between proper and improper *qiyās* is necessary, and that *qiyās*, understood properly, could indeed be applied to the cases they had thought it inappropriate.

The distinction on which Ibn Taymiyyah was unyielding is argued on the premise that true *qiyās*, like all methods of jurisprudence, must be based on texts, either explicitly or implicitly. The mark of validity for any ruling is the absence of any contravening legal statute, requiring or prohibiting a certain action, which statute itself must be founded on either a text or an affirmation by the Prophet.

A case in point is the Ḥanafīs' rejection of the legitimacy of considering rental contracts (*ʿuqūd al-ijārah*) under the method of *qiyās*. They had contended that rental contracts are "contracts of sales of benefits (*manāfiʿ*)," as distinguished from "contracts of sales of materials (*aʿyān*)," and as such they are illegal since benefits are potentialities not extant at the time of the contract, and since the sale of the inexistent is illegitimate. Because of the extreme need, however, they permitted rental contracts through discretion (*istiḥsān*), since in their opinion rental was "in contravention of *qiyās*)." Ibn Taymiyyah's opposition to their methodology is constructed on Qurʾānic foundation and rational argument. He cites the verse legitimizing the contract with a wet nurse (*ẓiʾr*): "فان ارضعن لكم فآتوهن أجورهن."[48] He takes the Ḥanafīs to task first for declaring that rental, or hire (*ijārah*), is contrary to *qiyās*, despite the explicit text of the Qurʾān, and, second, for arguing that the hire of a wet nurse is "not in accordance with the *qiyās* of rentals," pointing to the incoherence inherent in their having thus already admitted there is a valid *qiyās* for rentals, and at the same time excluding this type of rental.[49] He then categorically advances the thesis that rentals, including the hiring of a wet nurse, are commensurable with true *qiyās*. He says

> that they say rental is a sale of the inexistent, which is an illegal transaction according to *qiyās*, poses a confusing assumption consisting in the indiscriminate equation of rental with sale. If by sale they strictly mean the selling of material objects, the assumption is not valid; if they mean sale in a general way that may apply to the trade [of money] for an object or for a service, then they are accurate with respect to objects but not to services, since a contract for service is not identical with a contract of sale.[50]

He then continues with the argument, maintaining that the *Sharīʿah* permits a transaction of service, as well as of kind, even though the former is not existent at the time of the contract. In this case, the application of the analogy of "sale of kind" is improper, because it would mean a comparison of unequals. Furthermore, he is not convinced with the "inexistence" of an immaterial object, and states that as a Muslim he, too, would be obedient to the commandment to refrain from the sale, or rental, of the inexistent. He would not sell even at a very low price, a fugitive slave, for example, or a missing camel, and the like, since such a transaction constitutes an injustice against the purchaser if the item is not found, or against the seller himself if indeed it is found. Nor is the service of a wet nurse an inexistent object, even though it, on the one hand, appears to be a transaction of kind (her milk), and, on the other, is a contract of potentiality. It is appropriate to apply *qiyās*, he says, on account of the fact that contracting a wet nurse is an employment (or rental of labor) for a benefit that exists even in potentiality, though it appears to be a sale of kind. Her milk is a benefit rendered in kind, and is the nature of rental since it continues to be given in return for as long as she is hired. This, he concludes, belongs in the same category as the rental of a house, the rental of a tree for the fruit season, or the rental of a milk-producing animal. As such, *qiyās* is positively applicable in this case.[51]

Other cases which for Ibn Taymiyyah are eligible for the method of analogy, which proposition is rejected by the scholars, are the silent partnership in investment (*muḍārabah*), sharecropping contracts (*muzāra'ah*), restricted sharecropping contracts (*musāqāh*), i.e., for one irrigational season, and the like. Ibn Taymiyyah contends that such cases are eligible for *qiyās* by merit of their being partnership contracts; but the scholars had considered such relationships contrary to *qiyās* on the assumption that they were employment ("rental of labor") contracts for unspecified wages. Seen in the light of partnership, however, the two parties enter into a relationship wherein they agree to share the revenue proportionately, in which case no wages-service exchanges (*mu'āwaḍāt*) are involved. Hence their eligibility for *qiyās* application.[52]

Ibn Taymiyyah's entire effort in his theory of analogy was obviously dedicated to the profound thesis that "contradictions" (*mu'āraḍāt*) between certain legitimate legal opinions and certain pronouncements of analogy, as perceived by the scholars are due in large measure to their confusion of premises;

accurate application of analogy requires a full understanding of the nature of the legal problem, and a subsequent distinction between its implications and the implications of other problems that may be related in a general way, but may not be similar in nature.

One more facet of Ibn Taymiyyah's conception of *qiyās* needs to be brought to light, namely his insightful penetration into the *intent* of a legal precedent which, according to one authority,[53] distinguishes him among the jurists, and particularly above the Ḥanafī School. In contrast to the Ḥanafīs, Abū Zahrah states, Ibn Taymiyyah delves into the intent of a precedent of analogy. They had codified the causes of legal problems, and demanded that unless new ones had identical causes, *qiyās* could not be applied. Recognizing that precise identicality of circumstances in disputes is seldom as available as a judge may wish to find it, Ibn Taymiyyah proposed that similarity of occasion, and the general intentions upon which a precedent had been predicated, are sufficient grounds for applying the method of *qiyās*.[54]

(4) Other Sources and Methods: Although Ibn Taymiyyah's usage of other methods of jurisprudence is strictly done in the Ḥanbalī manner, it is appropriate that they be at least listed here for the record. These include legislation by extension (*istiṣḥāb*) [or "association"]. This method assumes the legal *status quo* of a person or an object unless his/its condition is changed. For example, the legal status of a missing person is "not presumed" to be changed, although the possibility exists that he is dead. However, by extension, he may not be assumed either dead or alive unless one of these conditions is ascertained. (Ibn Taymiyyah was careful to make a distinction between saying "the legal status is not presumed to be changed," and saying "is presumed not to be changed," the latter denoting a legal opinion already self-contradictory in principle).[55] At any rate, legislation by extension, says Ibn Taymiyyah, is applicable only in maintaining an existing legal status, such as a person's rights, but not in establishing a new status.

Another consideration in Ḥanbalī lawmaking, as acknowledged though somewhat hesitantly is that of "general welfare" (*al-maṣāliḥ al-mursalah*). By definition "general welfare" is legitimate; but this stipulation is added to safeguard its application: it is to be for the sake of deriving a legitimate benefit, as well as of driving away harm.[56] The derivation of benefit need not be limited to the preservation of health, wealth, honor, mental wholeness and religious purity, it should also include worldly endeavors that are not in contravention of the law. It is evident that Ibn Taymiyyah utilizes the principle of "general welfare" about which he is initially somewhat reluctant, perhaps for fear of being misconstrued, and turns it into a positive assertive note against the Ṣūfī attitude of renunciation of the world. Yet, perhaps, in a manner of objectivity, or perhaps merely for the sake of using Ṣūfī terminology, he suggests that the derivation of worldly benefits is "as legitimate as the aspirations toward illumination, transformation, serfdom, and humiliation, which without contravention of the Law, bring about religious benefits."[57] His very hesitation, however, is likely to have been a reaction against the Ṣūfī practice of seeking the benefits of "personal intuition (*dhawq*), inspiration (*ilhām*) and ecstacy (*wajd*)."[58] Equally important a reason for his less-than-enthusiastic acceptance of the "general welfare" principle is his desire for integrity, which stands in opposition to the economic and political permissiveness rampant in his age. He was aware of the human quotient of justifying the means for the sake of benefits derived in the end.

For this last reason also, Ibn Taymiyyah clearly sets the proper boundaries for applying the last principle: "utility" (*dharāʼiʻ*).[59] He states that this is a perfectly legitimate principle, as practiced in the Ḥanbalī School, because there it was utilized only in light of the rule that a legitimate end requires a legitimate means. No honorable end, which may rightly realize good benefits for its seeker, should be achieved through a means less honorable. The principle of *dharāʼiʻ*, therefore, should imply that the means assume the status of the ends when considered for legal transactions. Consequently, it searches both the motivations and the objectives. Illicit uses of the principle of "utility" are illustrated by entering into a marital contract with the intention of annullment or divorce for unspecified motives, or closing a sales contract with no intention of transferring the property title, for evading financial responsibility, and the like. Ibn Taymiyyah reviews some of the fruits of the proper utilization of this principle by the Ḥanbalīs. Among such results he lists, for example, the prohibition of food monopoly, and that of other fundamental necessities. On the basis of this prohibition, Aḥmad is reported to have ruled that if a person monopolized food, thus causing another person to die, the penalty of life ransom (*diyyah*) shall be exacted of him--even though he technically committed no murder, either deliberately or unintentionally. Nevertheless, being the cause by which a man died, he served as the means (*dharī'ah*) to his death. The severe penalty of *diyyah* is due, therefore, in order to counter the way (*dharī'ah*) of evil, and to promote the way of mutual cooperation. Countering the ways of evil is a means to put a halt to all manner of *strategem* (*ḥīlah*), or scheming, for the purpose of *in fraudem legis agere*.[60]

II. *His Independent Jurisprudence:*

Ibn Taymiyyah's objectivity, already evident in his departure from one school for another seeking after the truth,[61] is carried to its logical conclusion that where that truth leads, he would follow--beyond and above the traditions of the Schools, or the propositions of any individual. For him the ultimate source of divine truth is revealed in the Qur'ān and exemplified by the words and actions of the Prophet. And it is to that that he would be obedient:

> Praise be to God! It is the duty of men to obey God and His Apostle, and these [the *imams* of the Schools] are the leaders whose obedience God has ordered in the commandment "أطيعوا الله والرسول وأولى الأمر منكم"[62] However, (*innama*), their obedience is required in consequence of, or in subsequence to, (*taba'an li*) obedience to God and His Apostle, and not in independence of it. He also said "ان تنازعتم فى شئ فردوه لله والرسول ان كنتم تؤمنون بالله واليوم الآخر"[63] If a Muslim is encountered with a legal problem (*nāzilah*), he may seek the counsel of whomever he believes will counsel him in accordance with the law of God and His Apostle regardless of what his School may be. No Muslim is dutifully bound to follow any certain scholar in all that he says. Nor is any Muslim required to abide by the School of any certain person except the Apostle in all that he commands and discloses....To follow a person for his

> School by reason of inability to know the law without his direction is permissible, but not obligatory, if he is able to know the law apart from that manner. What is obligatory is to live in reverence for God insofar as it is possible, and to seek the knowledge of what God and his Apostle have commanded, and do it; but avoid that which is forbidden. God knows best.[64]

In addition to citing the aforementioned Qur'ānic texts, Ibn Taymiyyah substantiates his view of independent litigation with quotations from the words of Muḥammad, from the counsel of the four major jurisconsults themselves, and from the *Salaf*. The Prophet said, "Whomever God desires to bless, He shall cause him to understand religion (*dīn*)."[65] It follows that a man whom God does not cause to understand religion is not blessed. Therefore, it is the obligation of every man to seek this understanding (*fiqh*). *Fiqh* of religion consists of knowledge of the statutes and their reported evidences. If it is beyond a man's capacity to know all the detailed proofs, he is not held responsible for what he cannot know, but he shall be responsible for what he can know.

Abū Bakr is quoted by Ibn Taymiyyah also. He told the early Muslims "Follow me where I obey God; but if I disobey Him, you owe me no obedience." Ibn Taymiyyah's comment is that there is no human who is infallible in matters of religion and divine law except the Prophet; and no one has any obligation to follow other than the Prophet, and, by extension, those who obey his message. In this connection, the example is cited when in a discussion refuting usufruct marriage someone attempting to show his acuity said to Ibn ʿAbbās, "Abū Bakr and ʿUmar had ruled it illegal"; Ibn ʿAbbās replied, with exclamation, "Would that the sky nearly shower them with stones! Here I tell you God's Prophet, and you say Abū Bakr and ʿUmar!" The implication is: the Prophet's words always have infinitely greater authenticity than any man's.

Finally, the four jurisconsults themselves have attested that one may take or leave any or all, little or none, of what any man says, except the Apostle. Muḥammad's *Sunnah*, therefore, is the ultimate legal reference as it is the detailed actualization or embodiment of the Qur'ānic revelation; and as such, it transcends the *fiqh* of the Schools. Ibn Taymiyyah concedes, for example, that, on the issue of *tayammum* (i.e., utilizing sand, in place of water, for ablution) of the ritually impure,[66] some rightly followed Abū Mūsa al-Ash'arī's ruling which allowed it on the basis of a text.[67]

It is the duty of the Muslim to seek after authenticity in jurisprudence, which is most certainly assured in the texts. Mālik, for example, had said, in effect, "I am human; I err, and I also speak rightly. Examine what I say against the Book and the *Sunnah*." Al-Shāfi'ī also had said, in effect, "If you find a contending *ḥadīth* to be authentic, disregard what I say." Abū Ḥanīfah, too, was known to have said on a given occasion, "This is my judgment; if there is a better opinion, I shall be the first to accept it."[68]

Ibn Taymiyyah, a Ḥanbalī, justified his independence from Ḥanbalism and the other Schools by a quotation from Ibn Ḥanbal himself:

> Imām Aḥmad used to say, "Do not imitate me [i.e., follow my method of *fiqh*], or Mālik, or al-Shāfi'ī, or al-Thawrī; but investigate as we have investigated." He also used to say, "It is reprehensible for a man to be followed in his manner of religion. Therefore, do not let men imitate you in religion; for doubtless they would not escape error."[69]

Ibn Taymiyyah's definitive principle was that, unlike one who adheres to a tradition for its own sake, if a man exercise creative interpretation, and, on the basis of a profound text, change his position from one opinion to another, he is praiseworthy.[70]

A. *An Example of His Non-Partisan and Unique Contribution to Islamic Jurisprudence*

Most of Ibn Taymiyyah's legal interpretations and opinions were occasioned, as was the custom, by either specific court cases for which there had been no precedents, or by particular questions of law that were addressed to him by legal practitioners, or students of Islamic law. In any event, they were offered in the context of the social needs of the day. In this sense they were relevant to their situations, without being "situational" in the sense of limited application. Indeed, because these interpretations were based on the primary sources of law, namely the Qur'ān and the *Sunnah*, they have proven to transcend their time and their locale into a broader and more lasting influence.[71]

Of his numerous such interpretations, his *fatwā* on divorce has been selected here to represent and illustrate his independent scholarship as well as his integrity to his religious tradition. The issue of divorce (*ṭalāq*) has been chosen because it was keenly pertinent in Ibn Taymiyyah's time, and because it was also controversial. So controversial was his opinion regarding this social problem that his close friend the Sultan of Egypt and Syria, al Nāṣir Ibn Qalawūn, who had released him from prison eleven years before, was forced by the demands of the conservatives to imprison him once more in 720 A.H./1320 A.D.).

Ibn Taymiyyah's *fatwā* was induced by a widespread practice that he considered damaging to individuals and to society. That was the use of divorce as an oath, often intended not so much for the dissolution of the marriage relationship, as it was for emphatic assertion, for gaining credibility, for seeking a certain benefit, and the like. To vow the divorce of one's wife had, in practice, become equivalent to invoking the name of God in an oath, or to vowing to fulfill a certain religious duty or social act of mercy, such as performing the pilgrimage, emancipating a slave, feeding ten poor persons, etc. The result, in many cases, was that when a man's objective was achieved, he was bound by his vow which of course terminated the marriage.

Seeing that divorce as an institution was "the least desirable among what was declared by God to be lawful," where indeed it was undisputedly lawful, he ruled the divorce oath not valid, and, as an oath which "ought to be treated as a vow," it demanded an atonement (*kaffārah*). In his ruling, he took his stance outside the circles of the four major Schools; and, in fact, appears to echo the Shī'ī position in some respects.[72] For that he would not be apologetic, however, since he depends on the Qur'ān and the *Sunnah* for his understanding of law (*fiqh*).

Addressing himself to the issue, Ibn Taymiyyah presupposes the sanity and the sobriety of a man pronouncing divorce,[73] then divides it into three categories:

1. A pronouncement may be effectual (*munjiz*), when it is fully intended and unconditional. In this case, a man simply says to his wife, "You are divorced."

2. When divorce is not the ultimate end of a pronouncement which in this category would be made in the form of an oath, but rather another effect, such as a certain accomplishment, refraining from a certain action, or establishing the acceptability of a certain proposition, this may be called a divorce oath, or bid, and is not effectual. In this case, a man may say literally, "Divorce shall be upon me, I shall do so and thus," or "Divorce shall be upon me, I have paid so much for...," or "Divorce shall be upon me, that you do such and such...." By so doing, a man, in essence, wagers his marital relationship seeking after a certain end.

In response, according to Ibn Taymiyyah, the *imāms* differed in their opinion as to whether the divorce ought to take place if the condition is fulfilled. Abū Ḥanīfah, for example, replied in the negative. Some Shāfiʿīs said yes, divorce should take effect, and that that was the practice of their judicial system in Arabia, Iraq, Khurāsān, Hijāz, Egypt, Syria and Maghrib. Ibn Ḥanbal and some Mālikīs also agreed that the pronouncement should be made valid. A third possibility is that divorce would not be validated, but the oath, treated as a vow, must be fulfilled in a substitute way.

3. As to whether a provisional utterance of divorce should be sustained if it were intended by the man uttering it, and if the condition were fulfilled, the *imāms* affirmed it and society practiced it. In the face of the assumption that the stipulation would be fulfilled, but then it would become known that divorce was not in fact the intent of the man who had pronounced it, opinions varied. Some said that divorce should not be valid; others that it should be, regardless of the intent; and others yet that it should not be valid, but that an atonement of the oath should be exacted.

In this exposition of the different possibilities, we can see that the first category constituted no dispute for Ibn Taymiyyah. We recognize also that the second and third possibilities are similar, for the most part, and that only one significant difference would require separate treatment, namely, the question of intent which is raised in the third possibility but not in the second. Thus the issue is focused on two questions: does divorce take place, and, does the vow require a substitute form of fulfillment.

Ibn Taymiyyah replies that the vow to divorce should not incur divorce, even though the condition on which it depends be realized. As an oath, or a vow, it, however, demands substitution, since it should not be fulfilled in actual divorce. He advances, as a chief reason for his position, the argument that atonement is required in the event of unfulfilled vow, on the basis of the Prophet's *ḥadīth*: "If a man takes an oath, but discovers a different [course of action] to be the better way, let him bring off what is better and atone for his oath (or vow)."[74] The Qur'ān is also cited with respect to the formula of an individual's oath, and to atonement: "لا يؤاخذكم الله باللغو في أيمانكم ، ولكن يؤاخذكم بما عقدتم الأيمان ، فكفارة اطعام عشرة مساكين من أوسط ما تطعمون أهليكم أو كسوتهم أو تحرير رقبة فمن لم يجد فصيام ثلاثة أيام . ذلك كفّارة أيمانكم اذا حلفتم"[75] Both texts, Ibn Taymiyyah notes, refer to oaths in general, and are, therefore, applicable to any type of oath, whether it be in the name of God or other than in the name of God. Likewise, he invokes the specific Qur'ānic injunction: "قد فرض الله لكم تحلّة أيمانكم."[76] He then proposes that divorce itself is a serious matter, as is an oath; and that the two propositions ought not to be confused. The Qur'ānic *Sūrah* of Divorce, which opens with the verse: "يا أيها النبي ـ اذا طلّقتم النساء فطلّقوهن لعدّتهن وأحصوا العدّة ولتقوا ربكم. لا تخرجوهنّ من بيوتهنّ ولا يخرجن الا ان يأتين بفاحشة."[77] sets the fundamental boundaries (*ḥudūd*) of divorce which all Muslims are expected to know and to observe. The thrust of the *Surah*, it is clear, guards the goal of the happiness and harmony of the human race. It seeks social order, and safeguards the rights of individuals. It recognizes that, though it is sometimes necessary, divorce is not a desirable institution; and that if it must be pursued, the interests of all involved must be protected. Neither divorce nor the oath, implies Ibn Taymiyyah, should be approached lightly. And, if one commits the serious error of bringing the ominous prospect of divorce within the serious act of taking an oath, the damage of divorce should not be inflicted just to satisfy an oath that ought not to have enjoined it in the first place. Nor should a violated oath go unatoned.[78]

For Ibn Taymiyyah at least, there appeared to be no contradiction between his view and the traditional view; and rightly so, so long as we accept his premise that the pronouncement of divorce was used for achieving an unrelated purpose is to be considered together with other oaths.

The traditional view, as invoked and substantiated by Ibn Taymiyyah, and as has been confirmed by the texts cited above, holds a person responsible for his oath. The difference between Ibn Taymiyyah's view and that of the more common position of the Schools was, therefore, a methodological difference: his treatment of the divorce was appropriately concerned with its formula at least as much as with its intent, since the formula had been so common in social conversation that the implications were overlooked and the damage became greater than could be coped with. Identifying the oath (*nadhr*), he concludes that a similar requirement should be exacted upon him who breaches it. Considering the matter also in view of its practical consequence he concludes that the damage and disruption incurred by validating the vow would be far greater than breaching it; and therefore it ought not to be made valid, for the welfare of all the parties involved.

Of course, Ibn Taymiyyah was challenged on the grounds that a divorce oath should be considered on the same level as other oaths, such as an oath taken in the divine name. Al-Subkī,[79] a younger contemporary of Ibn Taymiyyah, and chief justice of Syria, criticized his theory on the grounds that an oath taken in the divine name and a vow made unto God are expressions of human intentions to perform an act that would please Him. Divorce may not be considered in the same manner as the pilgrimage or as acts of charity when they are pledged, says al-Subkī. Furthermore, he continues, the oath of divorce had not been considered among the legitimate oaths of Islam in the days of the Companions. It had crept into the community, along with other oaths and become conventional. Al-Subkī's argument utilizes the *ḥadīth* by Muḥammad which prescribes the only legitimate formula for oath, namely, the name of God.[80] He compromises this principle, however, by concluding that divorce which is not to be treated as an oath or a vow, should occur on the grounds that it must have been the intention of the person pronouncing it. In this treatment, atonement is, therefore, not required.

Al-Subkī's view appears more plausible with regard to the inappropriateness of requiring an atonement, since divorce as an oath cannot be established textually, or even from the records of the early Muslims up to seventy years following Muḥammad's death.[81] However, it must be remembered that the Qur'ān treats divorce as repudiation and this, when solemnly made, has the effect of an oath. Nevertheless, that divorce should be made to take effect only because a man had pronounced it but with no intention in fact of making it effective, is in the interest of neither the parties directly involved nor the Muslim Community at large. Ibn Taymiyyah's view that divorce in this context would not be valid was concerned with the well-being (*maṣlaḥah*) of society, and was textually supported. As for the atonement measure, it may have a punitive value for the careless individual who jeopardizes the serious social institution of marriage as well as his own familial relationships, and who appeals to an oath--be it legitimate or illegitimate--in frivolity. Moreover, atonement should have its positive religious and social values, too. For a man to make the pilgrimage or to fast three days in atonement for his frivolity does constitute an opportunity for growth in his personal piety and in social relations. Or, if he pays for his transgression by emancipating a slave, both he and society are the better for it. At any rate, the matter of atonement for an unmet divorce pronouncement must remain inconclusive since there is not a statutory text to support it. It is noteworthy that certain changes apparent in the revised divorce law of Egypt (Code 25, For 1929),[82] and of Syria (Code 59, dated September 17, 1953),[83] are recognizably influenced directly by Ibn Taymiyyah's non-traditional assessment of the phenomenon of divorce.

Ibn Taymiyyah was a creative and independent interpreter. Though he belonged to the Ḥanbalī School, he ranked with first-degree *mujtahidūn* for his originality of interpretation as well as his faithfulness to the sources of Islamic law. The sources he acknowledged were the Qur'ān, the *Sunnah, ijmā*ʿ and proper *qiyās*. When he was certain of the faithfulness of his interpretation to those sources, even though it might have differed from his school's or the others', he dared introduce it and face the consequences.

CHAPTER VII

IBN TAYMIYYAH'S SOCIAL IDEOLOGY

I. *The Muslim Community:*

The Muslim Community (*al-ummah al-islāmiyyah*, or, *jamā'at al-islām*) is defined in terms of an all-inclusive commonwealth, so to speak, which is held together by its faith in God and conformity to the words and example of his Prophet, Muḥammad. Though, ideally, this Community is one, in actuality it became subject to division due to regional particularisms and to the non-Arabic factions of Islam as represented by the *Shu'ūbbiyyah* movement as early as the third century after the *Hijrah*. By the time of Ibn Taymiyyah, not only was the Muslim Commonwealth divided into a multitude of independent Islamic states, but also internal religious and racial conflict was abundantly evident in the Syro-Egyptian empire, except insofar as the advent of the Crusades and the invasions of the Tatar had necessitated a unity of forces against common dangers. This need for such union, discipline and mutual understanding served to accentuate the originality of Ibn Taymiyyah's concept of the Muslim Community.

II. *The Meaning of Solidarity (Ta'āwun)*

One important element in understanding Ibn Taymiyyah's conception of the Community is the meaning of solidarity (*ta'āwun*) of the Muslims. He exposed a prevalent form of "solidarity"[1] that is inconsistent with Islamic idea: namely, a partisan kind of "solidarity of action which, in the name of promoting a united front, served to underscore multiplicity over against unity, and to advance the part over the whole." Ibn Taymiyyah's chief criticism[2] of that sort of solidarity which was advanced either for ethnic or ritual reasons, was precisely that it tended to militate against the greater unity of Islam; indeed it impeded the exercise of good social and political life. He pointed to the debilitating influences of such a notion upon the functions of the state: the partiality with which governors and agents were appointed by the Sultanate, the injustice with which the wealth of the communities was distributed, the complacency with which interceded requests (*shafāʿāt*) were granted by those in authority to win the favor of their political, ethnic or sectarian constituents. Ibn Taymiyyah likened the rigidity of doctrinal particularism to the exclusivism of the Rawāfiḍ who placed an excessive importance (*ghuluw*) on one component of a totality, and who put within the Community an element of dissension that was capable of impeding the expansive force of Islam. Such was the "solidarity" exhibited by these tribal groups who, when they were Islamized, continued to show dogmatic arrogance, notably through their esoteric views, and often placed themselves above the law of the state.

Ibn Taymiyyah, on the other hand, explained *taʿāwun* in terms of the solidarity that binds together all Muslim believers from Muḥammad to the Final Judgment, in a spirit of unity and brotherhood, in the same ideals and for the same ends. It is by this solidarity that the Community formed a grand entity, where each part is strengthened by the whole; where each generation, in the continuous tradition of strict narrow morality, owes a debt of regard to that which preceded it, and has an obligation of trust to transmit to that which follows; and where each group, ethnic or racial, is legitimately tolerated for what it contributes to the total unity.

Thus the concept of solidarity appears to have two distinct forms in Ibn Taymiyyah's thought, although he himself does not designate them by two special terms, and is to be understood by analogy. It is constituted by the recognition of the one God, the same Prophet, and an adherence to a common body of doctrine. Such a solidarity he calls a solidarity "of good action and of piety" (*birr* and *taqwā*). For Ibn Taymiyyah, one of the worthy principles of the [early] Muslim Community (*Ahl al-Sunnah wa-l-Jamaʿah*) lies in the unity of their doctrine, which principle he puts forward in his refutation of the contradictions of the philosophers, logicians and scientific positivists. Even the problematic of the existence of four major schools of *fiqh* interpretation is explained as possessing a basic, underlying unity as did the interpretations of the Companions who were themselves divided on certain points of doctrine. The actual divergences of the *madhāhib*, to which Ibn Taymiyyah devoted an entire treatise under the title *Ikhtilāf al-Ummah fī al-ʿIbādāt*,[3] is explained by the *ʿulamā*'s fragmentary knowledge of the texts, by their tendency to attach excessive importance to certain elements (*ghuluw*), and, in a more general way, by their errors in *ijtihād*, which in themselves are not reprehensible except as they become, and they do become, imposed upon the community as truths. Moreover, these errors are less weighty, at least theoretically, if one is to succeed in rediscovering for oneself the verse or the *ḥadīth* which would correct the error.[4] Ibn Taymiyyah further contends that such errors are not, at length, of great significance since the interpretations never concern themselves with the requirements and prohibitions (*wajibāt* and *makrūhāt*) of religion, nor are they uniquely such prescriptions that may be recommended alone.[5] And it is for these very reasons that Ibn Taymiyyah urges mutual sympathy and reciprocal tolerance among the followers of the *madhāhib* for the sake of the greater unity which ought not to be compromised.

III. *The Problematic of Ethnic Origin*

Nor is the problematic of the Arabhood (*ʿurūbah*) of the Islamic Community (*ummah*) such that it could not be surmounted. For it is true that Ibn Taymiyyah not only defended the position that Arab identity--of race and of language--is virtually synonymous with that of the Islamic Community, but vigorously demanded it.[6] His argument insisted that a true knowledge of Islam depends on the Arabic language, and that a full compliance with the religion requires a thorough mastery of the language. The language itself is part of the religious framework of Islam, since the knowledge of Qur'ān and the *Sunnah*, the understanding of which is required of every Muslim pre-requires precise knowledge of Arabic. Furthermore, since Islam is the religion of not only a corpus of doctrine but also of practical daily living, the language of the Qur'ān and of the *Sunnah* must also be the language of the mosque, the home, the street, the house of the legislature, the place of government and the market-place. He argues that since the use of a language has psychological and moral influences upon those who use it, great care must be taken to avoid the use of the languages of non-Arabs, and, rather, to preserve the purity of Arabic both in the homeletic address and in conversation. One of the significant benefits for Muslims of the use of Arabic exclusively is that it will aid them in emulating the early Muslims, and, in so doing, they gain a greater capacity for growth in wisdom, morality and faith. He says:

واعلم بأن اعتياد اللغة يؤثر فى العقل والخلق والدين
تأثيرا قويا ، ويؤثر ايضا فى مشابهة صدر هذه الأمة من
الصحابة والتابعين . ومشابهتهم تزيد العقل والخلق والدين[7]

Ibn Taymiyyah further prohibits the reading of the Qur'ān by any man, in a language other than Arabic, "whether he is capable of it or not." Likewise, he prohibits the translation of the Qur'ān, or any portion of it even if it is only one verse, into another language; because the translation of any text has the effect of weakening it, and for the Qur'ān particularly, it would disclaim its miraculous inimitability (*i'jāz*).

Ethnically, too, apart from the fact that the Prophet was one of them, the Arabs, according to Ibn Taymiyyah are a superior race. Superiority, for him, is marked by either the possession of useful knowledge (*al-'ilm al-nāfi'*) or [the example of] doing good (*al-'amal al-ṣāliḥ*). Knowledge, on the one hand, utilizes the mind which is the center of learning and understanding, and is capable of perfection which is the achievement of sound reasoning, which in turn is best served by the power of expression. The Arabs, he asserts, have proven their superior keenness of mind and power of expression. On the other hand, action is the extension of morality, which is the sum of the [conditioned] instincts of man. Ibn Taymiyyah contends that the Arabs' instinctive tendency toward the good, their generosity of hand and spirit, their bravery, and their faithful loyalty have been shown through the ages to be greater than those of other races. This was true even with Pre-Muḥammadan Arabs who were, like unplowed earth, "already capable of good work but latent in producing it." When Muḥammad was sent of God to proclaim Islam, he planted in that soil the best seeds which possessed the potential for the best fruit. He tilled it, and gathered in abundant and indescribable harvests, thus achieving the perfect combination of root and fruit.

Language and ethnic origin are elements of ultimate significance in the process of human thought and action, which for Ibn

Taymiyyah is part of the Sharī'ah which incorporates the thought modalities of the preceding generations of Muslims, and their manner. He observes that the Muslim Community holds this rule unanimously, "He who would achieve excellence, seeks the excellent way of the Arabs who went before."

Ibn Taymiyyah's construct of the Arab synonymity with the Islamic *Ummah* is based on Qur'ānic internal witness, in such verses as, "فاستمسك بالذى أوحى إليك، إنك على صراط مستقيم، وإنه لذكرك ولقومك وسوف تسألون"[8] and, "كنتم خير أمة أخرجت للناس تأمرون بالمعروف وتنهون عن المنكر"[9] He is completely confident in the divine wisdom of this choice, and reiterates, "الله أعلم حيث يجعل رسالته"[10]

Further evidence is traced in the Tradition: for example, after Al-Tirmidhī and Al-Bayhaqī, the Prophet is quoted as saying, "When He [God] created me, He made me the [best] choice (*khayr*) of His creatures; when He formed the tribes, He made me [a member] of the best of tribes; when He created the souls, He made me one of the best of their souls; then when He created the clans (*buyūt*), He made me of their best. I am, therefore, the choice of clans, and of souls."[11]

In the body of the law (*fiqh*), Ibn Taymiyyah finds ample evidence for the leadership of the Arabs in the political and religious affairs of nations, and suggests further that their Arabization is a religious imperative. This is because religion stands upon word and work. Arabic *fiqh* is the way that leads to the understanding of the word; and the *fiqh* of the example (*sunnah*) leads to the knowledge of its required action.[12] He quotes al-Shāfi'ī's statement in the *Risālah*,[13] "...[God] decreed that [His people] preach particularly unto them [the people of The Prophet] in their Arabic tongue, which is also their tongue. It is the duty of every Muslim to learn of the tongue of the Arabs all he can...." Ibn Taymiyyah points out that this was the ruling of other legists, "including Aḥmad Ibn Ḥanbal, Isḥāq Ibn Ibrāhīm, 'Abdullah Ibn al-Zubayr, Sa'īd Ibn Manṣūr, and others whom we have known or consulted."[14]

One last component of the discussion of the Arabhood of the Muslim Community, however, is, according to the argument of Ibn Taymiyyah, that it is less essential for a Muslim to be of Arab descent than it is for him to know the Arabic language. This is based on the saying of the Prophet, that "O People, The Lord is One; the father [Adam?] is one; religion is one. Arabhood (*al-ʿarabiyyah*) is neither father nor mother ["not geneologically inherited"]; rather, it is a tongue. He who speaks it is an Arab."[15]

IV. *The Problematic of Language*

It is at this very point, namely that Arabhood (*ʿurūbah, ʿarabiyyah*) is not racially defined, that Ibn Taymiyyah offers a convincing argument that serves to demonstrate that the Muslim Community is far greater than being merely Arab in ethnicity.

He begins his own counter-argument, so to speak, by demonstrating that being an Arab does not always guarantee one's eligibility for the faith and life of Islam. Arabs, he acknowledges, are divided; and some of them are of no avail [to Islam] (*ahl jufaʿ*). He cites the Qur'ān also: " الأعراب أشدّ كفرا ونفاقا ، وأجدر أن لا يعلموا حدود ما انزل الله على رسوله، والله عليم حكيم. ومن الأعراب من يتخذ ما ينفق مغرما وما يتربّص بكم الدوائر.."[16] It is as though the superiority of the Arab race, Ibn Taymiyyah implies, reveals itself in a negative way, i.e., if anyone is more capable of disbelief and hypocrisy, it is also the Arabs. In the Day of Judgment, they will use the exercise of their superiority in economic competence and their ethnic loyalty as their excuse for not believing the Prophet and his message. They will plead with him, the Qur'ān warns: " سيقول لكم المخلفون من الاعراب شغلتنا أموالنا وأهلونا فاستغفر لنا ، يقولون بألسنتهم ماليس فى قلوبهم . قل: فمن يملك لكم من الله شيئا ان أراد بكم ضرّا أو أراد بكم نفعا ؟ بل كان الله بما تعملون خبيرا . بل ظننتم أن لن ينقلب الرسول والمؤمنون الى أهليهم أبدا ، وزين ذلك فى قلوبكم ، وظننتم السوء وكنتم قوما بورا "[17] Ibn Taymiyyah's intellectual honesty drives him to point further to the unprejudiced witness of the Qur'ān: " ومن الأعراب من يؤمن بالله واليوم الآخر . . . ومن حولكم من الأعراب منافقون ، ومن أهل المدينة مردوا على النفاق . لا تعلمهم . نحن نعلمهم ، سنعذبهم . ."[18]

Likewise, conversely, non-Arabs (*al-ʿajam*), i.e., Persians, Romans, Turks, Berber, Abbysinians, etc., may be divided to believers and unbelievers, righteous and unrighteous. The Qur'ān, once more, is cited in favor of non-Arab believers: " هو الذى بعث فى الاميين رسولا منهم يتلو عليه آياته ويزكيهم ويعلمهم الكتاب والحكمة وإن كانوا من قبل لفى ضلال مبين . وآخرين منهم لما يلحقوا بهم . . . "[19] Ibn Taymiyyah's use of the Qur'ānic verse capitalizes on the universality of the message of the Prophet: The recipients of this message of necessity, include those who are "illiterate," which, according to Ibn Taymiyyah's reading of the context, refers to non-Arabs. The Prophet's point of identification with those is that he himself was unschooled. More importantly, God's purpose in the racial diversity within the order of his creation is clearly given: " يا أيها الناس انّا خلقناكم من ذكر وأنثى وجعلناكم شعوبا وقبائل لتعارفوا ان أكرمكم عند الله أتقاكم "[20] For one race to know another transcends all distinctions, and offers an opportunity for righteousness to flourish.

The Tradition is also called upon to vindicate the worth of non-Arabs. The Prophet is authoritatively reported to have said in a sermon, "'O People, behold, your Lord...is One; behold, your father is one; behold, there is no more merit in a black man than in a red man except insofar as piety is concerned. Have you not made [this] known?' They said: 'Yes.' He said: 'Let him who is present tell it to him who is absent.'"[21] Another *ḥadīth*, after ʿAmr, indicates at once the Prophet's consciousness of the Source of his message, and his conviction of the imperative bond between all believers. He said, "The sons of a certain man are not [necessarily] my relatives. God is my Patron, and [so are] the righteous believers."[22] Faith and righteousness are available to any man; as the Prophet said, "If religion is in Pleiades, it may be reached even by one of the sons of Persia."[23] The reference is explicitly to non-Arabs, and may be based on the Qurʾānic verse, " وان تتولوا يستبدل قوما غيركم .... "[24] as interpreted by Muḥammad himself to indicate Persian Muslims.

In this regard, Ibn Taymiyyah's conclusion is the same: the very existence of the Islamic Community depends on a kind of solidarity that is larger than the solidarity of its segments against one another. He reminds all Muslims of the Qurʾānic exhortation, " واعتصموا بحبل الله جميعا ولا تفرّقوا "[25] and places before them the Prophet's model for the unity of the *Ummah*: "The believers' mutual friendship, kindness, and caring is like unto that of the members of one body, wherein if one complained, the others suffer with fever, and rush in with attentive watching."[26] The Prophet's commandment is therewith reiterated, "Do not separate yourselves [from one another]; do not conspire [against one another]; do not harbor mutual hatred; do not nurture mutual envy [or jealousy]; [but] be God's servants and [one another's] brothers, as God has commanded you."[27]

Now that Ibn Taymiyyah has resolved with both scholarly integrity and personal fairness the superficial conflict between the Muslim Community and Arab racial identity, what of the problematic of language? He has shown great enough tolerance, without compromising the Islamic principle.

While he insists that Arabic is indispensable for the knowledge of Islam, as it is the language of the Qur'ān and the *Sunnah*, and as it is the emblem (*shi'ār*) of the *Ummah*, and that curious investigation of other languages could have its undesirable influence upon the mind of the investigator as well as upon the unity of the culture itself, Ibn Taymiyyah's argument of the interrelationship between the intention (*niyyah*) and the formula (*lafẓ*) in matters of religious ritual and law may be deduced to contribute toward an understanding of how the conflict of language and faith may be addressed. The intention fulfilled according to Ibn Taymiyyah is far more effectual than the verbal expression of it. Likewise, the intention to believe and to carry out the implications of the Islamic faith in the context of the Muslim Community is of more serious consequence than the verbal mastery of it.[28] Ibn Taymiyyah's notion of "solidarity," however, goes beyond a geographic, ethnic, doctrinal or linguistic solidarity. For him, it is an organic unity that supposes a common goal (*muqṣūd*), and the participation of every member of the community in the realization and fulfillment of that goal, within his limitations and without the distinctions of the external responsibility. It is that goal of this Community which will distinguish it as the greatest of all communities and nations; for it is a community of justice which commands the good and denounces evil (*al-amr bi al-ma'rūf wa al-nahy 'an al-munkar*).[29] It is the duty of each member of the community, as an expression of this solidarity, to uphold his fellow when he does good, and, insofar as he has influence, to correct him when he violates the law of the Community through verbal admonition and, in the event that he is not able, through the firm intentions of his heart. Each member of the Community is held responsible, as he sees the need, to offer good counsel (*naṣīḥah*), fraternal corrective direction (*wa'ẓ*), and an invitation to the right (*dā'wah*). This latter duty, namely the mission of every Muslim in which is seen by Ibn Taymiyyah the element of "prophetic calling" (*nubuwwah*), is of utter necessity to the life of the Community, if it is to achieve cohesion. This moral solidarity which is required of the faithful is the element capable of making this Community God's witnesses on earth (*shuhadā' Allāh fī al-arḍ*). This for Ibn Taymiyyah,[30] is the meaning of the Prophet's analogy of the "one body" wherein each member shows care for the other. It is the same idea inherent also in the analogy of an edifice, wherein the elements reinforce one another, and all adhere together by the Prophet, as the fingers are connected to and through the hand. Mutual expectations of Muslims are listed, not by way of enumeration but for the demonstration of inclusiveness, in the Prophet's saying: "Five obligations are owed by the Muslim to his fellow Muslim: To greet him if he meets him, to visit him if he falls ill, to wish him joyous victory over his enemies if he sneezes, to answer him if he calls, and to escort him [to his final resting place] when he dies."[31] Again and again, the Prophet is quoted to support the seriousness of this point; he said, "By Him in whose hand is my soul, no one of you is a believer until he desires for his fellow what he desires for himself,"[32] and he said, "The Muslim is the brother of the Muslim: he shall neither abandon him nor oppress him."[33] This bond commands mutual service and mutual support. The exhortation is repeated,[34] " واعتصموا بحبل الله جميعا ولا تفرّقوا " and God declared the Prophet's innocence of those who are divisive in the Community of faith, thus excluding themselves from it, " ان الذين فرّقوا في دينهم كانوا شيعا لست منهم في شيء . انما أمرهم الى الله"[35]

The entire doctrine of the *ummah*, or the Community, therefore, is set within the context of moral solidarity which is founded on the unity of God's purpose to advance the good and stop evil. When some men depart from any portion of God's commandment, division and hostility set in among them, Ibn Taymiyyah says. And when men are divided they become corrupt and perish; but if they band together for a common end, they are reconciled and prosper. In solidarity there is salvation (*raḥmah*), in division destruction (*'adhāb*).[36]

To do good and to refrain from doing evil, to exhort others to do good and to admonish them against doing evil, is the task before whom all members of the Community of faith and justice stand equally responsible and are mutually accountable. Before this divinely-assigned task, all distinctions are rendered of little consequence.

V. *The Political Problematic*

Thus far, it is to be recognized, Ibn Taymiyyah has been speaking in terms of the ideal Community. Such was also the character of the original Community of Muslims which consisted of the Prophet, the Companions and those who followed immediately. In that community there was true unity of belief and unity of purpose.[37] As such the Community called for no political distinction, since the individual virtue of its members was sufficient for the maintenance of social cohesion without the necessity to resort to force. However, since the Muslim Community became subjected to the disunity which results from ignorance and injustice, it could not survive without a hierarchical structure that assigned to everyone his place, or without the deliberate action of an overseer that could maintain order.

Ibn Taymiyyah, who was as practical as he was faithful to doctrine and to reason, provided, in the face of this necessity, a scriptural and a rational foundation for such hierarchy. From the very beginning, the Qur'ān has commanded obedience to God, to the Prophet and to those in authority, without providing a precise formula outlining the political order of authority. According to Abū Dāwūd, the Prophet has instructed that, if three men set out upon a journey, one of them be designated chief. The same prescription is found in these same terms in the *Musnad* of Ibn Ḥanbal, where ʿAbd Allah Ibn ʿUmar reports an action of the Prophet, designating one man of three travelling upon the desert as commanding authority among them. Ali, too, in the Sunnī tradition, long before the demands of the *Rawāfiḍ* could be anticipated, envisaged the necessity for a commanding officer. For Ibn Taymiyyah, political allegiance comes as no surprise, for it was also commonplace to the traditional *Ahl al-Salaf*. Henri Laoust cites, for an example, Sufyān al-Thawrī, of whom Ibn al-Jawzī had written a commendable biography, and whose ideas had quietly influenced Ibn Taymiyyah's thought. Sufyān held that the true servant of God is from the first responsible also to obey the state.[38] It was in this sense that Fuḍayl Ibn ʿIyād and Aḥmad Ibn Ḥanbal delighted themselves by repeating that "sixty nights under an unjust ruler are better than one without a ruler," thus preferring the discipline of the State to the tyranny inherent in the absence of authority.

Ibn Taymiyyah's rational justification for political structure, Laoust points out, is "directly borrowed from al-Muṭahhar al-Ḥillī: it dates back, in *Minhāj al-Karāmah*, to the philosophy of al-Fārābī and Ikhwān al-Ṣafā, and for that matter, to the *Republic* of Plato."[39] Those principal ideas [of the Ikhwān], Laoust continues, ring familiar: Men are made to live in society, for their solidarity and mutual aid are necessary for the fulfillment of their needs; yet their instinctive egoism incites every individual to claim for himself the exclusive right to profit, which right is demanded by society; society cannot survive unless a power superior to that of individuals is exerted to place each one within the limits of his individual rights.[40] In addition to his civil authority, Laoust notes, the head of state, according to Ibn Taymiyyah and others such as al-Ghazālī, has the responsibility of exacting the requirements of the law, and of leadership in the celebration of the feasts and the rituals (*shaʿāʾir*) of Islam. The secular branch is, therefore, indispensable for putting into practice the first requirement of law, namely that which consists of commanding the good and the forbidding of evil.[41]

To this point, Ibn Taymiyyah's idea of authority is fairly traditional. Yet he departs radically, but sensibly, in asserting that all authority need not be concentrated in one man. Islamic political universalism which is already affirmed in the Sunnī systems of doctrine of al-Fārābī, al-Juwaynī, al-Ghazālī and Fakhr al-Dīn al-Rāzī, had always demanded that the perfect state ought to encompass the whole of human affairs. Ibn Taymiyyah, for the first time in the history of Sunnī sociology sought to offer canonical justification for a "parcelling out" of authority. He argues that the Community, which was politically one at the time of the *Salaf*, need not necessarily remain as such. In fact, it had not continued to survive in unity: the vicissitudes of history had rent it apart into a multitude of independent principalities. Its real unity, therefore, resides in a place other than the fiction of a political unity--it resides in the solidarity of the religious avowals of each state, all of which having a sense of proper autonomy as well as an awareness of being a member of an organic whole. For Ibn Taymiyyah, *the ideal Community is a spontaneous confederation of states.*[42]

The question is raised as to how to reconcile this hierarchy with the equality in the sight of God (*musāwāh*) of all believers who constitute the social structure of Islam (*jamā'ah*). Ibn Taymiyyah finds the solution in the relationship which he established between individual and social aptitude, or capability (*qudrah*), on the one hand, and obligation, or duty (*wājib*) on the other. Human differences of race, birth, and seniority in Islam hold no weight in the sight of God. Only personal merit acquired through effective service rendered for his cause (*taqwā, 'ibādah*) counts in the sight of God. Each one does according to his own measure of ability. The social structure's function is to generate a sense of duty. The ruler is held accountable for more obligations than his subjects. If the entire social structure of action has any merit before God, it does so to the extent that it becomes a structure for duty.[43]

VI. *Excommunication from the Community*

The action of excluding (*takfīr*) a person from the community was for Ibn Taymiyyah a last resort in dealing with a transgressor. His view may be more clearly understood against the background of the historical development of the concept within the Muslim Community. Two opposed views had evolved with respect to determining a legislation to deal with the individual who commits a grave transgression (*fisq*), i.e., a transgression other than heresy, such as murder, theft, adultery, slander, etc. The Khawārij,[44] on the one hand, rigorously considered such a person outside the law without debate or appeal, and required the public powers of the community to demand him to recant publicly. The Murji'ah,[45] on the other, held that it was sufficient to apply a penalty, which could be determined by the law, constituting an objective reparation. Once penalized, the transgressor (*fāsiq*) is restored to the status of believer. He would continue to enjoy all the rights of the community, participate in all its ritual activities, and aspire to eternal reward. The Mu'tazilah,[46] who emerged as a result of the debate over this doctrine, originated a third understanding that became and remained peculiarly their own. They asserted that an offender, in his present life, occupies an intermediate position (*manzilah bayn al-manzilatayn*): because of his transgression, he is neither a believer (*mu'min*) nor an unbeliever (*kāfir*), and, in the hereafter, as a *fāsiq* he would reside eternally in hell.

For the Traditionalists (*Ahl al-Sunnah*), neither the rigid penal system of the Khawārij, nor the incomprehensible doctrine of the Mu'tazilah, nor the flexible and potentially inconsistent approach of the Murji'ah was adequately applicable.[47] Ibn Ḥanbal, although he was often considered intolerant and a fanatic partisan, reserved the act of exclusion from the community for only the Jahmiyyah, who denied the divine attributes. Even so, he took especial care to suggest a very general doctrine of excommunication, and demanded utter circumspection in declaring that a Muslim was one of them. "Moreover," records Ibn Taymiyyah, "he often asked God to accord them His mercy and forgiveness, because these heretics did not know that they had offended Him, and did not have a true awareness of their error." Ibn Ḥanbal does not excommunicate the Murji'ah who are not clearly distinguished from *Ahl al-Sunnah*, and calls for agreement on the excommunication of the Qadariyyah who reject determinism in favor of free will. He also assigns the ultimate penalty of capital punishment to the Qadarī who rejects the attribute of divine knowledge (*'ilm*).[48] Such a denier of the knowledge of God shall be considered as a *jahmī*, and shall be executed for his heresy, as a public example, in order to protect the weak members of the community, who may be susceptible to such error. This traditional tolerant view of the *Sunnah*, which is shared by most Ḥanbalīs, may be also identified in the thought of certain Ash'arīs, such as al-Ghazālī who justifiably could not recognize the influence of the Ash'arī school on the essential body of Islamic doctrine since indeed many Ash'arīs had been forced, upon contact with the Mu'tazilah view, into a stance of extreme intolerance toward any others who did not profess their same conception of the divinity.[49]

The framework of Ibn Taymiyyah's contribution to the issue of excommunication is properly that of the general tolerance of *Ahl al-Salaf*. No Muslim who confesses his faith (by pronouncing the *Shahādah*) and fulfills the duty of prayer, Ibn Taymiyyah says, may be excommunicated without being previously given an extremely prudent consideration. His position is clearly based on his conception of *ijtihād*. He says, neither the Qur'ān nor the *Sunnah* proceeded to offer a specific listing of the conditions of excommunication. The duty of the Muslim Community renders it imperative to allow for a harmony of divergent interpretations of the Law when they seem properly founded. No organization has the authority to legislate in the matter unilaterally, as a decision to excommunicate often bears the risk of not being the result of *ijtihād*. In this matter, the testimony of the sects is admissible as representative of an aspect of the truth. Islamic individualism grants each one only his conscience, enlightened by the Qur'ān and the *Sunnah*. Above all, however, it will be necessary to separate the question of principle from the question of action: For it could be decreed that whoever utters a certain statement is a *kāfir*, but unless and until positive evidence that an individual had actually made such a statement, no conclusion may be arrived at to excommunicate him. Furthermore, this is the rule that must always be invoked to follow in all the legal prescriptions which concern divine punishment (*wa'īd*). The objects of divine punishment may be known; but it is far more difficult, on the other hand, to say that a certain Muslim deserves such punishment, because one of the conditions required for ascertaining his guilt may be absent, such as in the case of a Muslim who may ignore some of the prohibitions, but whose good works are capable of compensating for his violations.

The conditions of excommunication for Ibn Taymiyyah, at least in theory, since he is generally tolerant on the issue, are the same as those which constitute the position of Ibn Qudāmah and other Ḥanbalīs: they include apostacy (*kufr bi Allah*), associationism (*shirk*), accusing God of lying (*takdhīb Allah*), insult (*sabb* or *shatm*) to God, or the Prophet, rejecting the Prophets, rejecting the revealed Scripture (i.e., the Qur'ān) or any one of their (the previous Prophets') books, or a portion thereof, rejecting any of the constitutive dogmas of Islam, or considering as lawful a prohibition which is agreed upon as such by consensus (*ijmāʻ*).[50] A slightly different ranking of these offenses distinguishes Ibn Taymiyyah from Ibn Qudāmah, for example. For him to insult (*sabb*) the Prophet's wives or Companions is a serious offense; to deviate from a constitutive doctrine of the faith is an equally grave sin; but to insult the Prophet is an unpardonable sin and deserves the punishment of death.[51] The abuse of slaves, for example, on the other hand, requires severe penalty, and repentance from this loathsome practice does not suspend the punishment.

In summary, Ibn Taymiyyah argues for the excommunication of the Jahmiyyah who deny the attributes of God, the Rawāfiḍ and the Ismāʻīlīs who reject the need for canonical law. Similarly, he allows no room in the midst of the Muslim Community for the hypocrites (*munāfiqūn*) to flaunt their incoherence with the plainly given divine commandments. Astrologers would qualify for excommunication "because they seek the events, and the stars, and resort to magic which is universally prohibited."[52] Nor are those who practice the cult of visiting the graves of their saints, and decorate the exteriors of their places of worship with symbols of heretical assent,[53] to be included in the Muslim Community.

VII. *The Status of Religious Minorities*

The Sharīʻah allows religious minorities (*Ahl al-Kitāb*, i.e., "the People of the Book," or, *Ahl al-Dhimmah*, i.e., "the People of the Covenant") to live in the midst of the Community under the conditions of allegiance to Muslim sovereignty and the payment of poll tax. Ibn Taymiyyah follows the Qurʼānic definition of *Ahl al-Kitāb*, namely, the Jews and those that follow the religion of the Torah, the Christians and those that follow the religion of the Evangel [the Gospel]. The Magians (*Majūs*) are considered an intermediate group between *Ahl al-Kitāb* and the associationists (*Mushrikūn*).[54] Although the tolerance of the early Muslims allowed confessional minorities to live in their community with a measure of security, Ibn Taymiyyah reflected the spirit of his time, which was characterized by an understandable feeling of religious xenophobia. Laoust, on this point, observes that, in spite of the precautions of his language, Ibn Taymiyyah's obvious aim was to advance a totalitarian concept of the community, and at length, to reduce the minorities through the strict restoration of the treaty of ʿUmar.[55] The pact, which ʿUmar concluded with the Christians of Syria in the presence of the Muhajirūn and the Anṣār, being the first precise legislation regulating the relationship of minorities to the Muslim Community, became, as Ibn Taymiyyah viewed it, the model for rules that followed, such as ʿUmar Ibn ʿAbd al-Azīz, and even the Caliph Hārūn al-Rashīd himself.[56]

By the time of Ibn Taymiyyah, the strict dictates which are explicit in that legal document had been so increasingly abandoned that he often denounced the entry of members of minorities, especially the Christians, into public political positions. He assigns a large share of the blame for this unlawful emancipation on the Faṭimīs of Egypt who "claim to be Muslims, but are in their essence, Rawāfiḍ, Bāṭinīs and Ismāʿīlīs bringing dishonor to the Sunnī element, and favoring the Jews and the Christians." He decries the entry of Christians into the service of the state under the Caliph al-Muʿizz and his minister al-Fāʾiz.[57] From that moment, he noted, they managed to abscond from dutiful taxation; they intermingled with the rest of the population; they blazed about an insolent light. They succeeded in occupying positions of power within the high places of government, of financial administration and of national security. They put their experienced skills for profit, and their crafty amiability, to work for their self-enrichment to the detriment of Muslims. They have notorious greed: they gamble in their own churches. The Jews, too, sell wines to Muslims in Cairo. In the public ceremonies of their cult they jostle one another ostentatiously where the banners of Islam are unfurled. Their religious practices, and even their edifices which were becoming increasingly numerous, were dangerously encroaching.[58] Such was considered, "in effect, a veritable threat to Islam" remarks Laoust, "and could invite only a hostile attitude, for they increasingly pledged their sympathy and their aid to its enemies; and every defeat for Islam was an occasion for their flagrant rejoicing. The Rawāfiḍ, the Franks and the Tatar found in them a favorable complicity for their conquests. Notably, the Rawāfiḍ, who had already stood, in word and action, by the side of the enemies of Islam in Khurāsān, in Iraq and in the Jazīrah where they furnished strong assistance to the Turks, were, from the fourth to the seventh century, in Syria and in Egypt, the defenders of the Christians. The sympathy they offered the Jews is of scandalous notoriety."[59] The threat of the religious minority, especially that of the Christians, menaced Islam indirectly, and Ibn Taymiyyah was always profoundly apprehensive of them. For the Christian ascetics had gained the empathy of their Muslim counterpart (*zuhhād*) and introduced them to the taste of monastic life (*khalwah*, or *rahbāniyyah*); the vow of celebacy was borrowed from them. The mass of the population in Egypt often participated in the celebration of Christian feasts; and one of their chief influences is at the root of the cults of saints and pilgrimages to local shrines. Ibn Taymiyyah's fairness compels him to point out that the Muslims themselves did not keep the stipulations of the pact.[60] To put an end to such deadly laxity, Ibn Taymiyyah finds no other way than to request the imām to apply the demands of 'Umar *ad ipsissima verba*.[61]

VIII. *The Obligations of Muslims Toward Minorities*

The pact of 'Umar with the Christians of Syria was a formal treaty conforming to the Islamic regulations of a legal contract. It is referred to by Ibn Taymiyyah as a "covenant" in the same manner that such other "covenants" or "contracts," e.g., of marriage, of sales, of a bequest, etc., are recognized. It imposes precise obligations on both parties, and is deemed legally binding. It is set in the framework of Islamic justice and good will, and is to be understood against the background of the Prophet's *ḥadīth* which suggests that an injury hurled upon a dependent is hurled against himself.[62] Other traditions, cited by Ibn Taymiyyah,[63] indicating the protection the Prophet had guaranteed for the *dhimmīs*, include, "God forbid you to enter into the home of the People of the Book without [their] permission, to beat them, or to take away their crops when they have fulfilled their obligations," and, "Behold, he who oppresses a *dhimmī* ('a covenanter,' i.e., a non-Muslim citizen or ally) cheats him or imposes upon him [a duty] which is above his capability, or usurps his possessions, I shall be his tormenter in the Day of Judgment." The exhortation for just relationships between the Muslims and *Ahl al-Kitāb* is thus clear; yet, Ibn Taymiyyah, without violating the rights of minorities, upholds the solidarity of the Muslim Community as the greater ethical responsibility, since to maintain that solidarity is the only guarantee of justice for minorities. Justice with respect to the religious minorities within the Community is not violated, implies Ibn Taymiyyah, when the words of ʿUmar are taken to heart: "humiliate them, but do no injustice to them" (*adhillūhum wa la taẓlimūhum*).[64] The probable meaning of this apparent paradox is, according to Laoust, "in the spirit of justice, the Muslims have the responsibility of according *Ahl al-Kitāb* a humiliating respect, to cause them constantly to be reminded of their irremediable inferiority, to be aware of their oppositeness (*mukhālafah*) and to be conscious of their own hostility (*muʿādāh*)."[65]

The Covenant of ʿUmar guarantees for *Ahl al-Kitāb* security of their persons, their families and their possessions, although it does not demonstrate the equal rights of the Muslim and the *dhimmī*. Muslims are obliged to extend themselves liberally in economic transactions. The People of the Book are permitted to join the Community's forces in combatting enemy attacks and if they do then the status of *dhimmī* falls down and they acquire the status of total equality. The state has the most serious obligation (*aʿẓam al-wājibāt*) of releasing Jewish or Christian prisoners. In his open letter to Sirjuwān, the Cypriot Archbishop and Head of State, Ibn Taymiyyah demonstrated how he personally put into practice this latter obligation. He states:

> All Christians know well how I have asked the Tatar to liberate our prisoners. The Tatar, nevertheless, liberated the Muslim prisoners only. Ghāzān and Qutlushā will accept; I have informed my prince of it. The Tatar, however, will deliver only the Muslims, and say, "We have only Christians whom we captured in Jerusalem; we refuse to release them." I have replied, "All Jews and Christians who are in your hands are our subjects. We must release them. We shall not wait, therefore; nor shall we leave in your hands even one prisoner, be he a Muslim or a *dhimmī*." We are determined to succeed in liberating a considerable number of Christians. That is our manner of conduct, and such is our generosity. God gives the recompense.[66]

Ibn Taymiyyah's tolerance for religious minorities, however, did not seem to go far beyond legal obligation. That that is so was essentially for the social and political order. Islam permits, for example, intermarriage with Jewish or Christian women (*kitabiyyāt*), so long as they are known to be upright (*muḥsināt*). Such intermarriage is indeed categorically permitted by the Qur'ān, or Ibn Taymiyyah would think it prohibited. At any rate, he strongly recommended in many legal decisions (*fatāwā*), given in Egypt, that such intermarriage be limited. "In the spirit of the Law," he argued, "Muslim men should not marry Christian women except in cases of need; and they should, likewise, consider it as reprehensible to obtain non-Muslim slave-women for concubines."[67] Similarly, Muslims should avoid a commercial partnership with Christians, since such partnership may contribute to their [the Christians'] prosperity, and consequently, perpetuate their infidelity,[68] and since their view of the extraction and the investment of profits does not correspond to the non-Muslim view.[69] Neither should Muslims participate in Christian feasts.[70] All in all, as may be seen in many of Ibn Taymiyyah's works, particularly throughout his *Kitāb Iqtiḍā' al-Ṣirāt*, the primary obligation of the Muslim is to uphold his own faith. If Ibn Taymiyyah's view toward religious minorities appears restrictive especially as seen against the background of a tradition generally more tolerant toward them, and against the background of the early Muslim Community which was not particularly insistent on being totally and forever homogeneous, one must understand that much of his bias was legitimized by the devastating effect of the Crusades, the infidelity of the Christian minorities within the land of Islam which is seen in their siding with the Tatars, as well as the very incoherence evident between their faith and practice in the Middle Ages.

CHAPTER VIII

IBN TAYMIYYAH'S SOCIO-POLITICAL THEORY: THE ISLAMIC STATE

Since the death of Muḥammad, the concept of *wilāyah* ("state" or "government") has been the concern of the entire Muslim Community. Ibn Taymiyyah's statement on the subject, though not innovative, offers a fresh understanding of the concept as it begins by re-thinking and re-defining the role of the State in the Community, as based on a thorough knowledge of the cumulative traditional view.[1]

In his own right, Ibn Taymiyyah was eminently qualified to offer this kind of new understanding because of his exhaustive familiarity with the arguments of the past, both traditional and radical. But the special historical circumstances of his time make his contribution all the more particularly significant.

In addition to the political chaos resulting from the Tatar invasions, beginning with Baghdad and moving westward to Syria, the Muslim Community itself had been divided into numerous independent states, each having its own political structure, and each continuing to exist under the threat of renewed attacks by the Crusaders and the Tatar. Islamic doctrine was, likewise, the object of impure influences of Greek philosophy and rational theology. The Law, too, which had enjoyed the vigorous revitalization of a liberated scholarship that exercised the sound and healthy freedom of creative interpretation, had now been rendered stagnant, or was at least stagnating into rigid and untouchable categories.

It is at this juncture that Ibn Taymiyyah's well-prepared intellectual activity in doctrine and jurisprudence was contributed to the Islamic Community, giving leadership of thought and action both in his own generation and to those that followed.

There was perhaps no greater need in the Muslim Community than the need for a clear definition of the status and the role of the State, especially now when the Syro-Egyptian Empire was under the foreign rule of the Ottoman Mamluks, which did not quite fulfill the requirements of Islam known and expounded by its scholars (*'ulamā'*, or *fuqahā'*).

Aware of this serious need, yet careful to maintain the present shaky peace, and keen to calculate the potential hazard to the Community in offering a rightful and straightforward criticism of the Mamluk government, Ibn Taymiyyah discharged his intellectual responsibility in a uniquely prudent methodology. His primary works which outline the nature and function of the Islamic State at once reveal his integrity of character and scholarship and seek to correct the prevailing misconceptions about the State by accentuating positively and objectively the implications of the idea of government through stimulating the consciousness of the community to an awareness of the rights and duties of its constituents. Thus, his *Al-Siyāsah Al-Shar'iyyah fī Iṣlāḥ Al-Rā'ī Wa Al-Ra'iyyah*, is a treatise on the meaning and the role of the State (or Political Theory);[2] his *Al-Ḥisbah fī Al-Islām* examines the extent of intervention by the State (or, public custodian, so to speak) in the economic affairs in the Community; and, *Minhāj al-Sunnah* includes his interpretation of the conception, the qualification and the obligations of religio-political leadership (*imāmah*) as well as the obligations of the constituency.[3]

Following his usual methodology, Ibn Taymiyyah was influenced in the formation of his political theory, first of all, by the fundamental principles set forth in the Qur'ān and the Tradition. His emphasis, however, was undoubtedly colored by his own opposition to the Shī'ī theory of religio-political leadership (*imāmah*) and of administrative leadership (*khilāfah*), and by the political circumstances of his age.

The general designation of the state (*wilāyah*) comprises the entire range of general public authority, and was used by Ibn Taymiyyah and others to include all levels of government within the Muslim Community, from the grand *imāmah* to territorial deputyship (*khilāfah*), to the lower echelons of government which may now be called *waẓā'if*, or [clerical, non-managerial] "jobs."

I. *The Need for Public Authority:*

Ibn Taymiyyah asserts[4] that public authority is indispensable in the social structure of human life. It is necessary according to both the Sharī'ah and reason. In the concluding chapter of *Al-Siyāsah Al-Shar'iyyah*, he says, "Let it be known that [the designation of] public authority is one of the most serious requirements of religion. Indeed, religion may not stand without it being there to uphold it, for men cannot realize their good without consolidation (*ijtimā'*), and consolidation is not possible without authority (*ra's*)." He offers a strikingly clear theological justification.

The concept of authority is rooted in belief in the unity of God and, in the unwavering purpose which is expressed in the commandment to propagate the good and to proscribe evil. In order for this to be done, with all that it entails, i.e., justice in social relationships, setting political goals and legal boundaries, collecting the *zakāt* and regulating the use of funds, etc., it is mandatory to assign such responsibilities to officials vested with sufficient power to fulfill them. Muḥammad had charted the pattern of even the minimal organization by instructing that one among three who may be travelling be designated in charge. The opinion of the *Salaf* is also involved as Ibn Taymiyyah cites the principle of Ibn Ḥanbal, as reported by al-Murūzī, "A ruler is indispensable for Muslims. Shall the rights of men be forsworn?" He argues that "Men cannot realize their good either in the present or in the life to come except through organization [or, consolidation] (*ijtimā'*) and mutual support (*tanāṣur*)...both are necessary for deriving benefits and driving away harm. For this reason, man is said to be instinctively social (*madanī*). When they are socialized (*yajtami'ū*)...they must have a commander (*āmir*, and, negatively, *nāhī*) for their common ends (*maqāṣid*)...."[5] Finally, the Qur'ānic injunction from which it may be inferred that the State is of a divine order is: "إنّ الله يأمركم أن تؤدّوا الأمانات إلى أهلها ، وإذا حكمتم بين الناس أن تحكموا بالعدل ،إن الله نعما يعظكم به،إن الله كان سميعا بصيرا . يا أيها الذين آمنوا أطيعوا الله وأطيعوا الرسول وأولى الأمر منكم،فإن تنازعتم فى شىء فردّوه إلى الله والرسول ، إن كنتم تؤمنون بالله واليوم الآخر. ذلك خير وأحسن تأويلا"[6]

The nature and objectives of authority, and the purpose of the State are outlined on the premise that authority (*wilāyah*) is a charge or a responsibility for care (*ri'āyah*) in a pastoral sense. This definition is derived from the Prophet's *ḥadīth*, "All of you are a shepherd; and every shepherd is responsible (*mas'ūl*, i.e., 'answerable,' 'accountable') for his flock."[7] The public official (*wālī*), Ibn Taymiyyah elaborates, is "a shepherd of men in the manner that a man may be a herder of sheep."

Then, authority is "a trust (*wakālah*); for rulers (*wulāt*) are trustees of the souls of believers after a fashion of partnership."[8] He specifies this general meaning further in the context of the extent of the authority of treasury officials, for example, he says, "Treasurers (*wulāt al-amwāl*) have not the power to apportion the funds as an owner may divide his property; rather they are custodians (*umanā'*), and representatives (*nuwwāb*), and stewards (*wukalā'*), and not owners."[9]

And thirdly, a "contract" is applied to the state as well as to its officials, thus authority is a contracted labor (*ijārah*), for the undertaking of handling certain public affairs, the two parties being the hired public official and the constituency. Ibn Taymiyyah substantiates this definition by citing an incident where a certain Abū Muslim al-Khūlānī said to Mu'āwiyah after appropriately greeting him, "...You are a hired hand (*ajīr*), employed by the Lord of these sheep. If you paint the scabby among them with tar, and treated their sick, and secured their first to their last within the fold, your master will pay you in full, but if you do not, he will punish you."

The purpose of the State, according to Ibn Taymiyyah is couched in terms of its subordination to the sovereignty of God. Its chief objective is, therefore, "to ensure that ultimate judgment (*al-dīn kulluh*) belongs to God, and that the word of God has final authority."[10] The State is, therefore, part of the divine scheme of justice, and is ordained for effecting it on earth. God said, and Ibn Taymiyyah quotes: "لقد أرسلنا رسلنا بالبينات وأنزلنا معهم الكتاب والميزان ليقوم الناس بالقسط" and, "وأرسلنا الحديد فيه بأس شديد ومنافع للناس وليعلم الله من ينصره ورسله بالغيب"[11]
God's just will is thus fully disclosed through the Prophets who brought the Scripture and the scales of justice, that it may be established. The mighty instrument of punishment (or establishment of boundaries) has also been given, so men may be

warned and conform to His word. Therefore, he who turns away from the Scripture, says Ibn Taymiyyah, shall be straightened out by rigorous force. The goal of the State, with all its subdivisions, therefore, is "the prescription of good and the proscription of evil, whether in the affairs of the greater authority of the war department (*wilāyat al-ḥarb al-kubrā*), that of the deputy-sultan, or in the lesser authority of the department of police, the department of administration, the department of finance."[12]

II. *The Duties of the* Imām *and the Political Functions of the State:*

Since the purpose of the State is to uphold the authority of the word of God by ensuring that men are enlisted in His true service (*'ibādah*) and to maintain the right religion upon earth by guaranteeing harmonious relationships among them, all of its divisions (*wilāyāt*) are created to serve the same purpose, within the jurisdiction of its responsibility. The just *imām*, being the head of the State, has the primary duty of guaranteeing the rights of individuals for the maintenance of social peace. He occupies a position of power (*shawkah*), of dominion (*mulk*) and of authority (*sulṭān*), and therefore must possess the ability (*qudrah*) to act. He has the charge of being a tutor (*wālī*) and of presiding at prayer; he is a representative (*wakīl*) of power. He is entrusted this responsibility by God, and therefore must do his best to fulfill it, for he will be judged at the last day by the Supreme Judge Himself.

The duties of the *imām* are viewed in the larger context of the function of the State. The State, in order to achieve its chief goal of maintaining the supreme authority of God's law and of maintaining social justice, delegates the various responsibilities to departments, or jurisdictions (*wilāyāt*), such as the department of war, the department of justice, and the department of the treasury. According to Ibn Taymiyyah, this delegation of authority is not specified in the canon, but is accomplished by convention (*'urf*). He follows generally an outline similar to that of Abū Ya'lā as delineated in the latter's *Al-Aḥkām Al-Sulṭāniyyah.* Ibn Taymiyyah's exposition of the function of the State, as may be found particularly in his *Al-Siyāsah Al-Shar'iyyah*, may be placed into the following categories:

A. *The Legal Function of the State:*

By this is meant the function of establishing justice, which is more comprehensive than a judicial role. In this function, two main responsibilities are assigned. First, is the responsibility of setting up the public law, i.e., the establishment of what is beneficial to the entire Community of Islam, that which is divinely required (*ḥudūd wa ḥuqūq Allāh*). In the context of urging the good and prohibiting evil, such regulations dealing with requirements and proscriptions would include pronouncements regarding the fulfillment or the negligence of prayer, almsgiving, fasting, the pilgrimage, telling the truth, honest relations, duties toward parents and blood relatives, relations with neighbors.[13] Secondly, comes the responsibility of legislation governing private rights, i.e., penal law; and it includes offenses of crime and misdemeanor,[14] such as murder, assault, robbery, adultery, slander, drunkenness, etc.

In this category of the legal function of the State are included, as will be seen later in greater detail, personal law, inheritance and commercial laws, etc. These are among the legal concerns of the State precisely because "justice in these dealings is in the best interest of cosmic justice (*qiwām al-'ālamīn*), without which neither this world nor the world to come may be good." Such matters of justice may be evident, as those instinctively understood, e.g., paying the price of goods purchased, the delivery of goods sold, the prohibiting of tipping the scales or reducing the measures, etc. Others may need to be made explicit by law. He continues to give examples of legislation, and in the end summarizes the spirit of the law by saying,

> The general proscriptions of the Book and the Tradition aim at the realization of justice and the prohibition of oppression in its most conspicuous forms as well as its minutest....[15]

The guiding principle for the legal function of the State is that it does not proscribe the dealings (*mu'āmalāt*) needed by men for their well-being, except as indicated in the Qur'ān and the Tradition, as it does not permit rituals (*'ibādāt*) other than those that draw them nigh unto God, except as indicated in the Qur'ān and the Tradition." For religion (*dīn*) is instituted by God, and that which is forbidden (*ḥarām*) is forbidden by God. In contrast, there are those whom God had renounced: "they have forbidden that which God did not, they have associated with Him that which was given no power, and have appropriated in religion that which God did not allow."[16]

B. *The Economic Function of the State:*

Ibn Taymiyyah's treatise titled *Al-Ḥisbah*, and approximately a third of his *Al-Siyāsah Al-Shar'iyyah* are primarily concerned with the function of regulating the economic life of the state and its procedures. As will be discussed in a later chapter, Ibn Taymiyyah's economic theory, too, derives from the overall responsibility of the State to command the good and to prohibit evil. This function concerns itself, however, with matters that are outside the jurisdiction of the judicial branch, except, of course, insofar as their execution is concerned.

For the time being, suffice it to say in this respect, that Ibn Taymiyyah's perception of Islam as a socio-political order and of the nature of human relations, is responsible for his concise delineation of the extent to which the State may participate in the economic viability of the Community. In so doing, he aimed at the higher purpose of rendering the Community morally just in the sight of God. Thus his concept of the State was that it was totalist, i.e., inclusive.

So far as the administration of public funds is concerned, Ibn Taymiyyah's view is clear: the State is responsible for the mutual fulfillment of the financial obligation of the officials (*wulāt*) and the subjects (*ra'iyyah*). This function is of the nature of the discharge of trusts (*adā' al-amānāt*) to whom they should be rendered. His rule is that "the agent (*waliyy al-amr*) shall collect the funds due [the State], allocate them where they properly belong, and shall not keep them from those who deserve them."[17] Ibn Taymiyyah discusses in detail the legitimate sources of State revenue,[18] and addresses himself to the question of penalty of those who evade their fiscal obligations, as well as those who offer bribes.

The legitimate expenses of the State, according to Ibn Taymiyyah are: public works, such as the fortification of ports, building and maintenance of roads, bridges, dams, waterways, etc., and public compensation, such as the salaries of public servants, i.e., governors, judges, legislators, revenue collectors, trustees and administrators, leaders of public prayer (*a'immat al-Ṣalāh*) and those who deliver the call to prayer (*al-mu' adhdhinūn*).[19] Taking his source in the saying of Umar, he states, "no one is more entitled to receiving these funds than he who must receive priority for having initiated the acquisition of funds and by whom the State is made secure, and he who has need." Then in dealing with the matter of the remuneration of administrators and comptrollers, he stipulates that they receive "what is sufficient, or what their work is worth." He says, "compensation (*'aṭā'*) shall be according to a man's usefulness, and according to his need for departmental funds and for charity also. Additional pay is not earned, by a worker, except to the measure that similar increments are deserved by his fellows."[20]

C. *The Military Function of the State:*

Whereas the objective of the just war (*al-qitāl al-mashrū'*), i.e., the holy way (*jihād*), is to render the whole of ultimate judgment (*dīn*) unto God, and to make His word supreme, Ibn Taymiyyah sees that military organization as the lawful duty of the State, and that participation in it is the duty of every male subject. Exemptions from the military service are granted to monks, shaykhs, the blind, or the chronically or permanently handicapped.[21]

The injunction to engage in military warfare is given in the Qur'ān: God said, for example "وقاتلوا فى سبيل اللـــه الذين يقاتلونكم ولا تعـــتدوا ان اللـــه لا يحب المعـــتدين"[22] The manner in which warfare is to be conducted is outlined in the Tradition: for example, it is unethical to kill an old man, a young child or a woman, according to the Prophet, says Ibn Taymiyyah. He adds, "God has allowed the killing of however many are necessary for restoring morality, for, as God said, "الفتنـــة أكـــبر من القتـــــل"[23] i.e., schism is more serious than killing, and it is, therefore, lawful to kill, which, admittedly, itself is evil, in order to put an end to the schism of the unbelievers (*kuffār*) but only in the event of their obstruction of true religion. Ibn Taymiyyah does not permit the killing of unbelievers simply because they are unbelievers, although "some allow it," he says.[24] His stance is reasoned on the premise that so long as non-believers who do not obstruct the religion of God (*dīn Allah*) harm only themselves; it is those who plot against the security of Islam and its State should lawfully be fought and destroyed.

Military action is also the lawful duty of the State for the purpose of defense. The State has the right to enlist all eligible men, and to solicit the non-military assistance of its other subjects through other means, such as financial contributions. Those eligible who refuse conscription are themselves the potential enemy, and may be fought by the others.

In addition, the State has the obligation to declare warfare on warring enemies until they either surrender to the Islamic State, or, humiliated (*ṣāghirūn*), they pay poll-tax. Others within the ranks of Islam who conspire to reject any of the demands of religion, such as the *zakāt*, or other religious deviants, such as *Khawārij* in the day of Muḥammad, may be fought by the consensus (*ittifāq*) of the Muslims.[25]

It is the duty of each eligible subject to enlist in the armed forces of the State, or to support them financially if they are absolutely incapable of military service. This is incumbent upon all, and must take priority over other legitimate commitments, such as prayer, almsgiving, the pilgrimage.[26] In contrast, according to Ibn Taymiyyah who bases his legal opinion on that of Aḥmad Ibn Ḥanbal, the Jews, Christians, *Khawārij* or the apostates (*ahl al-riddah*) should not be conscripted nor should their aid be solicited.[27]

D. *The Moral and Religious Function of the State:*

From the time of the Companions, the State has been considered by all Islamic thinkers not only as an agency for directing the legislative, judicial, and economic affairs of the Community, but also for regulating its religious and moral life--as its ultimate *raison d'etre.*

This, according to Ibn Taymiyyah, is what is meant by holding the word of God supreme, and by rendering ultimate judgment, or religion (*dīn*) wholly unto God. It implies that the State has the responsibility of propagating the doctrine of the unity of God which is a liberating force from the slavery of paganism.

It also implies that the State is entrusted with the promotion of truth and good as revealed in the Qur'ān. To this end, Ibn Taymiyyah says, the State must be prepared to "do battle with those who resist its efforts to manifest the religion of God," basing his conviction on the injunction: " وقـاتلوا فى سبيل الله الذين يقاتلونكم "[28]

His view is balanced, however, by the conviction also that there is no coercion in religion, thus allowing for the coexistence of the non-Muslims of *Ahl al-Kitāb* in Muslim territory, so long as they do not obstruct *da'wah*. There is no harm to Islam, only to themselves, if *Ahl al-Kitāb* take the posture of acquiescence (*sākit*) toward Islam. If they were to be disruptive by proclaiming counter-doctrines (*bid'ah mukhālifah*), they must be penalized, for a tradition says, "Error concealed will harm no one except the errant, but if revealed and was not renounced, will cause broad damage."[29] The Sharī'ah dictates, says Ibn Taymiyyah that the *kuffār* (i.e., those who activate the *bid'āh*) should be fought, but does not require the destruction of those who do not actively spread it."[30]

The State fulfills its function of regulating moral life by eliminating the abhorrent evils (*munkarāt*) which corrupt the mores of the Community, and which have been proscribed by the *Sharī'ah*, and by preparing a suitable climate for morality to flourish. The State has the attendant duty, therefore, of setting the boundaries of morality, which according to Ibn Taymiyyah, is vastly more important than the obligation of outlining economic policy. In morality, as in other disciplines of human relationships, the State has the power to curb individual freedoms for the sake of the common good.[31]

Thus, this function may be met by the State through the establishment of both positive and negative legal measures, a concern for which Ibn Taymiyyah devoted a full section in his work *Al-Siyāsah al-Shar'iyyah*. Under the title of Penalties (*'uqūbāt*), he explains that penal systems in Islam are devised in order to direct men in the way of meeting their moral duty, and of abstaining from reprehensible action. For this, the Law facilitates the way of good, and obedience, aids individuals to follow in it, and provides incentives for realizing it. For example, it permits horse-racing, camel-racing and archery for the sake of charity, as was done under the sponsorship of Muḥammad and the Rāshidūn Caliphs. Likewise, the Law strictly sets the limits before error and evil, and vigorously opposes them.

It is not necessary for evils or for controversies to occur before legal measures may be taken. The State should legislate on anticipation, i.e., before a crime and its consequences take place, Ibn Taymiyyah suggests. This is preventive and precautionary law.

In strictly religious terms, the State is responsible for ensuring that no innovation upon the Qur'ān or the *Sunnah* be brought into being. Likewise, it must guard the *ijma*' against embellishments and distortions. It must guarantee that imposters are penalized. It must protect the traditions of the Prophet against misreporting, paraphrasing, contradiction, negation, and expansion. The State is required, according to Ibn Taymiyyah, to check "exaggeration in religion," e.g., the deification of humans, the rejection of the names and the miracles of God, permissiveness in Law, the distortion of the Qur'ān, the denial of the omnipotence of God, the manifestations of magic and witchcraft, the elevation of prophets and religious teachers to sainthood, and the expectation of miracles from them, etc.

To urge the good and to proscribe evil, says Ibn Taymiyyah, demands "understanding, patience, and insight," in order to discern what is for the good, and in order to recognize what is possible to achieve. Ibn Taymiyyah sets forth this general rule: When there is a conflict between that which promotes the welfare [of the Community] and that which advances evil, between that which is meritorious and that which is degrading, or when these are indistinct, the more worthy should be favored....When prescription and prohibition are needed to achieve a certain good and to combat a certain evil, the opposite alternative should be considered. When all aspects of the matter are considered, then a decision should be made in light of the cumulative result. If it is seen that, in the end, less good is forfeited and more evil accrued, that course of action is not only "not recommended," but indeed prohibited. This process must conform to the scales of the Law (*Sharī'ah*).

III. *The Basis of the* Imāmah

Ibn Taymiyyah's theory of chief authority (*imāmah*) is basically traditional, or Sunnī, in principle, though distinctly characteristic of his own methodology. The classical view recognizes the indispensability of *imāmah*. Scholars, however, have held varied positions on the nature of its indispensability, based on the manner in which each one approached the issue. Al-Ash'arī, for example, considered *imāmah* as a legal requirement (*shar'iyyah*), while the Mu'tazilah saw it only as a rational necessity. Al-Ghazālī sought in vain to draw explicit support for the *imāmah* from the Qur'ān and from the Tradition; and, failing that, he concluded that that which is necessary for the fulfillment of an obligation is itself obligatory. And since religion (*dīn*) is inseparably connected to the temporal world (*dunyā*), a social order maintained by chief authority is necessary. It was al-Taftazānī who vigorously insisted that *imāmah* was founded on consensus (*ijmā'*).

The opposite Shī'ī theory of *imāmah* as expounded by al-Ḥillī, whom Ibn Taymiyyah attacks in *Mihāj al-Sunnah*, insisted that the appointment of a supreme head of state (*imām a'zam*) was not only a rational necessity and a legal requirement of the Community, but also a divine necessity of grace (*luṭf wājib*). Al-Ḥillī views *imāmah* on a par with prophecy, with regard to indispensability, and of the highest consideration (*ashraf*) of all Muslim concerns. Like prophethood, *imāmah* is the instrument of God's design of the salvation of men in that it is intended to lead men toward the good, and to teach them the way from error (*ghalaṭ*), forgetfulness (*sahw*) and evil (*khaṭa'*). Although *imāmah*, according to al-Ḥillī, does not possess the gift of prophecy (*nubuwwah*), it exceeds in its importance the rank of prophethood in that it serves the function of intermediation between God and man, through the work of interpreting that which God had revealed through the Prophet.

Ibn Taymiyyah's view demonstrates that the Islamic State, though ideological and totalist, is not sacred as with the Shī'āh. Its base remains common sense and utility. For him there is no apotheosis of the State. In his refutation of al-Ḥillī's theory[32] and in contradistinction to the inadequacies of classical Sunnī methodologies, Ibn Taymiyyah asserts, in the first place, that the Qur'ān and the Tradition alone do not offer a detailed prescription of the specific modalities required for the life of the Community. While profoundly acknowledging the supreme political authority (*imāmah*) of Muḥammad as divinely established, his understanding of the sovereignty of God impels him to affirm that even prophethood itself is not incumbent upon Him as a necessity of grace (*luṭf wājib*). The divine commissioning of infallible prophets, like, to an extent, the designation of *imāmah*, is an act of divine mercy. It is to be recognized, however, as is the case in the various Traditional Schools, Ibn Taymiyyah explains, that the political authority of the Rāshidūn was relative and conditional (*muqayyadah*), as contrasted to that of the Prophet, which was absolute (*muṭlaqah*). The Prophet, he continues, had commanded the Muslims to follow the manner of the first four Caliphs, and not to depart from them or innovate upon them, for every innovation is a deviation.[33] Thus Abū Bakr was specifically designated by the Prophet to succeed him in regulating the political affairs of the Community, then others were chosen to serve. Ibn Taymiyyah suggests that the choice of the four *imāms* was attributed to their distinctively superior character (*afḍal al-Muslimīn*), which was borne out subsequently by their brilliant political competence. They were unitary in their authority; their state was universal. And so, ideally, ought to be the Muslim Community: a single domain wherein every evolutionary development is a triumph of the multiplicity over the unity, and every reform to the extent of its effectiveness is a restoration of the unity. For Ibn Taymiyyah, this same principle, which controls the evolution of dogma and law, is the determining factor in the social and political governance of Islam.[34] But now, realistically in view of his present political conditions, Ibn Taymiyyah declares that the Community is divided; and to demand that a unitary authority be established would place the Community before two unsavory alternatives: either to succumb to a task profoundly exceeding its capability, or to profess the legitimacy of an institution which, seen from the vantage point of its actual functionality, is no more than "a formalistic and constrictive fiction," which he would seek to shatter.

IV. *The Investiture of the* Imām

Ibn Taymiyyah was less concerned with the general procedures of the appointment of the head of state than he was with the refutation of the Shī'ah's misguided conception of the whole matter, as shown particularly in the work of al-Ḥillī. As such, however, Ibn Taymiyyah's position may be deduced, although not in great detail.

Of the two major methods for the designation of an *imām*, namely, the appointment by a clearly revealed text (*naṣṣ*), on one hand, and election (*ikhtiyār*), on the other, the Shī'ī view[35] held that "only God may and should designate, by an explicit text, the infallible *imām*, whose mission is to be the supreme preserver of the Law, and the only intermediate authority between God and men." In *Minhāj al-Karāmah*, al-Ḥillī cites four Qur'ānic verses and a dozen traditions by the Prophet to make the case for the choice of Alī as *imām*.[36] Ibn Taymiyyah offers a point-by-point reply in his *Minhāj al-Sunnah*. Continuing the Shī'ī argument, al-Ḥillī insists that as 'Alī was appointed by God through a revealed text, each *imām* should designate his successor through a directive (*waṣiyyah*), because only he is in a divinely-privileged position to discern an infallible *imām* who will perpetuate his mission. Ibn Taymiyyah[37] recognizes this rule as the reason for the wide divergence in the listings of the Zaydīs, the Rawāfiḍ and the Ghulāh of their *imāms*, and, building on the scholarship of al-Nawbakhtī and other heresiographers, rejects them all.

The Sunnī practice in this respect has followed the method of election (*ikhtiyār*), which Ibn Taymiyyah adopts in principle as the more practical of the two. However, while the principle of *ikhtiyār* by the Sunnīs is satisfied when there is a consensus, or near-consensus, of the electoral body, known as "*Ahl al-ḥall wa al-'aqd*" ("those authorized to bind and to loose"), Ibn Taymiyyah asks for popular ratification (*mubāya'ah*) of the designated nominee. His criticism of an exclusive election by an electorate is based on his concern that the prerogative of the latter to act in behalf of the Community assigns it an awesome authority, and deprives the Community of its own. As such, the designation of an *imām* by an electorate is in this case no more mediate, than his appointment by an immediate text after the manner of the Shī'īs. Ibn Taymiyyah energetically rejects the admission of the notion of the juridical supremacy of a body being given exclusively the right that belongs to the public. He likens such a body in this case *Ahl al-ḥall wa al-'aqd* to a class of clergy which is totally incompatible with Islam. For him, as was later grasped by some recent modernists,[38] the power of the Community (*sulutat al-ummah*) rests with the public. He is, Laoust comments,[39] "historically too loyally informed and juridically too realistic" to allow his doctrines to open a door for power struggle to exist, through the acceptance of the notion of divine appointment of the *imām*, or an elitist election. Rather, he simply subjects the procedure to "a minimum of canonical principles."[40]

Ibn Taymiyyah adheres to the method of ratification (*mubāya'ah*), wherein authority is constituted, not at its point of origin, namely by an electorate, but at the point of public endorsement. It is at this juncture that binding ('*aqd*) takes place. And, in this respect, the designation of the *imām* is "like any such contractual transaction, as that of a sale, or of a marriage."[41] It should be treated, as should other contracts, in light of its ensurance of mutual benefit of the two parties, i.e., the *imām* and the people. "For the *imām*, it should ensure the effective power of and the infinite happiness resulting from his leading his constituency in obeying the will of God, and, for the subjects, social peace and the constitutional guarantees of the law."[42] This is understood when the Community--not the *imām*--is perceived as the keeper of the law (*ḥafiẓah 'alā al-Shar'*); and for this Ibn Taymiyyah urges the *imām* to consult (*mushāwarah*) the people, and the subjects to counsel (*munāṣaḥah*) him.[43]

V. *The Qualifications of the Head of State as Politico-Social Values of the Community*

Ibn Taymiyyah takes a realistic, and singularly admirable, position with respect to the requirements of the *imāmah*. His view at once vigorously opposes that of the Shī'ah, which prerequires the infallibility ('*iṣmah*) of an *imām*, and criticizes traditional orthodoxy when it narrowly and unequivocally stipulates that an *imām* must be a descendant of the Qurayshī tribe.

To begin with Ibn Taymiyyah's apparent departure from the Sunnī stance, it should be noted that he does not exactly oppose it. For, indeed, one of his criticisms of the Khārijī position is for their wavering on this point. But, in fairness to them, he also agrees with them in part. He argues that the Khārijīs are in error in not demanding that the *imām* be a Qurayshī, if they mean to apply their thesis to the Rāshidūn Caliphs, but that they are canonically in the right when their theory is applied to the caliphate after the death of ʿAlī with whom the era of Sunnī legalism was ended. Defending his case, consequently achieving a well-founded position, he replies to his Sunnī critics in the great classical manner of the tradition with the Prophet's commandment in the *ḥadīth* to obey an Abyssinian slave, though he be mutilated, if he makes his witness to the Qur'ān.[44]

In addition to opposing the possibility of a potential clerical or priestly class, Ibn Taymiyyah further makes his point by asking the traditionalists how they can really mean that the *imām* must be of Qurayshī descent when they themselves are not in agreement on the issue. Some allow, he writes, that the *imāmah* be open to all the descendants of Fakhr Ibn Mālik Ibn al-Nadhr, a proposition adopted by *Ahl al-Sunnah*, the large majority of the Murji'ah and some Muʿtazilah. The Rāwandīs impose the descendancy of Al-ʿAbbās Ibn ʿAbd al-Muṭṭalib as a precondition of *imāmah*. The Shīʿah insisted that *imāmah* may be legitimate only if the *imām* were a descendant of ʿAlī-Ibn Abī Ṭālib. A descendant of al-Ḥārith Ibn ʿAbd al-Muṭṭalib would have to admit that the caliphate is not the exclusive right of one of the sons of ʿAbd al-Muṭṭalib, but that all his sons could legitimately qualify for it: Abū Ṭālib, Abū Lahab, al-ʿAbbās and al-Ḥārith. A certain author who had lived in al-Arman wrote a major work on the thesis that the *imāmah* had rightfully been returned to Banū ʿAbd Shams, Ibn Taymiyyah notes. Finally, Ibn Ḥazm, testifying that he had personally seen a treatise by the son of ʿUmar himself in which the author affirmed that the *imāmah* was not lawful unless it is kept within the lineage of Abū Bakr and of ʿUmar.[45] This divergence of opinions, for Ibn Taymiyyah, renders the notion of limiting the right to *imāmah* to the Qurayshī tribe a practical impossibility.[46]

In response to al-Ḥillī, too, Ibn Taymiyyah reflects the

same attitude of desiring to be practical. Al-Ḥillī, continuing the thought of his master al-Ṭūsī, relates the requisite of infallibility of the *imām* to the task for which he is appointed. It is only an infallible *imām*, al-Ḥillī argues, who can cause justice to rule over men, and defend the weak against oppression. Only he can guide the Community and inspire every member to live by the rules which serve his interests. In response, Ibn Taymiyyah states that not only is the Community permitted to depart from the infallibility rule but it is incumbent upon it to go against it, since it is also the preserver of the doctrines of the law (*ḥāfiẓ al-Shar*ʿ), which task is humanly impossible to fulfill literally. He contends that the Qur'ān and the Tradition, separately or together, do not give sufficient evidence for requiring infallibility. The *ijma*ʿ in most cases is impossible to know. Moreover, those who compose it are themselves not infallible, and it is, therefore, altogether illogical to demand a quality which does not exist in any one of its parties. Therefore, consensus is not an effective measure to apply to the problem of infallibility.

Al-Ḥillī is criticized further on account of his failure to be thorough-going in his investigation. He barely touches upon the other modes of law-making, Ibn Taymiyyah observes. He contends that analogy (*qiyās*) is far too serious an instrument to allow for strictly personal conjecture (*ẓann*). By analogy, Ibn Taymiyyah asserts that infallibility of the *imām* should not be required for the interpretation and conservation of the law, as it was not required at its revelation by the Prophet, though it was present in him.

The inconsistency of al-Ḥillī is also exposed when infallibility is set in a context of relativity. Al-Ḥillī argues that every fallible man commits injustices, and no unjust man is worthy of *imāmah*. Hence, the *imām* is the best man of his time. Ibn Taymiyyah resists this messianic view of the *imāmah* and replies that, inversely, the best man of his time should be thoroughly knowledgeable of the law, but that does not guarantee his fulfillment of it. When such a situation occurs in the Community, there exists with it the constant possibility of revolt.[47] In sum, Ibn Taymiyyah is unwilling to adopt the exaggerations of Shīʿīsm which seek to extend the Prophet's actual infallibility to the prerequisites of *imāmah*.

His greater contention against the Shī'ah doctrine is the latter's distortion of the nature of the relationship between the head of state and the constituents. He agrees with al-Ḥillī that, without a doubt, every community needs a chief; but the chief, Ibn Taymiyyah argues, is ineffectual without the aid of his subjects. Indeed, he asserts, the *imām* has a greater need of his people's aid than they have for his. To rule, says Ibn Taymiyyah, is eminently a cooperative enterprise. The relationship between the subjects and their rulers is likened to that between the members of a caravan and their guide, the believers at prayer and their leader, the pilgrims and their chief.[48] In his rule, the chief of state must depend on agents (*nuwwāb*).[49] Thus, if the doctrine of the Shī'īs is one of authority, and that of the Sunnīs is one of elitist consensus, Ibn Taymiyyah's doctrine is a doctrine of cooperation (*ta'āwun*).

Ibn Taymiyyah notes, too, with a lengthy historical documentation that the Shī'ī succession, beginning with 'Alī whose rule was the product of the first schism (*fitnah*), had been the weakest, in spite of its doctrinal idealization. He directly relates this phenomenon to the illusory conditions under which Shī'ī *imāmah* was conceived. In view of blunders of the present *imām*, the Shī'īs would maintain that the quality of infallibility exists in their expected *imām* (*al-imām al-muntaẓar*). Ibn Taymiyyah recognizes in this "absent and lost" messianic figure, as in the *imām mahdī* of the Rawāfiḍ, a mystic element which caused them to follow "false and ignorant" leaders (*mutawallī*), thought by them to be infallible.[50]

To idealize, and so to idolize the *imām* is "to commit a sin against God," writes Ibn Taymiyyah. The *imām* simply has a double function: he is the model to be emulated, and, at the same time, the agent for the execution of the law. These two qualities have been combined most pronouncedly in the Rāshidūn Caliphs."[51] For the fulfillment of his double function, the *imām* need possess, as the most important priorities of his characteristics, justice (*'adālah*), and piety (*wara'*), both of which are necessary for the avoidance of the abuse of power.

Ibn Taymiyyah's conclusion is fairly modest; it reflects an attitude of openness and realism. His rule is that no more moral qualities should be required of an *imām* than are expected of a witness for his deposition. To make the point, he ventures, "Much less justice should, in effect, be required of the ruler than of his witness."[52] The reason: the testimony of the witness may be alone responsible for the demise of the man or the Community, whereas the matter of rule, being a collective responsibility, offers a greater chance for justice to flourish.

VI. *The Structure of the Islamic State*

The State needs a support structure that will ensure its effectiveness. Such a system of support consists of two chief forces, namely, an apparatus of agents to whom the *imām* may relegate the responsibilities of the State, thus dividing the labor into manageable compartments, and a set of expectations to be fulfilled by the general public itself. This principle is, from the outset, implicit in the very title, as well as in the outline, of Ibn Taymiyyah's work on the principles of the State (i.e., *Al-Siyāsah al-Shar'iyyah Fī Iṣlāḥ Al-Rā'ī Wa Al-Ra'iyyah*); and it is explicit throughout the discourse. These two elements of support may be summarized as follows:

A. *The Political Apparatus:*

Because neither the Qur'ān nor the Sharī'ah outlines the political structure of the Islamic State, it became the practice of the Muslim Community to accord the chief of State the prerogative of determining how many and what agencies are needed for its operation, of appointing their personnel, i.e., his agents (*nuwwāb*), and of bestowing on them the powers and privileges necessary for their effectiveness under his command. He is guided in his decisions by the opinions (*alfāẓ*), the circumstances (*aḥwāl*) and the custom (*'urf*) of the Community.[53] This principle applies in the selection of judicial, military, and economic officials as well.

There may be an overlap of responsibilities, too; Ibn Taymiyyah suggests: for example, "the department of War of Egypt and Syria, at present, has jurisdiction over laws of compatible nature [with its own laws], such as the amputation of the hand of a thief, the penalization of war criminals, as well as personal disputes for which no legal representatives (*kuttāb*) or witnesses exist....The department of justice (*wilāyat al-Qaḍā'*) has the assignment of adjudication in matters involving legal representatives (*kuttāb*) and witnesses, personal rights, as well as estates and public bequests (*wuqūf*), custody of orphans, etc.[54] In other countries, such as *al-Maghrib*, the department of war, for example, has no juridical responsibility. It merely executes the decisions of the judges.[55] Ibn Taymiyyah thus reflects an attitude of flexibility which transcends the ancient Sunnī rigid tradition which in matters of state government relied nearly entirely on legal precedents and on *'urf*.

For Ibn Taymiyyah, two chief posts seem to occupy a clearer and more dominant place in his discourses outlining the political structure of Islam. They are the judge (*qāḍī*)[56] and a public guardian, or probate officer (*muḥtasib*).[57]

The position of judge is one primarily concerned with arbitration. A judge is the sole authoritative interpreter of the law. He derives his authority directly from the *imām*, and his competence is determined by him.

The public guardian (*wālī*), like any agency of the State, participates in the task of commanding the good and proscribing evil. He is assigned the responsibilities of instructing the people to hold the five daily prayers at their established times, and of punishing those who do not fulfill their duty of prayer by beating and imprisonment, or by execution, although he himself does not administer capital punishment. He contracts (*yata'āhad*) the *imāms* [of prayer], and the *mu'adhdhinīn*, and takes the necessary action if any of these exceeds his limits of authority or responsibility. If he is unable to restore order in their prescribed work, he may prosecute them before the agencies of war, justice or any others that have appropriate authority.... He is charged with urging the people to hold the Friday prayer, and other public prayers, to speak the truth, to pay their debts, to refrain from lying, from dishonesty, and from cheating in weights and measures, in industry, in trade transaction, and in religion.[58]

Both judge and public trust officer are expected to possess the *imām*'s characteristics of keen statesmanship and flexibility, which are capital among the qualifications insisted upon by Ibn Taymiyyah.

Like other public servants, the *qāḍi* and the *muḥtasib* need be knowledgeable (*'ālim*), just (*'ādil*) and competnet (*qādir*). Although in his spirit of openness, Ibn Taymiyyah rules that in particular situations certain combinations of these qualities may make it permissible to relax the requirement of the third, he states that the absence of any of these qualities precipitates disturbance (*khalal*) of the social order.[59] Moreover, other qualities should be sought in all candidates for public office; they include personal and technical aptitude (*quwwah*, or *qudrah*) and loyalty (*amānah*). With respect to judicial authority, *quwwah* conveys thorough knowledge of the Qur'ān and the *Sunnah* as well as the personal ability to carry out one's judgment. In the arts of warfare, it implies experience, courage, and the cumulative knowledge of war strategy and tactics. *Amānah* derives from fearing God, and implies courage and resoluteness in the application of the requirements of the law without heeding the slanderous and confused noises of public opinion. The public servant's character is also enhanced by the complementary qualities of mercifulness, of fortitude, of patience and the avoidance of violence. "The exercise of authority," Ibn Taymiyyah states, "is not established on coercion (*qahr*) and awe (*rahbah*) as these may suggest, but on charity (*iḥsān*), and on generating willingness and desire (*raghbah*) [to comply]."

The supervision of the State employees and their performance of the necessary social duties (*furūḍ al-kifāyah*) is the responsibility of the *imām*. It is his obligation to set up measures of control and to implement the penalties they entail. One such explicit measure is the prohibition of taking or accepting gifts from the citizens. Neither shall a public officer appropriate for himself a portion of the income due to an orphan or an heir of an estate. In addition to the ultimate punishment on the Day of Reckoning when such an unfaithful recipient of illegitimate income will "wear it upon his neck like shackles (*ghulūl*)," he is to be made to return it to its rightful owner, and be penalized in proportion to the amount embezzled or received in bribe; such penalties may amount to discharge, imprisonment, confiscation of unearned income, and the like. The enslaving effects of such illegitimate monies are likened to those of a long flat brick put in the official's mouth to seal it. To accept a bribe is, in effect, to refuse to do one's duty without an added benefit. Ibn Taymiyyah rules that this constitutes a double wrong: the wrong of unwillingness to do one's duty and the wrong of receiving illegitimate income.[60]

Public officials are appointed by the *imām* on the basis of their suitability for the task, without regard of their social status. Ibn Taymiyyah, putting the goal (*maqṣūd*) of the task before any other consideration, contrasts the motivation and the process of the selection of public servants by the *imām* to that of the kings (*mulūk*) of the world. The latter, he says, have their goals set on worldly gain, without regard for religion (*qaṣd al-dunyā dūn al-dīn*). For that they prefer to select who can aid them in achieving their goals. In Islam, the goal of the State is to permeate the world with the right and the good of religion. That goal, therefore, demands the best suited (*al-aṣlaḥ*, or *al-afḍal*) of men.[61] When there are several candidates of equally suitable qualifications, the *imām* seeks divine appointment by casting lots (*qur'āh*) after appropriate, vigilant consideration.

All public officials, Ibn Taymiyyah suggests in the opening of *Al-Ḥisbah* must be selected with a view toward their example in prayer and warfare, these two being the highest obligations of any Muslim.

B. *The Obligations of the Citizens:*

The responsiveness of the subjects to their rulers is a major factor in the support structure of the Islamic State. Ibn Taymiyyah's understanding of solidarity (*ta'āwun*) implies, in addition to the Muslims' mutual assistance, an affirmation of support (*i'ānah*) for their political leaders.[62] The chief manifestation of this support is the attitude of obedience (*ṭā'ah*).

To be obedient to those in authority is not only commanded by God, but also is itself an extension of the believer's obedience to Him and to His Prophet.[63] The distinction made by Ibn Taymiyyah, however, is that it is the duty of every Muslim to respond in absolute obedience to God, and to the Prophet who revealed His divine will, whereas obedience to political authorities is limited to the extent that it is in harmony with the obedience of God and the Prophet, and of one's conscience.[64]

Abū Bakr, in a famous sermon, required the Community to obey him insofar as he himself is obedient to God.

Obedience, the primary requirement of the Muslim toward his rulers, is not only commanded by the Qur'ān and exemplified by the life of the Community, but is also rationally demanded in the simple principle that it is necessary for the maintenance of the unity of the *ummah* and of its social peace. Historically, Ibn Taymiyyah argues, Muslims ordinarily showed political loyalty more in times of victory and prosperity than in defeat.[65]

Ibn Taymiyyah emphasizes the Sunnī requisite of voluntary loyalty, however. He says that nothing of the nature of passive resignation is implied in the Islamic notion of political obedience; on the contrary, it is required of every Muslim to participate actively in the cooperative life of the Community. The *imām* has the obligation of sharing his ideas most completely openly with the subjects. Likewise, other public servants must perform their duties under the dictates of the same ideals, insofar as they are able within the limits of their functions. The subjects are similarly expected to express their response.

This openness constitutes the framework for the citizens to offer their counsel (*naṣīḥah*). Again, counsel, which is therefore an element in the construct of active obedience, is not only recommended, it is demanded by religion. This is the implication of the *ḥadīth*: "Religion is the counsel."[66] Traditional Islam insisted on it as the way to active participation in government and an antithesis on the one hand to secretive disloyalty (*kitmān*), and to open revolt (*khurūj*) on the other.

Counsel with leaders as well as with fellow citizens belongs with the general duty of all Muslims to fulfill their duty of the proclamation (*da'wah*) of the way of God and the Prophet, and of mutual correction (*wa'ẓ*) within the Community. Indeed, this duty extends beyond national boundaries, for it was in this spirit, as is pointed out by Laoust, that Ibn Taymiyyah objectively, and for no personal gain, offered his counsel to the monarch of Cyprus on his relations with his subjects.[67] Ibn Taymiyyah thus followed the lead of Muḥammad who had offered his counsel to the emperors of Byzantium and Ethiopia.[68]

Obedience is the obligation of the Community toward its political leaders; but to what extent? Ibn Taymiyyah acknowledges the right to dissent, but cautions that it ought to be exercised with extreme restraint. He reviewed the theories of the *'ulamā'* with regard to the disobedience of the *imām* if he proves himself morally deviant (*fāsiq*), or ignorant (*jāhil*). Some[69] would totally refuse to obey the *imām* and would go as far as demand his ouster by armed revolt; others make the distinction between the *imām* and his agents, which distinction is rejected by Ibn Taymiyyah, since an agent is a representative of the *imām* in his respective authority.[70] Ibn Taymiyyah places social peace above the exercise of the right to dissent. He says, "it is the duty of Muslims to obey their ruler whether he is impious or ignorant," to the extent that their obedience does not contravene the commandments of the Qur'ān and the *Sunnah*, and argues, in consonance with his own principle, that it is far more important for the witness to be just in his testimony against the ruler.

The impiety of political leaders should not interfere with the conduct of the State of the affairs of the nation, Ibn Taymiyyah contends. And, lest his view be misconstrued to mean a laxity in his theory with regard to the moral responsibility of the State, he makes a distinction, however less persuasively, between the private conduct of the *imām*, and his competence to handle the affairs of the State in accordance with the moral requirements of the Qur'ān and the *Sunnah*. At any rate, his view of placing political harmony in the Community above all else may be better appreciated, once again, in the context of its political circumstances of his day.

In summary, Ibn Taymiyyah's political theory reveals an advanced concept of civil government which stands in contradistinction to the European theocratic notion of the Crusades, and, at the same time, to the rule of force the residue of which was still represented by the Mamlūks of Egypt and Syria. Civilian, to be sure, this political structure offered by Ibn Taymiyyah still depended in the main on divine sovereignty, and on a view of the Islamic Community which places it under the mandate to realize the divine will upon the earth. The application of this calling, however, is to be devised entirely by the people.

The State is an instrument not only for social control, but indeed for the cultivation of an environment in which can flourish the truth and the good, and for the coordination of social efforts which seek to bring about such an environment. Such efforts are not limited to politics and economics but extend to the areas of the life of faith and of moral integrity. It is the place where true freedom is ensured for self-actualization through solidarity and mutual aid, both of which may require the sacrifice of absolute individual freedom in favor of realizing the goal of urging the good and refraining from and proscribing that which is reprehensible.

CHAPTER IX

IBN TAYMIYYAH'S POLITICO-ECONOMIC ETHIC

I. *The* "Ḥisbah"

The principle of commanding the good and admonishing against evil, as has been seen, permeates the social structure of Islam. The area of the economic life of the Community being perhaps the most tangible expression of it, is, of course, governed by that principle. In terms of the economic direction by the State, as in the case of political and moral life, this principle is translated into the realm of interdependence and support. The Qur'ān has prescribed that faithful believers are entrusted with a mutual consultative and admonitory responsibility in matters affecting the quality of their daily conduct:[1]

" والمؤمنون والمؤمنات بعضهم أولياء بعض يأمرون بالمعروف وينهون عن المنكر"

Interdependence and support may be achieved through one or a mixture of two ways. One way, rather idealistically conceived, is a commitment to total voluntary participation of every member of the Community toward the realization of its goals. This would presuppose a conception of man that would render him completely unselfish, highly sensitive to common objectives and totally committed to achieving them at any cost to himself. It would also imply, on the presumption that each member of the Community is equally thus-minded, that no organization is necessary for realizing such a goal. The other course to be followed is the establishment of a structure which would regulate the economic interaction of the Community and ensure that its higher goals are kept in sight.

The recognition of the existence of evil itself, which to resist is part of the double priority set before the Muslim Community, necessitates the adoption of the second means of achieving economic stability, without sacrificing the notion of the voluntary participation of the Community to achieve that priority. Indeed, it is this balanced view, which on the one hand realistically recognizes the human tendency toward placing the self in first consideration, and, on the other, expectantly trusts man's instinctive sociability, that has been held, though to varying degrees of balance, by the Muslim Community since its inception.

Such a structure for the regulation of the politico-economic affairs of the Community has generally been known in Islam as *al-ḥisbah*. In medieval Islam, which embraces Ibn Taymiyyah's period, *al-ḥisbah* referred to more than an economic authority of the State. It often had jurisdiction over judicial and moral concerns as well. It included then what may now be assigned to common pleas courts, departments of police, departments of sanitation and municipal services, boards of health, departments of housing, welfare, education, as well as ministries of commerce and general economic affairs.

Thus, *al-ḥisbah*, an administrative and supervisory authority composed of specialized employees through whom the State oversees individuals' religious, moral, social and economic activities was ordinarily recognized[2] as an instrument for "prescribing good if it appeared lacking, proscribing evil if it were evident, and for arbitration (*iṣlāḥ*) among men." Ibn Taymiyyah's more specific definition of the function of *al-ḥisbah* is "the prescription of good and the proscription of evil as may not come under the jurisdiction of rulers (*wulāh*), judges (*quḍāh*), or state auditors (*ahl al-diwān*)."[3] The division of labor among these particular authorities is merely conventional (*ʿurfī*), according to time and place.[4]

Ibn Taymiyyah's politico-economic methodology may be characterized, in the light of his functional definition of the *ḥisbah*, as one primarily concerned with its general principles which shape its actual applicability. In this regard, he may be classified with the jurists and historians[5] who traced its canonical foundations and defined its jurisdiction *vis-à-vis* the pragmatists[6] who produced mere manuals for the effective utilization of the various crafts and commodities. A sample of the latter category provides an interesting contrast to the content of Ibn Taymiyyah's conception of the *ḥisbah* as may be found in his work thus titled. The following is such an excerpt from al-Qurashī's manual, *Maʿālim al-Qurbah Fi Aḥkām Al-Ḥisbah:*

> ...also the disposal of refuse on the roadside, and the scattering of watermelon seeds, or sprinkling water [in a public path] which bears

> the hazard of [causing a person to] slip and fall, and leaving rain mud-puddles in public roads, all of these are reprehensible (*munkar*) ...and the authority official (*muḥtasib*) is charged with seeing that the people take responsibility for them....

and,

> ...it is the duty of the *muḥtasib* to hold bakers accountable for the adulteration of the dough with tumeric and saffron which [deceivingly] rose-color the bread, or with pea flour, or bean meal. He shall require them not to bake [their bread] unless it has been leavened, for unleavened bread is heavier, both in the scales and in the stomach....[7]

Ibn Taymiyyah, though constantly practical in his doctrinal and legal deliberations, offers, rather, a framework of fundamental principles, with sufficient practical illustrations, for the politico-economic conduct of the State. And, as is implied by the deliberate title of this chapter, the economic activity of the Community, according to Ibn Taymiyyah, is discussed in the total context of the political function of the State,[8] thus reflecting the cohesion with which he conceived the relationship between the different parts of government to the purpose of the whole.

Ibn Taymiyyah's treatment may be considered unique even among the classical works of *al-ḥisbah* because of his typical method of first presenting the various views and discussing the different schools of jurisprudence, then either selecting the view or the combination of views that he deems most consistent with his understanding of the Qur'ān, the *Sharī'ah* and the *Sunnah*, or introducing his own definitions and interpretations in accordance with these sources. So whether the view he presents is the result of his own creative interpretation (*ijtihād*), or a reinforcement of a previously introduced idea, it is his personalized conception, and is reached after diligent study of the Qur'ān and the *Sunnah*.

Nor is the treatise merely an academic commentary on the subject of *al-ḥisbah*. Ibn Taymiyyah's practicality consists of his raising the practical issues of the economic function of the State. The major issue thus raised apparently for the first time in such detail and with important implications for the present and the future of Islam is the extent of the State's authority to control the economic life of the individuals within the Community. For example, he addressed himself to questions of private property rights, the law of supply and demand, labor as an economic asset, wage and price controls, etc. Herein lies the uniqueness of Ibn Taymiyyah's politico-economic methodology; and it is on this aspect, rather than a discussion of the details of a comprehensive view of his various writings which may be related to the Community's economic life, that this portion of this study proposes to focus.

It is very significant, at the outset, to consider Ibn Taymiyyah's politico-economic theory in its proper context.

Ibn Taymiyyah takes, as his point of departure, the principle of economic freedom. Unless economic freedom is real and actual, to raise the issue of private property, labor or wage-price controls would be utterly superfluous and inane. Obviously there can be no controls unless freedom is presupposed. Controls constitute the legitimized exceptions to the rule of economic freedom. Ibn Taymiyyah's argument for free enterprise is framed in statements such as this: "The people are in charge of their own wealth; no one dares take it, or any portion of it, away without their consent, except in particular and necessary situations."[9] He says, with respect to price controls, "If the merchants are selling their commodities at somewhat higher prices than ordinarily known, but without taking advantage (*ẓulm*) of the public, whether this price increase is due to shortage in supply or increase in population, it would be unwarranted and unjust to force them to sell at the same prices."[10] "It is an injustice (*ẓulm*) to force men to sell when they do not have to sell and to prohibit them from selling when they are legally entitled to sell: and injustice is illegal and forbidden (*ḥarām*)."[11] He cites other, supportive opinions such as those of Mālik, Ibn ʿUmar, al-Qāsim and others, when he defends the merchants against unwarranted price controls by the State when they are doing all their duty to be fair. Likewise, he cites the opinions of some of the same jurists in instances warranting price control, such as Mālik's conclusion under given circumstances, to impose price ceilings on meat dealers.[12] The principle of freedom is evident in this insight: "If the consumers' needs are met by the merchants' sincere efforts to sell at fair prices, it is not necessary to impose price controls; but if the needs are not met by the merchants, then it becomes necessary to impose just controls, i.e., prices that are neither depreciated nor inflated."[13]

The tension, therefore, between the economic freedom of the individual and the intervention of the State constitutes a positive and healthy relationship that aims at maintaining the mutual freedom of all members of the Community, as is clear in Ibn Taymiyyah's discourse. For economic freedom is inseparably related to the principle of economic justice.

Justice constitutes the overriding quality that makes possible any cohesion in the life of the community. It gives logical consistency to both freedom and control in the economic arena. Within its mold, all Ibn Taymiyyah's socio-economic views fit together. One of the frequently-used terms of his economic theory, for example, is that of "equivalent compensation" (*'iwaḍ al-mithl*). It is used in relation to required labor, for example, to indicate the measure of an individual's earning if he were to perform a task needed by other members of the Community, or the extent of his liability if he were to refuse the performance of it. He says, "If the authorized official (*waliy al-amr*) require craftsmen to exercise their skills in order to meet the needs of the public, such as farming, tailoring or construction, he shall specify commensurate wages (*ujrat al-mithl*). Underpayment of such specified wages by the consumer shall not be permitted; nor shall the craftsman demand more if he were to do the work."[14] "If people need the skills of farmers, weavers or builders, it is incumbent upon the authorized official to order such craftsmen to do the work; and if they were to refuse they shall be required to pay [a fine of] equivalent compensation, but not more, as it is also unjust to require them to work for less than their work is worth."[15] Obviously, while freedom is not compromised, it is curbed in deference to an overarching notion of justice that would not permit for example malicious labor strikes. Here the arbitration of the State is, therefore, part of a checks-and-balances system of justice which does not exist for the sake of taking one side of an issue against another, but rather for bringing harmony between elements of potential conflict, and for the insurance of the healthy survival of the Community's economy.

Moreover, justice (*ʿadl*) is seen by Ibn Taymiyyah, not only as an instrument to be utilized in the resolution of economic conflict, but indeed as the fundamental framework of the solidity of any society, regardless of its confessional position. At the opening of his treatise, he quotes, among others, a Qurʾānic verse which asserts the truth that the very purpose of divine revelation, through a variety of means, was indeed that justice be established among men: "لقد أرسلنا رسلنا بالبينات وأنزلنا معهم الكتاب والميزان ليقوم الناس بالقسط"[16] He attests to the universal unquestionability of the noble consequences of justice, and to the historical and sociological phenomenon of the survival of just societies *vis-à-vis* the extinction of their decadent counterparts. "This is why it is said," he notes, "'God upholds the just state, though it be errant (*kāfirah*), but abandons the unjust, even though it be believing.'"[17]

In his stark realism, Ibn Taymiyyah declares that the well-being of the Community is more possible in a framework of "justice which may be tainted by some forms of iniquity, than in a framework of inequity which may not necessarily participate [actively] in deeds of evil." For this it is said, he concludes, that God establishes the just state, but not the unjust though the latter be Muslim, and it is also said that the world would survive unbelief if justice prevails, but would not survive oppression even in the presence of *islām*.

Justice, therefore, is the ordering principle (*niẓām*) of all things. "If the world is to thrive, it will be through justice, though this [alone] may not guarantee salvation on Judgement Day (*ākhirah*); but without justice it will not stand, even though its inhabitants may have enough faith to deserve eternal reward."[18]

Ibn Taymiyyah then outlines the effects of injustice upon men. It generates among them "hatred, envy, and the desire for the demise of others." For this to take place is natural due to instinctive covetousness among human beings. "It is part of human nature to desire for oneself the things that others have acquired, whether legitimately, or illegitimately, to elevate oneself above others, and to prefer one's own well-being to that of others, to covet what others possess and even wish them the loss of their prosperity. Even if the latter is not actively thought, there is in human nature sufficient desire toward self-elevation, corruption, self-aggrandizement and jealousy which has the same effect of actually coveting the property of others through desire."[19]

Justice is the safeguard of freedom for the individual (*al-fard*) as well as society (*al-jamā'ah, al-jumhūr,* or *al-'āmmah*). It is conceived as the principle which guarantees and defends social and economic rights.

Within the context of freedom and justice, we proceed to examine Ibn Taymiyyah's conception of the role of the State in the economic life of the Community, in the specific areas of labor, commerce and personal property, as representative issues in the overall scheme of his politico-economic ethic.[20]

A. *Labor--A Socialist View:*

According to the revelation of the Qur'ān and its exemplification by the *Sunnah*, the doctrine of work, in Ibn Taymiyyah's view, is a social and moral element in the construct of the Islamic Community, in addition to its being the individual's function in its economic scheme.

As such it is regarded as an obligation upon every capable individual for the welfare of the entire Community. It is agreed upon as a social necessity among the thinkers and the jurists of Islam such as al-Ghazālī, al-Jawzī, al-Shāfi'ī and his school and Ibn Ḥanbal and his school, all of whom are cited by Ibn Taymiyyah. The utilization of various skills is required for self-sufficiency, so to speak (*farḍ al-kifāyah*), or for economic independence. Social self-sufficiency, in its technical usage, implies the responsibility of an entire society toward providing the necessary skills for meeting every social need. The significance of this notion lies in the fact that if a society lacks a necessary skill whether by reason of its absence altogether or the refusal of those who have it to exercise it, the entire society is to blame. To put it positively, the economic independence of a society, like its political strength, is the collective duty of its members. In this light, Ibn Taymiyyah stresses the obligation of utilizing one's skill as particularly serious, by virtue of one's possession of such skill, and as necessitated by social need.[21] "The use of physical skills (*manāfiʿ al-abdān*) is as much an obligation as the imparting of knowledge, adjudication among men, the [public] fulfillment of confessional testimony, the commending of good and the prohibition of evil."

The practical implications of this doctrine are, first, that labor may be required by law, which requirement would have to be reinforced by the State authorities, and, second, that in the event that this should become necessary, wage controls may be imposed, to guard against potential mutual exploitation. Consistent with his own method, Ibn Taymiyyah illustrates his principles in this manner: he says, for example, "If soldiers stationed at the battlefront need to have their lands farmed, farmers should be required to do this work for them. Soldiers, for their part, shall not exploit farmers, since farmers were recruited to work for them."[22] Similarly, wage controls are conceived in the context of social need. He says, "Society needs the skills of farmers, weavers and builders, as people must have food to eat, clothes to wear and dwellings to inhabit. When the authorized official (*waliyy al-amr*) compels (*ajbara*) skilled workers to meet the people's needs for their industries, such as farming, weaving, and building, he is to set an equitable pay (*ujrat al-mithl*) which neither the consumer may lower, nor the worker raise. This kind of control is obligatory."[23] The extent of need determines the wage, Ibn Taymiyyah continues. For example, a pay scale would have to be consulted when a need exists for milling grain, preparing the dough, making the bread for a private consumer, as opposed to the purchase of grain, then completing the process for the purpose of marketing bread for profit, he says. This discussion of pay scales Ibn Taymiyyah calls "pricing labor (*tasʿīr al-aʿmāl*), which seems more comprehensive, and more positively practicable, than mere "wage control." In this regard, labor, like money, is viewed as a social commodity which is traded in the marketplace for the benefit of all. As such it ceases to be merely a personal possession, separate from the realm of social interaction, and becomes subject to social regulation, in terms of both demand and cost.

B. *Commerce and State Control:*

The tension between personal freedom and the economic independence of the State is perhaps more pronounced in the case of commercial transactions (*bay' wa shirā'*) than in the issue of labor, since the latter constitutes a matter of personal survival, whereas the former leaves a wider margin for such tension to exist. That is to say, it may not be as critical for a merchant constantly to market his commodities or to maintain an index of attractive prices as it may be for a laborer to keep a steady practice of his skill. In the face of this and other possibilities, Ibn Taymiyyah, like other jurists of Islam, recognized the necessity for regulating commerce by indicating, in the first place, what may constitute a legitimate means of gaining an income, and then, some of the circumstances under which commercial control by the State may be necessary.

Legitimate means of gaining income are indicated negatively in *al-Ḥisbah* and other works of Ibn Taymiyyah, by stating the unacceptable ways of obtaining it, which ways should be banned by the State. Among these he cites "usury (*al-ribā*) in its simple or compounded forms, gambling (*al-maysir*), such as selling chances (*bay' al-ghirar*), or setting exorbitant prices (*najash*) [literally, 'price gouging']."[24] Some of these transactions have been unanimously recognized by Islamic interpreters of *Sharī'ah* as illegal; others have been debated. It seems, however, as is evident in the example of the Prophet, the Companions and those who followed, that all these modes of generating income should be prohibited, Ibn Taymiyyah says.[25]

As for the legitimate means of receiving income, particularly in commercial transactions, i.e., selling and buying, Ibn Taymiyyah sees several circumstances which warrant the controlling intervention of the State.

First among the situations necessitating economic control is the demand, or the public's need, for a certain commodity. The type of control of which Ibn Taymiyyah is speaking here is that of compelling merchants to sell the commodity in question, especially if it is food. "It is within the prerogative of the authorized official to coerce (*yukrih*) a person to sell his goods for a fair price (or, its market value, *qīmat al-mithl*) when it is needed by the public; as when he has in his possession food which he does not need while others are hungry, he shall be compelled to sell it for what it is worth. For this reason, the jurists have said, "he who is forced by the predicament of need (*iḍṭurra*) may take food from another without the latter's choice, but for its fair price; and if the owner refuses to sell it for only what it is worth, he does not deserve more."[26]

Of prices, Ibn Taymiyyah said they may be divided to fair and unfair. Fair prices should be imposed when merchants refuse to sell the commodities needed by the public for their known prices. Price control in this case "means no more than imposing the fair price" on a commodity; for merchants "should abide by what God requires of them." Ibn Taymiyyah reiterates this Ḥanafī qualification: "price control ought not to be imposed, however, unless without it the public is hurt."[27] He also calls for support on the Shāfi'ī opinion, which under conditions other than public demand is least favorable toward price control.[28] His judgment, at any rate, is made on the premise that the need of the public is of the nature of the divine right (*haqq Allah*),[29] which, in the idiom of Islamic law, means "public right."

Economic control is further necessitated in the presence of "monopoly" (*iḥtikār*), which is defined by Ibn Taymiyyah in terms of "hoarding a needed commodity and refusing to sell it altogether" for the purpose of creating a greater demand which, in turn, would justify a price increase.

Ibn Taymiyyah, citing a *ḥadīth* which says "No one but an evil man monopolizes,"[30] calls this sort of dealing "an oppression of the consumers," and justifies the intervention of *waliyy al-amr* for making the commodity in question available to the public at its fair price. He even concurs with Abū Ḥanīfah's opinion that placing the commodity under the custody of the State for the purpose of making it available in the open market to avert public harm, is a legitimate course of action.[31]

Two other occasions necessitating the State's economic intervention are related. They are: the case of merchants conspiring to fix prices at high levels; and that of monopolizing certain trades or products. The former is called *tawāṭu'*, and the latter, *ḥaṣr*.

In the case of the sellers' connivance to refuse to sell below a certain price, price control becomes inevitable in order to protect consumers against preposterous profits. Conversely, consumers who may boycott a certain group of merchants are prohibited from collective purchasing for the purpose of dividing up the purchase among themselves at lesser costs.

Hasr, i.e., selective merchandising, may result in an abhorrent type of monopoly of the market, ultimately costing the consumers abominably high prices. Ibn Taymiyyah states: "...a worse evil [than selling at unfair prices] is when such a way exists whereby food, or any other commodity, is sold by a certain group of persons, that if someone else [not belonging to that group] sells it he is prohibited [by the merchants] either by force, as he may have to pay a large sum of money, which is an act of oppression, or simply by not being allowed to continue to sell, since his activity constitutes a competition that threatens to spoil the profits of the consolidated merchants. In such a case, price control is necessary."[32] This view would appear to oppose the idea of partnerships and, in the context of Ibn Taymiyyah's social conception of labor, it is easily understood. For a unionized group of merchants to exist, for the obvious purpose of laying a strong hold on commodities, is an oppression on two accounts: it is oppressive to the original owner who will have no one to whom he may sell other than the union, and it is oppressive to the consumer who does not have the freedom to choose a more suitable price than that set by the union. Ibn Taymiyyah, consistently practical, consents that "if all of the evil cannot be eliminated, as much of it as possible should be resisted. Therefore price controls are undebatably requisite in these cases. The cardinal rule is that set prices must be fair, and this is required by the *Shari'ah*. The rule of fairness would further demand that as in some cases coercion to sell *may not* be permitted unless it is rightfully well-founded (*bihaqq*), coercion to sell *may* be permitted if it is rightfully well-founded.[33]

From this argument, it is easy to see Ibn Taymiyyah's consequent rejection of "the middle-man." He considers such a position as a function of artificial usefulness created only for the exploitation of both the grower, or the original owner of a commodity, and the consumer. By buying the commodity from the grower at a sub-normal price, since the latter has no way of knowing the market value of his goods, and by selling them at prices higher than they are actually worth, the middle-man, who is not needed in the first place, will have not only made a handsome profit for himself with minimal effort, but will have also inflated the economy considerably.[34] To support his opinion that such practices should be outlawed, he cites the Prophet's prohibition of the middle-man from intercepting at modest costs the goods of the farmers before the latter arrive at the market-place to sell their own goods, and by the same token, his prohibition of an urbanite from selling, through a second transaction, to a farmer or shepherd. The *ḥadīth* used specifically dictates that individuals should derive their own profits directly from the others, i.e., without the interference of a third party.[35]

Ibn Taymiyyah also addressed himself to the phenomenon of underselling. Not only should price controls be imposed when prices are set too high, but when they are deliberately lowered by some merchants to undercut the others--"dumping" in modern economics. However, he approaches this critical question with great caution, and with some additional considerations. One such consideration is the agreement of Ibn Ḥanbal, Mālik and al-Shāfi'ī that pricing under the current market rate makes often for a healthy competition, and does not frequently constitute loss for those who practice it. They are unanimous in concluding that the vender's freedom to reduce the price should not be curbed. Ibn Taymiyyah, mindful of this unanimity, agrees that in certain categories, such as in the case of the one who brings his commodity into the marketplace (meaning the peddler who has no overhead) and especially grain peddlers of wheat and barley (these being basic, necessary commodities for human consumption) should be exempt from price controls. Others, however, following Ibn Taymiyyah's fairness rule, should be subject to having their low prices normalized.[36]

How does the State arrive at setting equitable price controls, and when are such controls mandatory? Ibn Taymiyyah satisfied himself with a practice prescribed by a certain Ibn Ḥabīb, wherein the *imām* gathers together representatives of the vendors and asks them the current rate of their respective trade items. Then, he calls in others who will be asked for the same information in order to verify the figure quoted by the first group. When this is done, the *imām* negotiates with the merchants toward a price that is at once profitable for them and acceptable to the public, until they reach a mutual agreement, without the coercion of the vendors. Then it is up to them to use the guideline voluntarily. The advantage of this method is that it proves profitable for the merchants, satisfactory for the consumers and beneficial for the entire economy as it activates the market and subsequently renders the monetary system more stable.[37]

When a merchant refuses to utilize the suggested prices voluntarily, Ibn Taymiyyah demands that he be "ordered to do what is dutiful, and penalized if he does not..."[38]

In review, Ibn Taymiyyah criticizes those who insist on arbitrary and absolute price controls, who assert that by so doing, the public is protected against the unbounded greed of the merchants. He points out the inequity of this generalization. In addition, he notes the inconsistency in this camp with its rejection of coerced selling under any circumstances. He also refutes the argument of lawmakers who arbitrarily and absolutely reject price controls, merely onthe basis of Muḥammad's affirmation that God is the one in supreme control, when he said, "God is the appraiser, the withholder and the generous giver..."[39] Ibn Taymiyyah argues that the Prophet's statement was offered in a specific context, and is, therefore, not to be used as a general pronouncement. Furthermore, it had nothing to do with illegitimate abstention from sale, or with demand for unfair price. He proceeds to set the *ḥadīth* in its proper context, and continues to show historical evidence of how, in the times of Muḥammad, the economic conditions of Madīnah generally did not warrant price controls. Using the Tradition, he cites the Prophet's ruling to arbitrate a price in the case of co-ownership of a slave, one of whose owners wished to sell and the other desired to buy his share. If price arbitration was permitted by the Prophet for the sake of selling a share of a slave, how much more, Ibn Taymiyyah contends, it is necessary to determine the prices of the basic needs of food and clothing.[40]

Thus Ibn Taymiyyah arrives at the solution that price arbitration and control are an economic measure which may be exercised under certain circumstances, and which should be exercised as necessity dictates.

C. *Property and Its Expropriation*

The question of State expropriation of personal property is related to the issue of price and wage control. For while the dispossession of property for an adequate compensation by the State is not implied in the principle of sale by coercion, it may be considered synonymous with it, depending, of course, on the particular situation.

Where the expropriation of property is to be considered synonymous with sale by coercion, it, too, is considered an exception to the *Sharīʽah*, according to Ibn Taymiyyah, after al-Shāfiʽī. For, as has been already shown,[41] "The people are in charge of their own wealth; no one dare take it, or any portion of it, away without their consent, except in particular and necessary situations." It is with respect to these particular situations that Ibn Taymiyyah addresses the question of expropriation.

His guideline of public, as well as private, necessity prevails here also. The example of the need for food when it is available in excess in someone's possession by another who is hungry has been cited as an occasion legitimizing coerced sale of it.[42] Even when the need is not as dire as in the case of hunger, but is nevertheless real, it dictates coerced sale. Ibn Taymiyyah cites, as a yardstick, the controversy between two men, who came to the Prophet for arbitration in their conflict. One had owned an estate in which the other had owned a tree. The former was annoyed by the frequent trespassing of the latter whose excuse was his ownership of the tree. The Prophet commanded him either to sell it or to deed it voluntarily to the other man. When he refused, he authorized the estate owner to cut the tree down. Ibn Taymiyyah concludes from this incident that the need for food, which is more urgent than the removal of the nuisance caused by the external ownership of a tree, would likewise necessitate its coerced sale.[43] Needs for other than food legitimize forced sale of property: these include, the payment of debts or alimony, and the priority of a co-owner, over a stranger's right, to buy his co-owner's share of their property. All, however, are so authorized by Ibn Taymiyyah under the fair price rule.

Another occasion for expropriation is the need for the

usefulness of an object. Under the condition of this need the object in question, says Ibn Taymiyyah, ought to be made available for its equitable rental value. Such objects, for example, may be an inn, a space in the marketplace, or a public bath. If the owner reserves the right not to lease it, he shall be required, in the face of public need, to forfeit his right.[44] Ibn Taymiyyah then tells this rather amusing illustration: if a certain family were forced by their need to live in a certain man's house (which presumably had available space), and could find no other, he is obliged to lease it to them. If they had need further for warm covers, cooking utensils, or gardening tools, it is incumbent upon the owner to extend such objects free of charge, if he himself is not in need of them. Ibn Taymiyyah's conclusion, which goes further than that of Ibn Ḥanbal who advocates paying the fair rental value of such items, is based on the Qur'ānic verse: "فويل للمصلّين الذين هم عن صلاتهم ساهمون، الذين هم يراءون، ويمنعون الماعون"[45]

Here, Ibn Taymiyyah may have outdone his own rule of fair compensation, and thus may have broken it in the interest of socialistic altruism. For how in the case of extreme need for basic nourishment does he consistently require that forced sale be accompanied by payment of the fair market value, and at the same time suggest the free use of another man's property? It is possible, though unlikely, that he extended to this situation the traditional rule of free lodging and hospitality for a stranger. If he literally meant every detail of his parable, then he has been inconsistent with his own methodology as well as the precedents of the jurists.

It appears, however, that he became somewhat over-zealous in making a legitimate point, namely, that nothing which may be useful at present for a fellow human being should be withheld from him now in favor of possibly making it available at a later point for a greater personal gain. This explanation appears to be consistent with Ibn Taymiyyah's overriding principle that in the economic exigencies of the Community, the higher good of all should be sought above personal accumulation of wealth, through mutual cooperation and through collaboration.

PART FOUR: SUMMARY AND CONCLUSION

CHAPTER X

THE ENDURING CONTRIBUTION OF IBN TAYMIYYAH

Ibn Taymiyyah's contribution, as has been reflected in the preceding chapters, was veritable and sizeable. In many respects, it may be considered "reformative" in its very affirmation of normative Islam, i.e., the ideals and life-patterns revealed in the Qur'ān, interpreted and exemplifed in the life and work of Muḥammad, and demonstrated effectively in the early Muslim generations. The thrust of Ibn Taymiyyah's legacy was as such directed toward the understanding of revealed Islamic truths and their application in the realm of human conduct.

As we review his contribution, we are confronted with several questions. One of these questions is whether, in his thought formulation and development, Ibn Taymiyyah's ethics was influenced by his theological doctrine or *vice versa*. Another question is how was he so consistently able to affirm the compatibility of revelation and reason at the same time that he identified strongly with the most conservative of the four Schools, i.e., the Ḥanbalī School, and also sought to destroy the arguments of rational philosophers? Another, yet related, question may be, is there any contradiction between the fact that he belonged to the most conservative of the *Madhāhib* and the fact that his ideas are increasingly gaining recognition as "reformative"? Finally, in assessing the worth of his contribution, is he to be considered a success or a failure?

It is appropriate that a response to these questions be offered prior to the recapitulation and evaluation of his contribution.

First, it is of primary importance to note that the fundamental ethos of Ibn Taymiyyah's life-work as a theologian-jurist was a firm conviction of the unity and uniqueness of God, combined inseparably with a certainty of the call and mission of a demonstratively obedient (*muslim*) community. For him, these two aspects were intertwined because the God who disclosed his nature and character in the Qur'ān also indicated therein His divine pattern for human action. Since, therefore, there is to be in Islam no line of demarcation between dogma and law, between theology and jurisprudence, between religion and life, as it were, the interdependence between the expression of community solidarity and the affirmation of the unity and incomparability of God constituted a formidable component in Ibn Taymiyyah's theological-ethical system. For this reason, it is not easy to judge whether his conception of God led him to reassert this understanding of the *ummah* or the reverse. It is most likely, however, that, based on their inseparability within revelation, the twin themes were never apart in the development of his ideas, as he was at once in constant contact with the texts of the Qur'ān and the Tradition, and beset by the human conditions of the *ummah*. For Ibn Taymiyyah, as for normative Islam, the problem of priority does not exist in addressing religion and ethics.

Secondly, as Ibn Taymiyyah called his fellow Muslims to return to the fountainhead of revelation as embodied in the Qur'ān, and at the same time challenged them to utilize the faculty of rational knowledge, he was in fact calling them to participate in the very reality that is Islam. For him to accept fully the authenticity of the whole of revelation was not a mere exercise of his conservative Ḥanbalism; it was to be truly Muslim. And to be truly Muslim also required conviction and rational certainty. He believed, upon study, that revelation was not meant to be unintelligible, nor merely received without rational inquiry. By definition, revelation was communicative, and as such was self-interpretive. He argued that if a particular text lacked clarity, there are ample other texts within revelation which are given to shed light upon it. If the meaning remained unclear, it is through no fault of revelation, but through the finitude and insufficient development of reason. At any rate, the authentic sayings of the Prophet and the life of the early Muslims give ample demonstration of revelation. This was the basic principle in Ibn Taymiyyah's hermeneutics. As for applied ethics, he suggested that the *ijma'* (consensus) of the *ummah* and the utilization of proper *qiyās* (analogy) are certain to give substance to the use of reason (i.e., "common sense," with reference to ethics) in appropriating revelation. In this way,

Ibn Taymiyyah's criticism of the philosophers was not because they utilized reason, but because they resorted to the categories of Greek rationality, as in the case of Ibn Sīnā, as an alternative to understanding revelation. They depended on deductive methodology; he insisted on inductive learning. Likewise, he allowed no other alternatives to understanding revelation, such as allegorical (*Bāṭinī*) interpretation, as well as dependence on illumination (*kashf*) of the Ṣūfīs. Even al-Ghazālī's compromise between intellect and esotericism expressed in this principle of illumination, was totally rejected by Ibn Taymiyyah as less than the full exercise of rational ability through *ijtihād*.

Thirdly, as a confirmed conservative, Ḥanbalī jurist, was his product "reformative"? Yes. He was an orthodox Muslim in the fullest sense of that characterization. He worked vigorously to return the Community to the basic givens of Islam. Against the doctrinal and social phenomena of legalism, the esotericism, the mysticism and the blind dogmatism of his day, he strove to restore an open and healthy Islam. Therein lies his "conservatism"! Seen against the predominance of the dogmatism of the Ḥanafīs, that is, the "liberals" of his time, his was by far a more reformative Islam. As a Ḥanbalī, too, he was able to step outside his affiliation when intellectual integrity required him to do so.

Was Ibn Taymiyyah a success? Was he a failure? His success may be questioned on the grounds that he had only one disciple, notably, Ibn al-Qayyim al-Jawziyyah, and that for four hundred years there was no echo of his voice. That he had only one scholarly follower of note is not necessarily a discredit to Ibn Taymiyyah. After all, he arose in an age too intellectually lazy to be quickly moved to accept the challenge of his demanding kind of disciplined scholarship, especially in the sciences of the Qur'ān and of *Ḥadīth*. Be that as it may, he at least turned the attention of his contemporaries to what normative Islam demanded. As for the development of Ibn Taymiyyah's ideas through the work of Ibn al-Qayyim, a separate study should prove both interesting and valuable.

Concerning the silence of history for four centuries about Ibn Taymiyyah's work, this is attributable to several factors. Among them are these: a) the dominance of other Schools of law, particularly the Ḥanafī School, overshadowing the Ḥanbalī School; b) the prevalence of the Turkish language in the political life of the Middle East as it had come within the orbit of the Ottoman Empire, and c) the rigidity of Islamic dogma and law, accounting for the opposition of revivalist or innovative ideas and resulting in hostility against original thinking.

Now as to whether Ibn Taymiyyah is to be considered successful may be ascertained from a summary review of his contribution, focusing on its social factor, and from a reference to his impact on the future.

I. *His Contribution and Its Social Worth*

The contribution of Ibn Taymiyyah would be more readily recognized and acclaimed had he proposed a tailored "program" for specific and detailed social action dealing with the conditions of his time. Yet, had he had such a plan, his would have been a mere "movement" that might have had instant appeal, or a kind of opposition serving to popularize and/or place in contempt both the movement and its author, or both. Such a movement might have, at any rate, become a transitory response to the prevalent, insidious maladies that had befallen Islam. It might have been judged a success or a failure precisely because it would have been specific, narrowly conceived, and only temporary and contextual.

That Ibn Taymiyyah proposed no programmatic scheme of social reform does not mean, however, that he did not offer specific reformative ideas for the Islamic society. For indeed he spent his whole juristic career writing, on the basis of original *ijtihād*, legal opinions (*fatāwā*) pertaining to social conduct. He wrote on the social implications of such personal evils as drunkenness, adultery, theft, violence and the like. He wrote on social institutions like marriage, property, contracts, government, public finances, etc. He discussed all these and more, as we have seen in the preceding pages, specifically and in great detail. Yet, it is evident that his concern was greater than simply addressing issues. His entire system of thought was so socially oriented that every realm of his intellectual, legal and demonstrative activity was aimed at a more lasting social change. At the same time he addressed the root causes of the social conditions which prevailed in his day. In this manner he provided a *foundation* for change rather than a *program* designed for symptomatic and temporary relief. Let us now recapitulate his contribution:

1. Strange as it may seem, the expression of his social concern took as its point of departure the very doctrine of God: the one, transcendent and incomparable God whose nature is not to be confused with that of any other being, and whose sovereignty is not shared by any of His creatures. The unity of God as understood in its proper meaning by Ibn Taymiyyah, left no room for either any such belief or any such practice as may manifest a dependence by any segment of the Muslim Community upon any other power to produce or to conduct to personal or social well-being. The conduct and the social interaction of daily life by Muslims must be firmly, unequivocally, and uncompromisingly grounded in the oneness of God whom they worship and whom they serve. This God is not only the Creator of all the things that are, but is also the supreme Ruler and Law-giver. He is in need of no help in governing the universe because He is a God of infinite mercy and of supreme justice. The demands of His laws are, therefore, reasonable and just and as such do not depend on the intervention or the intercession of other powers or associations for fulfillment. This was Ibn Taymiyyah's idea of God as revealed in the Qur'ān and as proclaimed by the Prophet. That Muslims had become susceptible to the *Ṣūfī* practices of seeking aid, God's or otherwise, through acts of visiting the tombs of the pious dead, for example, was abhorrent to Ibn Taymiyyah. It meant not only a reduction of the reality of God's sovereignty to a mere superstition, but also an escape from individual and social responsibility to fulfill what God requires and to realize His will. It meant also a defiance, in effect, of God's just law (*Sharī'ah*) and a deviation from moral responsibility in personal social life. To uphold the doctrine of the unity of God was to destroy the notions of the healing power of a palm tree in the village of Manfūḥah, for example, or the easy blessings to be bestowed on one's life through a visit to a certain cave in Dar'iyyah, or to the tree of Ḥanafī or to the gate of al-Mutawallī, in Egypt. And to destroy such notions as these was, for Ibn Taymiyyah, to liberate the Muslims from the oppressive

domination of false beliefs in order to release them for creative obedience to the God who Himself is the Creator of their potential to serve Him among their fellows. This liberation is carried further by Ibn Taymiyyah, from superstitions that inhibit and stifle, to a liberation from a similar, unquestioning obedience to those who, having a position of leadership or authority in matters of doctrine and practice, distort the requirements of religion for the common man. It was against this sort of corruption that Ibn Taymiyyah asserts vigorously that God alone is Author of faith and Giver of law. He alone approves or proscribes. His word alone is the rule of faith and life, and not the words of men. Neither theologian nor legist has binding authority in what is lawful or unlawful; only the Qur'ān and the *Sunnah*. "Our *imām* is the Qur'ān and the *Sunnah*," he said, "and he who fulfills the requirements of *ijtihād* has the right--nay, the duty, to practice it according to his understanding of the texts." For this reason, Ibn Taymiyyah lamented the discontinuation of creative interpretation by his time, and considered that no greater intellectual or practical disaster (*nakbah*) had befallen Islam, since its residual effect had been the cessation of scholarship, the termination of progress, the stifling of understanding, the indulgence in perpetuating tradition for its own sake, as well as excessive imitation, and rivalry, in the interpretations of doctrine. It was thus the affirmation of Divine unity primarily that Ibn Taymiyyah lifted up against the jurists, the theologians and the *Ṣūfī* leaders. In so doing, he turned the attention of conscientious Muslims of his generation and of succeeding generations to the doctrine so fundamental to a viable social structure for Islam.

2. The ethical counterpart for this theological doctrine of God's unity and uniqueness is the unity and uniqueness of the Muslim Community. Although this correlation may appear to suggest some incarnational overtones in Ibn Taymiyyah's construct, any such intention was totally and deliberately excluded in the formation of his ideas. The modality here is one of practical application of what the Muslims believed and understood about the one God in the expressions of the nature and the purpose of their community. Theirs, asserted our theologian-jurist, is a singleness of calling and a singleness of will--to do God's

revealed will. Theirs is a solidarity that ought to be manifest in an unswerving faithfulness to the task of understanding the requirements of revelation, as each member searches the meanings of the Scripture and seeks guidance from the example of the *salaf*. Theirs is to be a cohesiveness of intent and of action to fulfill these requirements.

3. The absolute uniqueness of the nature and character of God and the call to solidarity are communicated through the instrumentality of the Qur'ān as given to and through Muḥammad. Though a man among men, Muḥammad's infallibility is affirmed by Ibn Taymiyyah in accordance with the unquestionable character of the Prophet's mission and with the finality and inerrance of his message. This affirmation, however, is not simply an expression of due praise and devotion for the Prophet and his message; it aims ultimately at demanding utter obedience to him inasmuch as the purpose of his message is the realization of God's will in human life, that is, in the social dimensions. In God's service, which is accomplished in obedience to the Prophet of revelation, is the completion of religion. And service, by definition, is an outward manifestation of concern for one's neighbor, an act of social extension of one's faith. Applied corporately, it is the collective interaction of love and devotion in concrete and visible form, toward the fulfillment of God's will.

4. That God's revelation of His nature and His will is complete and amply clear in the Qur'ān is argued convincingly by Ibn Taymiyyah. Yet, in order to make certain that revelation implies and requires application, i.e., action, and in order to impress upon Muslims the vitality of this revelation for every age, he demands that the response to revelation should be fraught with an active search on the part of every Muslim, into the meaning of revelation. This is the reason that fresh and honest *ijtihād* is insisted upon by Ibn Taymiyyah, because he believed that new and disciplined interpretation is bound to suggest meaningful response in the life of the individual and of the community. It is appropriate, therefore, to understand this argument as a defense for the social dimension of *ijtihād*.

5. The purpose of *ijtihād* is to reinforce belief with proper understanding and conviction, and with appropriate

response. Proper understanding of revelation, therefore, is the key link between *īmān*, i.e., the response of the inmost being to God's revelation, and *islām*, i.e., the outer response to divine revelation as motivated by *īmān*. It is noteworthy, therefore, that Ibn Taymiyyah's definition of *islām* (and, indeed, of Islam) is one of active, assertive relational (or, social) manifestation of faith in God. Too, the very meaning of "godliness" (*taqwā*) is understood in this same light. To be godly, he states, is "to do all that God commanded out of a sense of obligation, and out of a sense of positive desire (*ījāban*), and to refrain from what he prohibited..." To heed what God said above all else is, as has been shown, to acknowledge His absolute unity.

It is in this very action that *'ibādah*, or, *'ubūdiyyah*, i.e., service, and *islām*, i.e., an incarnate affirmation of God's will in human life and relationships and not a passive surrender, are explained by Ibn Taymiyyah. With such active, affirmative characterization of the human response to revelation, there is no ambiguity in Ibn Taymiyyah's explication of his understanding of the doctrine of determinism/free will. And against the vast spread of social evil in his time, due to the widely espoused notions of determinism, Ibn Taymiyyah's voice was clearly audible. He proclaimed that man is the author of his actions, that human ability and capability for carrying out actions are real, that natural law is at work in every aspect of creation, that cause and effect are a reliable component in the order of creation, that reason is God-given, that human will is an active force in the development of personal and social events, and that there is no conflict between the natural order and the moral order, the divine will or the human will for those who receive and believe God's revelation.

Through these assertions, Ibn Taymiyyah sought to shatter the *ṣūfī* system of doctrine which had minimized to an insignificant degree, if not completely eliminated, the possibility of ethical action. His ideas exposed the inefficacy of the mystic notions of illumination (*kashf*), which had been substituted for rational knowledge, of non-being (or nonentity, *'adam*), which had become the *ṣūfīs'* escape from the responsibilities of serious and meaningful existence (*wujūd*), of passive acquiescence (*qismah*) which had taken the place of ethical obligation (*taklīf*), of monastic devotion (*ta'abbud*) which had been mistaken for service (*'ibadah*), of ineffectual and neglectful trust (*tawākul*) which had replaced active, obedient certainty and dependence on God's immutable laws laid down in His creation (*tawakkul*), and so forth. Here again Ibn Taymiyyah's overriding concern was the practical implication of affirming God's unity (*tawḥīd*) overtaken in the *ṣūfī* system by blind obedience (*ṭa'ah*) to the *shaykhs*, which was contrary to reason and to revelation.[1]

6. Ibn Taymiyyah stated the obvious, namely that revelation, in addition to disclosure of God's unique character, imparted His *Sharī'ah*, i.e., God's "clear way," by which men could please Him. The *Sharī'ah*, he explained, is a system of morality designed for a new society as well as for a new type of individual. To fulfill the *Sharī'ah* is to perform the essential acts of Islamic devotion which, in each case, have a social import. Thus:

a. Prayer, which constitutes the highest ritual obligation in Islam after public confession of faith (*shahādah*) is not merely an act of private, pious devotion; it is an act of commitment and of servitude. Great stress is placed by Ibn Taymiyyah on punctuality in individual prayers, because of the essential fellowship of all Muslims when they are joined at the same time, though in different locations, for this purpose. This union signifies solidarity of purpose and solidarity of action by the Muslim Community. As well, it has a utilitarian, social, value: namely, when business transactions are suspended at the same time for this purpose, no member of the business community stands to lose an opportunity for a sale or a service! The supremely visible unity in the act of prayer is that of the Friday prayer. Herein is celebrated in common a singularity of intent and of action to hear anew what God commands through the delivery of the sermon, and to renew through the common presence and participation the affirmation of the social cohesion inherent in the *ummah* of Islam. The act of common prayer is the single-most visible expression of solidarity. Its neglect threatens to jeopardize justice, according to a *fatwā* by Ibn Taymiyyah. Also, because there is no distinction in Islam between religious and secular life, as has been shown and will be recapitulated, the act of common prayer is the first manifestation of the function of the state. Ibn Taymiyyah asserts that it is a *sunnah* that the chiefs of state who, by nature of their political function, are the military leaders of the community should also be its *imāms* in prayer. In prayer, private or public, every dimension of life takes on a holy character: the entire earth, where Muslims prostrate themselves in servitude and worship, becomes a mosque, just as much as the mosque stands in the midst of the city, and as the prayers syncopate the daily routines of social life.

b. Likewise, fasting, which is considered as the act of practical devotion *par excellence*, is viewed most significantly by Ibn Taymiyyah in terms of its social value, for the ultimate purpose of realizing God's will on earth. The social factor is the underlying element in his discussion of fasting as "the obligation of the *ummah*," rather than merely the duty of individuals. The reason is obviously that it serves as a mode of spiritual discipline for the nation, and thus as both an act of national devotion, and an opportunity for increased social sensitivity on the part of its individuals, since fasting is a primarily personal act. But Ibn Taymiyyah took issue with the practice of fasting as a mode of asceticism, and considered it reprehensible if it weakened the physical or moral strength which the Muslims must maintain in good reserve, especially when they must face *jihād*, or "holy war." Because *jihād*, too, is an essential obligation for the Muslims, their strength should not be jeopardized or compromised, even if that meant exemption from fasting. For this reason, Ibn Taymiyyah in one of his *fatāwa*, considered it legally permissible, after the manner of the Qur'ān and the *Sunnah*, to break the fast at the time of the invasion of Damascus by the Tatar.

c. The pilgrimage, being one of the essentials of Islam, is treated seriously by Ibn Taymiyyah, but with two particularly significant social considerations. They are: the reaffirmative value of universal community solidarity as Muslims come to Makkah and al-Madīnah from every part of the earth, and the social realism of its availability or inavailability to Muslims. That the pilgrimage renews one's personal faith is not doubted by Ibn Taymiyyah, but the advantage is multiplied in the context of the gathered community. The symbolic act of a community determined to obey and to realize God's will in its time and places of habitation is keenly observed by Ibn Taymiyyah. Yet, he suggests, out of a compassionate social concern for those who may not in a life-time be able to perform the pilgrimage, that revelation did not require it as an absolute obligation. He gives two reasons: first, that religion is not to be regarded as a taskmaster demanding more than what is within the capability of its adherents, as God does not require of man what he is not capable of doing, and, second, that the higher demand, if a choice must be made, is *jihād*. *Jihād*, therefore, serves as a point of reference for the requirements of the *Sharī'ah*.

d. The *Zakat*, or material stewardship, which is accepted universally by Muslims as the most conspicuous form of social compassion, is more than a program of assistance to the poor. It is the extension of one's commitment materially to one's neighbor in order for the latter to be enabled to do his own active part in the realization of God's will, i.e., in serving Him with his fullest ability. In the act of giving, the Muslim performs a triple socio-religious duty: he fulfills the requirement of the *Sharī'ah* for himself; he helps fulfill his brother's own potential as a creation of divine purpose; and he helps his brother fulfill the divine will in his community. In his small but valuable work *Al-Ḥisbah*, Ibn Taymiyyah interpreted a greater social worth of *Zakat*, namely the opportunity for the state to develop a responsible canonical fiscal structure, which he views, after the model of Abū Bakr, as "one of the constitutional obligations of faith." Through and through, he stresses, and guards against the abuse of, the social value of such a structure, as may be inferred from his admonition of the rulers against the misuse of funds, and his exhortation of the Muslims to refuse, if necessary, to pay *Zakat* if they knew that public officials would misuse it!

The purpose of the state is to guard the *Sharī'ah*; and the purpose of the *Sharī'ah* is to show the Muslim *ummah* the way of the right. The purpose of the community of Islam is to uphold the *Sharī'ah*; and the *Sharī'ah* is sufficient for all the purposes of life and government. The *Sharī'ah* is to be the guiding principle of the rulers and of the scholars; it dictates the framework within which to operate, but always has at the center of its interest the welfare of the community. And it was on the basis of this affirmation that Ibn Taymiyyah gave a new development to the juridical idea of "public interest" (*maṣlaḥah*). In the sphere of human relations (*mu'āmalāt*), the principle of *maṣlaḥah* is to be applied: everything which conduced to human welfare, and was not specifically proscribed, was "not only allowed but even by implication enjoined." For this reason, argued Ibn Taymiyyah, the task of *ijtihād*, i.e., of deciding what conduced to social welfare, could never cease. And this was a fundamental component in the ethical system of Ibn Taymiyyah.

As applied to government, for example,[2] this principle implied that while the Mamlūk rule in Egypt may be legitimate, there is room for new ideas how that rule might be carried on. He saw that good government depended on an alliance between political and military leaders (*amīrs*) and interpreters of the law (*'ulamā'*). For the Mamlūk government of Egypt, where the political leaders were the Turks and the scholars were Arab, this meant that the rule should not be in the hands of a foreign power alone. But, far from suggesting a change limited to his own time and locale, Ibn Taymiyyah's was a greater concern. His proposal was of a principle that required that no government should be in the hands of any limited group: "the claims of justice and unity must take precedence over those of any natural ties, whether friendship, ethnic solidarity or blood relationship." On the basis of that principle, "it is a duty for everyone who directs any part of the public affairs of the Muslims...to employ the most suitable person he can find in each position which is under his control...if he rejects the worthiest and most proper candidate in favor of another, because that other is his relation, friend or freedman, or because they belong to the same country, legal sect, religious order or ethnic group--Arab, Persian, Turkish, Anatolian--or because he has accepted a bribe or service from this man, or for other reasons, or because of some personal animosity toward the worthier candidate or some enmity between them, he cheats God and His Prophet and the faithful."[3]

This concept of the public good, as thrusted by Ibn Taymiyyah to the forefront of the considerations of the state, continued to lay hold on future thinkers of similar historical experience, such as Ibn Khaldūn, Muḥammad Ibn ʿAbd al-Wahhāb, Muḥammad ʿAbduh, and others. They, too, acknowledged in their respective times the essential role of a common good and a divine law in maintaining the stability and prosperity of state; and, like Ibn Taymiyyah, they affirmed that, because there is no distinction in Islam between religion and life, the stability of the state was a sign of the health and solidarity of the community, and that, in turn, was a concrete indication that God's will is being wrought in the social order. A stable state meant that law and morality were upheld in society, because the state was free from impediments and is able to perform its function of overseeing the performance of all duties commanded by God and of defending the *ummah* against its enemies. All of these involved power and political authority. Thus the Islamic community, if it is to be viable, must take the form of healthy Islamic states; and political and social action is also a way of serving God: "it is a duty to consider the exercise of power as one of the forms of religion, as one of the acts whereby man draws near to God."[4]

Such was Ibn Taymiyyah's contribution for his own time. At least this is what we can know of it, since many of his works have been destroyed. The value of the portion of his contribution of which we can be aware we know is immense.

II. *The Influence of Ibn Taymiyyah on the Future*

The extent of Ibn Taymiyyah's impact on Muslim Society, as we have observed, may never be fully known, but, recognizably, it is great. One cause for our incomplete knowledge of his influence is that, in spite of the wealth of his material many of his works are not available, and many others have yet to be discovered.[5] Another cause is the long silence of history about Ibn Taymiyyah, for reasons previously suggested. It was four hundred years before some of the ideas of Ibn Taymiyyah were echoed in the life and work of Muḥammad Ibn ʿAbd al-Wahhāb (1081-1166 A.H./1703-1787 A.D.). That history was thus silent about Ibn Taymiyyah should by no means imply that he had no influence upon it; or else how could ʿAbd al-Wahhāb, also a Hanbalī, have enunciated with such clarity the conceptions expressed so long before his time? We know, and this writer has seen in the British Museum in London, a number of manuscripts of works by Ibn Taymiyyah that are said to be copied by Muḥammad Ibn ʿAbd al-Wahhāb. Neither do we dare suggest that our medieval leader's thought has completely achieved its potential reach; for we do now see in our present generation[6] and may continue to see in the future some fruits whose seeds were unmistakably planted by him, although admittedly he does not receive his due credit for his role in the process of their evolution.

We do know, however, that there is a strong parallelism between the thought of ʿAbd al-Wahhāb and Ibn Taymiyyah's. We are aware of the resemblance, in many respects, between ʿAbd al-Wahhāb's movement and subsequent reform movements in Islam. Thus, if it is said that the Wahhābī mvoement was a pioneer and an enabler of the more recent reformist forces in Muslim society, it ought not to be forgotten that a yet more aggressive step taken by Ibn Taymiyyah had paved the way for all of them.

To reiterate, Ibn Taymiyyah, who was a typical representative of orthodoxy, leveled his wrathful criticism against the *Ṣūfīs* who by this time had assimilated a multiplicity of ideas, beliefs and practices that were foreign to the revelation of Islam, such as the worship of saints, the veneration of tombs and the like. Similarly, the philosophers who depended totally on rational processes for the formulation of their faith, thus challenging revelation and subordinating it to reason alone, were the object of his attack. Yet, Ibn Taymiyyah's contribution, as has been clearly discussed, has not been merely a negative reaction to the ideas and practices of his day:

> There is discernible in his writings a positive movement of the mind and spirit which genuinely seeks to go behind all historic formulations of Islam by all Muslim groups, to the Qurʾān itself and to the teaching of the Prophet.[7]

Likewise, his critique of existing orthodoxy, as reflected in the attitude of blind traditionalism of the *ʿulamāʾ*, shows a bold and assertive desire on his part, not so much to tear down, but to construct afresh the concepts of the Qurʾān and the *Sunnah* for the faith and life of the Muslim Community. As such he had acted as "a liberalizing force" against the authority of medieval schools; and he did so through the exercise of original reflection on and interpretation of the Qur'ān and the *Ḥadīth* in a manner that corresponded to the style of the early Muslims. Insisting that to be a believer, and to be a believing community, required an honest understanding of the will of God as revealed in the Qur'ān and embodied in the *Sunnah*, and a commitment to implant God's will in the context of daily living, Ibn Taymiyyah integrated the obligations toward divine worship, individual righteousness and social justice into the indivisible concept of *'ibādah*, or "service" to God. And it is within this context that the overall thrust of his career, as well as the particular emphases of his various treatises and *fatāwā* are to be viewed: religion and life, pious faith and social morality are inseparable.

Muḥammad Ibn 'Abd al-Wahhāb, rising in the eighteenth century in Central Arabia, and drawing his inspiration from the teaching of Ibn Taymiyyah through the Hanbalī School to which they both belonged, focused his energies, not on the dangers of Westernism that potentially threatened Islamic Arabia, but more seriously on the centrality of the theology of unity for Islamic revival. He demanded that the unity of God and the solidarity of the Muslim Community be the foundation of Muslim faith and life. His emphasis on a theology of unity was unmistakably a reaction to *Ṣūfī* practice. He proclaimed pointedly that association (*shirk*) is evil regardless of "whether its object be a king, a prophet, a saint, a tree or a tomb."[8] The worship of saints is no less evil than to worship idols, he declared. Genuine Islam was demonstrated in the exemplary life of the early Muslims (*al-salaf al-ṣāliḥ*). Later additions and innovations, such as mysticism and asceticism, philosophy and polemic theology, cult and ritual, were foreign to the Qur'ān, he insisted. He issued to his generation a call to repentance and a challenge to shed off tribalism and to unite into the knowledge of the *Sharī'ah* for a life-style emulating the *salaf*. He courageously attacked the system of government of the Ottoman Empire on the grounds that "the Islam that the Sultan protected was not the true Islam," and that, by implication, the Sultan was not the true leader of the *ummah*.[9] He thus conceived of a Muslim state in which the *Sharī'ah* constitutes the body of law, and in which the people may live as the faithful community of that law. The *īmām* possessed full authority of leadership, with the counsel of the *'ulamā'* of the *Sharī'ah*, and of the community. Unity of all Muslims (*vis-à-vis* the tribalism of *'abbāsiyyah*) was stressed, although insistence on the Arab (*vis-à-vis* the Turkish) consciousness of the State was not compromised. He appealed to the ruling dynasty to join forces with him to win the world to genuine Islam. The call was met with the enthusiasm of that influential dynasty of Ibn Sa'ūd which united with Ibn 'Abd al-Wahhāb that by the end of the eighteenth century the Wahhābīs (who called themselves Unitarians, or *Muwaḥḥidūn*) were in control of central Arabia and the Persian Gulf; and a little later they had spread toward Iraq and occupied the *Ḥijāz* and were threatening Damascus.[10] They developed programs of social, economic and educational emphases in a communal life pattern upholding the ideals of unity and solidarity among themselves as a token of God's unique sovereignty over them and His unequivocal endorsement of their cause.

The Wahhābi call, resounding the social and theological affirmations of Ibn Taymiyyah, had veritable echoes beyond the *Ḥijāz* and the Arabian Peninsula. It had great exposure among Muslims of other lands largely and initially through the opportunity of the pilgrimage. We read of a small community in Zanzibar that embraced anew these principles of pure Islam, shedding off *Ṣūfī* practices, such as the visitation of tombs, and the like. We also know now of some of the great movements of India, Pakistan, Algeria, Morocco and Yaman through the respective efforts of Al-Sayyid Aḥmad, Al-Sanūsī, and Al-Imām Al-Shawkānī. We know, too, of the great doctrinal and social reformation ideas of Muḥammad 'Abduh, of Egypt, based on his "theology of unity," as well as those of his disciple, Muḥammad Rashīd Riḍā, also of Egypt, as evidenced by his prolific writings, especially the voluminous commentary on the Qur'ān, known as *Tafsīr al-Manār*. No doubt, too, the programmatically radical ideas of Ḥasan al-Bannā and his followers of al-Ikhwān al-Muslimūn (Muslim Brothers), of Egypt, have been inspired, if not indeed in doctrine, certainly at least in motivation, by this cumulative influence of Ibn Taymiyyah.

Ibn Taymiyyah's contribution was thus comprehensive and far-reaching. It emerged from a passionate concern for the expression of faith in social action, and was deeply rooted in sound doctrinal perception and grounded in brilliant intellectual integrity. By the example of his own life and action he demonstrated for his generation and those which were to follow a life of devotion, a depth of scholarship and an irrefutable manner of social witness.

Was he a success or was he a failure? We are not privileged to judge the extent of his success; but we are in no doubt about the immensity and the breadth of scope of his positive contribution. In addition, by evidence of his influence as it has begun to be felt in the more recent past, we do have the certainty of hope that his impact will ultimately be greater than we are now able to realize.

INTRODUCTION

NOTES

[1]It is generally agreed that Ibn Taymiyyah produced some 300 works, only less than half of which are extant.

CHAPTER I

NOTES

[1]See Ibn al-Athīr, *Al-Kāmil fī al-Tārīkh*, Vol. XII, pp. 137-138. Cf. also Ibn Kathīr, *Al-Bidāyah wa al-Nihāyah*, Vol. XIII, p. 86 f., and Al-Suyūṭī, "Akhbār Muʿāmalat al-Sālaṭīn fī Miṣr," in *Ḥusn al-Muḥāḍarah*, Vol. II, pp. 60 ff.

[2]Ibn Kathīr illustrating the bloody mercilessness of the Code quotes from ʿAlāʾ al-Dīn al-Juwaynī, an excerpt from the Code, as follows: "Whosoever commits adultery must be executed, محصنا او غير محصن, also, the homosexual, he who tells a premeditated lie, he who performs magic, he who interferes with two persons in conflict, thus supporting the one against the other, he who urinates in stagnating water and he who swims in it, he who gives food or drink to a prisoner, or clothes him without permission or he who finds him should he escape but not return him...." Vol. 13, p. 118.

[3]As quoted from his *Al-Muqaddimah* in M.Y. Musā, *Ibn Taymiyyah*, pp. 46-47.

[4]*Khuṭaṭ al-Maqrīzī*, Vol. 2; pp. 358-360 (al-Maqrīzī died in 845 A.Ḣ.).

[5]See *Shadharāt al-Dhahab*, Vol. 4, pp. 290 f.

[6]See Ibn al-Salāḥ's *Fatāwā*, pp. 34-35.

[7]For a summary description of these *Shīʿī* sects, see Abū Zahrah, *Ibn Taymiyyah, Ḥayātuh wa-ʿAṣruh*, pp. 168-172.

[8]*Maʿārij al-Wuṣūl*, p. 3.

CHAPTER II

NOTES

[1]His full name as stated by one authority (Abū Zahrah) is Aḥmad Taqiyy al-Dīn Abū al-'Abbas Ibn (al-Shaykh) Shihāb al-Dīn Abu al-Maḥāsin 'Abd al-Ḥalīm Ibn (al-Shaykh) Majd al-Dīn Abū al-Barakāt 'Abd al-Salām Ibn Abū Muḥammad 'Abd Allah Ibn Abū al-Qāsim al-Khiḍr Ibn Muḥammad Ibn al-Khiḍr Ibn 'Alī Ibn 'Abd Allah. His family name, Ibn Taymiyyah, has generally been assumed to be taken from the first name of his great, great-grandmother, who had been named by her father after a young child whom he had seen at the time of his pilgrimage. Taymiyyah, the grandmother, had a reputation for great piety and preaching ability.

[2]T. H. Weir (*Encyclopedia of Islam*, I, p. 287) suggests that Ḥarran, which was visited by Ibn Jubayr in 1184, was in Ibn Taymiyyah's time no more than a small market-town quite stripped of its ancient wealth.

[3]Ibn Rajab, *Ṭabaqāt*, 111, p. 167.

[4]See Henri Laoust, *Essai Sur Les Doctrines Sociales et Politiques de Taḳi-d-Dīn b. Taymiya* (Cairo: L'Institut Francais d'Archeologie Orientale, 1939), pp. 7-8.

[5]*Ibid.*, 9.

[6]A chief Ḥanbalī scholar and apologist often designated as *The Shaykh,* and author of *al-'Umdah,* of *al-Muqni'* and of *al-Mughnī*. See Laoust, *loc. cit.*, n. 1.

[7]*Loc. cit.*

[8]As quoted by Abū Zahrah, *Ibn Taymiyyah: Hayātuh wa 'Usūruh* (Cairo: Dār al-Fikr al-Arabī, 1952), pp. 18-19.

[9]*Ibid.*, p. 21

[10]P. 139.

[11]*Loc. cit.*

[12]He bases this conclusion on the premise laid in an economic explanation of the decay of Baghdad given by Poliak. See Laoust, *op. cit.*, p. 12.

[13]Ḥanbalism was introduced to Damascus by the chief justice of Baghdad, Abū Ya'lā al-Shaykh Abū al-Faraj 'Abd al-Wāḥid (d. 486) who had gone there by way of Jerusalem. Cf. Laoust, *op. cit.*, p. 13.

[14]Laoust, *op. cit.*, 15, N. 1, points out the significance of a Ḥanbalī title, brought by Ibn Qudāmah, namely that for about three centuries, from the 5th to 8th, the Ḥanbalīs had referred to the leaders of their school as *qāḍi* ("jurisconsult," "justice"), which was his title that was also used to designate Abu Ya'la, and later Taqiyy al-Dīn.

[15](*Al-Mughnī*, edited with an important introduction by M. Rashīd Riḍā, was published in Cairo by Al-Manār Press, 1341; and *Rawḍat al-Nāẓir*, edited by Ibn Badrān and published also in Cairo by al-Salafiyyah Press, 1922.)

[16]*Op. cit.*, p. 15.

[17]*Op. cit.*, p. 16, n. 1.

[18]As will be seen below, the practice of *ijtihād* had already begun to become so restricted that by Ibn Taymiyyah's time it was virtually non-existent.

[19]M. Y. Mūsā, *Ibn Taymiyyah* (Cairo: Al-Mu'assasah Al-Miṣriyyah Al-'Āmmah, 1962), p. 73.

[20]From Kamāl al-Dīn al-Zamlakānī, as quoted in Ibn al-Athīr, *Al-Kāmil fi-Al-Tārīkh*, IV, pp. 131-132.

[21]See, for example, Ibn al-Athīr *Al-Bidāyah wa al-Nihāyah*, XIV, pp. 12 and 19.

CHAPTER III

NOTES

[1]Ibn Taymiyyah's concise commentary on the Ikhlāṣ *Sūrah* reflects the basic significance of this theme to his entire theological-ethical construct. One evidence of the fundamentality of the theological principle of divine unity to the author's subsequent works is its very publication in numerous editions.

[2]See *Majmū'at al-Rasā'il al-Kubrā* (Cairo: M.'A. Ṣubayh, 1966). Vol. II, pp. 321-349.

[3]Laoust notes that this second "proof" of Ibn Taymiyyah's argument for the existence of God points to His sovereignty over the order of creation which constitutes "a hymn to the existence of the Creator." He also suggests that this idea, called "al-tajallī" by the Salāmiyyah, is borrowed by Ibn Taymiyyah and further developed by Ibn al-Qayyim al-Jawziyyah. See H. Laoust, *op. cit.*, 153, n. 1.

[4]*Ibid.*

[5]See n. 1, above, and the annotated bibliography, below.

[6]*Sūrah* CXII. Translated, it reads, "Say: He is God, the One and Only; God the Eternal, Absolute; He begetteth not, nor is He begotten; And there is none like unto Him."

[7]See *Al-Risālah Al-Tadmuriyyah* (Beirut: Al-Maktab Al-Islāmī, 1971), pp. 9-16.

[8]*Ibid.*, 43-44.

[9]*Ibid.*, 29.

[10]*Ibid.*

[11]Examples of the Mu'tazilah interpretation, as cited by Abū Zahrah, *op. cit.*, 262-263, reflect how, in their effort toward deanthropomorphization, they went into great lengths to affirm the unity of God in a negative discourse.

[12]*Al-Risālah Al-Tadmuriyyah*, pp. 7, 8 and 9.

[13]*Ibid.*, p. 12.

[14]See his treatise, *Al-Iklīl Fī Al-Mutashābih Wa al-Ta'wīl* (Cairo: Maktabat Anṣār al-Sunnah, 1947), p. 22.

[15]*Ibid.*, p. 28.

[16]*Majmū'at Al-Rasā'il Al-Kubrā*, Vol. I, p. 249.

[17]*Ibid.*, pp. 419-421.

[18]*Op. cit.*, p. 159.

[19]*Majmū'at Al-Rasā'il Al-Kubrā*, Vol. I, pp. 440-465.

[20]Ibn Taymiyyah suggests that the speaker in the reference in the first person plural is God. See *Ibid.*, Vol. II, p. 34.

[21]*Ibid.*, p. 160.

[22]See his chapter on the Divine Attributes in *Majmū'at Al-Rasā'il wa al-Masā'il* (Cairo: Al Manār Press, 1922-30), pp. 37ff. In the hierarchization of the attributes, see his *Jawāb Ahl al-'Ilm Wa al-Kalām* (Cairo: Al-Salafiyyah, 1956-57), pp. 84ff.

[23]*Ibid.* See also, Laoust, *op. cit.*, p. 163.

[24]See *Sharḥ Al-'Aqīdah Al-Iṣfahāniyyah* (Cairo: Maktabat Kurdistān Al-'Īlmiyyah, 1911), p. 7ff.

[25]See *Tafsīr Sūrat Al-Ikhlāṣ* (Cairo: Maktabat al-Khanjī, 1905), pp. 62-69. (Cf. Laoust, *op. cit.*, p. 173.)

[26]*Tafsīr Sūrat Al-Ikhlāṣ*, pp. 50-54. It is noteworthy that the title of this commentary as it appears in the appendix of *Minhāj al-Sunnah* bears the subtitle "The Doctrine of the Incomparability of God with His Creatures."

[27]*Ibid.*, p. 52.

[28]*Majmū'at Al-Rasā'il Al-Kubrā*, Vol. I, pp. 113-116.

[29]See "Al-Irādah Wa al-Amr," *ibid.*, I. 323-390; "Marātib Al-Irādah," *ibid.*, II, 69-86; and "Al-Qaḍā Wa l-Qadar," *ibid.*, II, 87-96.

[30]On this point, see the section titled "The Best of What Has Been Said Regarding Will, Wisdom, Determinism, etc." which is concerned with the refutation of any notion of "motivation" in creation. *Mujmū'at al-Rasā'il Wa al-Masā'il*, Vol. 5, p. 119.

[31]*Op. cit.*, p. 177.

[32]*Sūrah* LI (*Al-Dhāriyyāt*): 56, "I have only created Jinns and men, that they may serve Me."

[33]*Sūrah* XXI (*Al-Anbiyā'*): 92 "...I am your Lord and Cherisher: therefore serve me (and no other)."

CHAPTER IV

NOTES

[1]Scholars such as al-Nasafī in his catechism advance the idea that revelation is the logical consequence of divine wisdom. Al-Taftazānī, in his commentary on al-Nasafī's work inferred a suggestion of an inevitability or obligation ("*wājib*"), on the part of God, for self-disclosure. See also *Sūrahs* IX: 61; XVIII: 46-47; XXXIII: 45-48; XXXVI: 6; etc.

[2]See *Minhāj Al-Sunnah Al-Nabawiyyah Fī Naqḍ Kalām Al-Shī'ah Wa Al-Qadariyyah* (Cairo: Maktabat Dār al-'Urūbah, 1962), Vol. IV, pp. 149ff; *Mujmū'at Al-Rasā'il Wa Al-Masā'il*, Vol. V, pp. 64ff; and *Majmū'at Al-Rasā'il Al-Kubrā*, Vol. I, pp. 20f.

[3]*Majmū'at Al-Rasā'il Wa Al-Masā'il*, Vol. V, pp. 69f.

[4]See *Kitāb Al-Nubuwwāt* (Cairo: Al-Matba'ah al-Salafiyyah, 1966), p. 168.

[5]*Minhāj Al-Sunnah*, Vol. V, pp. 149; *Majmū'at Al-Rasā'il Al-Kubrā*, Vol. I, p. 20.

[6]See Al-Tūsī's argument in his classical work *Fuṣūl Al-'Aqā'id*, p. 52.

[7]Cf. *Al-Jawāb Al-Saḥīḥ* (Cairo: Matba'at al-Madanī, 1959-60), Vol. I, p. 9.

[8]Several of Ibn Taymiyyah's works (e.g., *Al-Risālah Al-Qubruṣiyyah*, *Al-Jawāb Al-Saḥīḥ*, and *Mi'rāj Al-Wuṣūl* advance the thesis that what is true of Muḥammad was true of previous prophets who, according to the Qur'ān, bore one and the same message from God to diverse peoples and at various times. This theme is analogous to the idea of the unity of God in relation to the diversity of the divine attributes. Muḥammad, however, as is clearly revealed in the Qur'ān, is the "seal of the propehts," and his message is universal.

[9]Laoust, *op. cit.*, p. 186.

[10]*Ibid.*

[11]*Sūrah* V (*Al-Mā'idah*): 70, "O Apostle! Proclaim the (Message) which hath been sent to thee from thy Lord."

[12]*Sūrah* V (*Al-Mā'idah*): 95, 102, "...our Apostle's duty is to proclaim the message in the clearest way..." See also *Sūrahs* XIV: 4; XLVI: 9.

[13]*Sūrah* XVIII (*Al-Kahf*): 109, "Say, 'If the ocean were ink (with which) to write out the words of my Lord, sooner would the ocean be exhausted than the words of my Lord, even if we added another ocean like it, for its aid.'"

[14]*Majmū'at Al-Rasā'il Wa Al-Masā'il*, Vol. III, pp. 154-165.

[15]*Ibid.*, p. 165.

[16]*Ibid.*, p. 110. Explanation in the last parentheses is mine.

[17]As quoted by Abū Zahrah, *op. cit.*, pp. 213-227.

[18]I.e., "Al-Tabyān Fī Nuzūl Al-Qur'ān," in *Majmū'at Al-Rasā'il Al-Kubrā*, Vol. I, pp. 213-227.

[19]Such verses as XIX: 193; XXXVI: 5; XXXIX: 1; XLV: 2; XLVI: 2, etc., are cited to give weight to this deduction.

[20]*Sūrah* XXIII: 18.

[21]*Op. cit.*, p. 47.

[22]*Op. cit.*, pp. 105-115; see also pp. 55-92.

[23]In this regard, Al-Ghazālī's theory is more plausible. In summary, it suggests that the task of interpretation is necessary and must be assumed, but only by a qualified person. A qualified scholar's interpretations are still reliable when they conform to the interpretations of the *salaf*, who themselves have utilized *ra'y*. Cf. *Iḥyā' Uṣūl Al-Dīn*. I, 260-265.

[24]*Tafsīr Sūrat Al-Nūr* (Cairo: Al-Matba'ah Al-Munīrīyyah, 1939), p. 36.

[25]*Muqaddimah Fī Uṣūl Al-Tafsīr* (Cairo: Al-Matba'ah al-Salafiyyah, 1965-66), pp. 93-104.

[26]*Sūrah* III (Al-'Umrān): 164, "God did confer a great favor on the believers when He sent among them an apostle from among themselves, rehearsing unto them the signs of God..."

[27]*Sūrah* XLI (*Ha-Mīm*, or *Fuṣṣilat*): 2, "A revelation from God, Most Gracious, Most Merciful."

[28]These documented traditions, in Arabic, read as follows: "الإيمان أن تؤمن بالله وملائكته وكتبه ورسله واليوم الآخر، وتؤمن بالقدر خيره وشره" and, "الإسلام أن تشهد ألّا إله الّا الله وأن محمّداً رسولُ الله، وتقيم الصلاة وتؤتى الزكاة وتصوم رمضان وتحجّ البيتَ إنْ استطعتَ إلى ذلك سبيلاً"

[29]*Al-Īmān*, pp. 2-10.

[30]*Ibid.*, p. 6.

[31]*Sūrah* IV (*Al-Nisā'*): 131, "Verily, We have directed the people of the Book before you (O Muslims) to fear God..."

[32]See "Al-Waṣiyyah Al-Ṣughrā," *Majmū'at Al-Rasā'il Al-Kubrā*, Vol. I, pp. 234-235.

[33] *Sūrah* III (*Al-'Umrān*): 64, "Say, 'O People of the Book! Come to common terms as between us and you: That we worship none but God: That we associate no partners with Him; That we erect not, from among ourselves, Lords and patrons other than God.' If then they turn back, Say ye, 'Bear witness that we (at least) are Muslims (bowing to God's will).'"

[34] For a concise treatment of the meaning of *kufr* in the Qur'ān see Marilyn R. Waldman's "The Development of the Concept of *Kufr* in the Qur'ān," *Journal of the American Oriental Society*, Vol. 88, No. 3, July-September 1968.

[35] *Al-'Ubūdiyyah* (Beirut: Al-Maktab Al-Islāmī, Second Printing, 1969), p. 47; See also p. 117.

[36] *Ibid.*, p. 113.

[37] *Ibid.*, pp. 88, 90, 92 and 95.

[38] *Ibid.*, p. 101.

[39] *Ibid.*, p. 114.

[40] *Sūrah* I (*Al-Fātihah*): "Thee do we worship and Thine aid do we seek."

[41] "There is no God but God."

[42] Important writings on this subject include Ibn Taymiyyah's *Qā'idah Jalīlah Fī Al-Tawassul Wa Al-Wasīlah* and *Risālat Shadd Al-Riḥāl*, etc.

[43] *Majmū'at Al-Rasā'il Wa Al-Masā'il*, Vol. I, pp. 40-43.

[44] *Sūrah* IX (*Al-Tawbah*): 113, "It is not fitting for the Prophet and those who believe that they should pray for forgiveness for pagans, even though they be of kin after it is clear to them that they are companions of the Fire."

[45] The *ḥadīth* reads: "يا معشرَ قريش اشتروا أنفسكم من الله، لا أغنى عنكم من الله شيئاً، يا بَنِي عبد المطّلب لا أغنى عنكم من اللّه شيئاً، يا عبّاس لا أغنى عنكم من الله شيئا، يا صفيّة عمّة الرسول صلّى الله عليه وسلّم لا أغنى عنكِ من الله شيئا، يا فاطمةُ بنتَ رسول الله سلينى من مالى ماشئْتِ لا أغنى عنكِ من الله شيئا." See *Qā'idah Jalīlah*, p. 5.

[46] *Ibid.*

[47] *Majmū'at Al-Rasā'il Wa Al-Masā'il*, Vol. I, p. 22.

[48] See, e.g., *Sūrah* XXVIII (*Al-Qiṣāṣ*): 70 and *Sūrah* LXIV (*Al-Taghābun*): 1, etc.

[49] *Qā'idah Jalīlah*, p. 112.

[50] *Ibid.*, p. 113.

[51] *Majmū'at Al-Rasā'il Wa Al-Masā'il*, Vol. I, p. 54.

[52]*Ibid.*, pp. 55 and 59.

[53]E.g., Abū Zahrah, *op. cit.*, 326.

[54]*Ibid.*

[55]Abū Zahrah cites the example of the son of ʿUmar who is said to have visited the Prophet's grave "a hundred times or more," and was seen touching the seat of Muḥammad's pulpit then placing his hand on his own face. *Ibid.*

[56]Ibn ʿAbd al-Hādī, *Al-ʿUqūd Al-Durriyyah* (Cairo: Matbaʿat al-Hijāz, 1938), p. 235.

[57]See *Qāʿidah Jalīlah*..., p. 106. The texts are: "اذا سألتم فاسألوه بجاهي، فان جاهي عند الله عظيم" and, "فمن زارني بعد مماتي فكأنما زارني في حياتي."

[58]*Majmūʿat Al-Rasāʾil Wa Al-Masāʾil*, Vol. I, pp. 3-9, and Vol. V, pp. 128ff.

[59]*Ibid.*, p. 130.

[60]See his discussion on "solidarity in righteousness and godliness," ("التعاون على البر والتقوى"), *Ibid.*, Vol. I, p. 232.

[61]*Ibid.*, p. 9.

CHAPTER V

NOTES

[1]Muhammad Isma'īl 'Abduh, "Mushkilat Al-Jabr Wa Al-Ikhtiyār" *Usbū' Al-Fiqh Al-Islāmī*. Edited by Muḥammad Abū Zahrah. (Cairo: Al-Majlis Al-A'lā Li Ri'āyat Al-Funūn Wa Al-Ādāb, 1961), pp. 761-826.

[2]See *Ibid.*, pp. 763-764.

[3]See, e.g., *Sūrah* LXXXI: 28-29 and *Sūrah* IV: 70-80.

[4]M. Y. Mūsa, *op. cit.*, pp. 77-79 and 82-83.

[5]Edited by Aḥmad Al-Azharī. Cairo: Matba'at al-Mawsū'āt, 1944.

[6]The report, according tothe *Saḥīḥ* of Muslim in part after 'Abd Allah Ibn 'Amr, and in part after Ibn Ḥanbal, reads:

" خرج رسول الله ـصـ على أصحابه وهم يتناظرون فى القدر، رجل يقول
ألَمْ يقلِ الله كذا ؟ ورجل يقول ألم يقل الله كذا ؟ فكأنما فقىء فى وجه حب
الرمان فقال أبهذا أمرتم؟ إنما هلك من كان من قبلكم بهذا، ضربوا كتاب الله
بعضه ببعض. وانما نزل الكتاب يصدق بعضه بعضا لا يكذب. انظروا ما أمرتم به . . ."

See *Muwāfaqat Saḥīḥ Al-Manqūl*...in the margin of *Minhāj Al-Sunnah*, pp. 24-26.

[7]*Ibid.*, pp. 16, 17.

[8]*Ibid.*, p. 18.

[9]*Qadā*, literally, means "decree"; *jabr*, "inescapability," "inevitability," "force" or "coercion." *Qadar* originally meant "supreme capability," hence "decree," and it is sometimes used in that sense, but later in the development of the problem the term was used by the determinists to describe the rationalists who, they said, attributed *qadar*, i.e., "supreme capability," to man rather than God. Therefore, those affirming absolute human free will came to be known as the *qadarīs*.

[10]*Ikhtiyār* signifies "choice"; *qudrah*, "capability"; and *qadar* when it is not synonymous with *qaḍā* refers to human capability. See n. 9, above.

[11]Al-Shahrustānī. *Al-Milal Wa Al-Niḥal* I, 108-112. See Abū Zahrah, *Tārīkh Al-Madhāhib Al-Islāmiyyah*, Vol. I (Cairo: Dār Al-Fikr Al-'Arabī, n.d.), pp. 71-75, for a historical review of these schools of thought.

[12]Al-Shahrustānī, *op. cit.*, p. 147.

[13]According to Abū Zahrah, *Ibn Taymiyyah*, pp. 201-209.

[14]*Ibid.*

[15]Ismā'īl 'Abduh, *op. cit.*, 774.

[16]*Ibid.*

[17]*Sūrah* XLII (*Al-Shūrā*): 11, "...there is nothing whatever like unto Him, and He is the one that hears and sees (all things)."

[18]*Sūrah* XVI (*Al-Naḥl*): 74, "Invent not similitudes for God: for God knoweth and ye know not."

[19]*Op. cit.*, 775.

[20]The title of this work, being translated, means "Rejecting [that there exists] a Conflict Between Reason and Transmission [of Revelation]" indicates Ibn Taymiyyah's purpose for writing it.

[21]Al-Shahrustānī, *op. cit.*, pp. 108-112.

[22]See Abū Zahrah, *Tārīkh Al-Madhāhib Al-Islāmiyyah*, pp. 171-172.

[23]Al-Ash'arī *Maqālāt Al-Islāmiyyin*, I, p. 312.

[24]As quoted in *ibid.*

[25]See n. 3, above.

[26]Abū Zahrah, *op. cit.*, pp. 184-185.

[27]*Muwāfaqat Saḥīḥ Al-Manqūl*, I, p. 197.

[28]*Op. cit.*, I, p. 147.

[29]*Op. cit.*, pp. 186-187.

[30]Max Horton in *The Philosophy of Islām* as quoted in *ibid.*, and also Ignac Goldziher, *Le Dogme et La Loi de L'Islam* (Paris: P. Geuther, 1958), pp. 83, 84.

[31]*Op. cit.*, p. 794.

[32]*Op. cit.*, pp. 55-56.

[33]See n. 3, above.

[34]'Alī Ḥasab Allah, *Muḥāḍarāt Fī 'Ilm Al-Tawḥīd* (Cairo: Dār al-Fikr al-'Arabī, 1970), pp. 77-79.

[35]Meaning "Clarification."

[36]See Abū Zahrah, *op. cit.*, p. 271.

[37]Based on the text of *Sūrah* XXXVII (*Al-Ṣāfāt*): 96, "But God has created you and your handiwork."

[38]Based on the text of *Sūrah* LII (*Al-Ṭūr*): 35, "Were they created of nothing, or were they themselves the creators?"

[39]Based on the text of *Sūrah* VII (*Al-A'rāf*): 178, "Whom God doth guide, he is on the right path; Whom He rejects from His guidance, such are the persons who perish."

[40]Abū Zahrah, referring to Ibn 'Asakir, in *op. cit.*, pp. 270-273.

[41]See *Ibid.*

[42]Reference is made to a work by al-Imām al-Liqānī, titled *Sharḥ Al-Jawharah.* Ismā'īl 'Abduh, *op. cit.*, p. 803.

[43]Al-Shahrustānī, *op. cit.*, pp. 127-127.

[44]*Ibid.*, pp. 119-127.

[45]By 'Abd al-Raḥīm Ibn 'Alī (known as Shaykh Zādah); see n. 42, above.

[46]Ismā'īl 'Abduh, *op. cit.*, pp. 807-808.

[47]*Dar' Ta'āruḍ Al-'Aql*, p. 20.

[48]*Ibid.*, p. 46.

[49]*Muwāfaqat Saḥīḥ Al-Manqūl*, II, p. 112.

[50]*Dar' Tā'aruḍ Al-'Aql*, pp. 38-43.

[51]See *Ibid.*, pp. 142-143 and 197-199.

[52]*Ibid.*

[53]Al-Shahrustānī, *loc. cit.*

[54]See Al-Juwaynī's *Al-'Aqīdah Al-Niẓāmiyyah*, as quoted by Ismā'īl 'Abduh, *op. cit.*, p. 799.

[55]*Minhāj Al-Adillah*, as quoted in Ismā'īl 'Abduh, *loc. cit.*

[56]*Majmū'at Al-Rasā'il Al-Kubrā*, II, 89, on the basis of the text of *Sūrah* IV (*Al-Nisā'*): 150-151, "Those who deny God and His apostles, and (those who) wish to separate God from His apostles, Saying: 'We believe in some but reject others' and (those who) wish to take a course midway--they are in truth (equally) unbelievers; and We have prepared for unbelievers a humiliating punishment."

[57]*Majmū'at Al-Rasā'il Wa Al-Masā'il*, II, pp. 87-155.

[58]Based on the text of *Sūrah* VI (*Al-An'ām*): 50, "...I follow what is revealed to me...'Can the blind be held equal to the seeing?' Will ye then consider not?"

[59]*Sūrah* XXXVIII (*Ṣād*): 28, "Shall we treat those who believe and work deeds of righteousness, the same as those who do mischief on earth?..."

[60]*Sūrah* XLV (*Al-Gāthiyah*): 21, "What! Do those who seek after evil ways think that We shall hold them equal with those who believe...?"

[61]*Muwāfaqat Saḥīḥ Al-Manqūl*, I, pp. 41-43.

[62]*Minhāj al-Sunnah*, I, p. 270; *Minhāj Al-I'tidāl* (Cairo: Al-Matba'ah al-Salafiyyah, 1955), p. 125.

[63]*Majmū'at Al-Rasā'il Wa Al-Masā'il*, I, pp. 126-128; Cf. *Majmū'at Al-Fatawā Al-Kubrā* (Cairo: Vol. II, pp. 24-26.

[64]It seems that Ibn Taymiyyah implies that God, in His law-giving will, discloses a positive act of willing, whereas evil occurs also according to God's will but in a negative sense of merely permitting it to occur.

[65]*Majmū'at Al-Rasā'il Wa Al-Masā'il*, p. 128.

[66]E.g., *Sūrahs* III: 49-51; XIV: 2 and 23; IV: 64; X: 10; etc.

[67]*Minhāj al-I'tidāl*, pp. 117-140.

[68]*Muwāfaqat Saḥīḥ Al-Manqūl*, I, pp. 90-91.

[69]*Majmū'at Al-Rasā'il Wa Al-Masā'il*, Vol. V, p. 126; *Minhāj al-I'tidāl*, p. 121.

[70]*Sūrah* XXXVII (*Al-Ṣāfāt*): 96, "But God hath created you and your handiwork!"

[71]*Majmū'at Al-Rasā'il Wa Al-Masā'il*, Vol. V, p. 144.

[72]*Ibid.*, pp. 156-158.

[73]*Minhāj Al-Sunnah*, Vol. I, pp. 264-266; *Minhāj al-I'tidāl*, p. 120.

CHAPTER VI

NOTES

[1]Some modern scholars translate this technical and legal term as "legislation of expediency," which may be equivalent to the forced meaning of *ijtihād*. The term as used by Ibn Taymiyyah, however, conveys the faithful interpretive effort of him who assumes its task. For the use of a restrictive translation, see, for example, Professor Khurshid Ḥāmid's rendering of a quotation from Ibn Taymiyyah in Abū al-A'lā al-Mawdūdī's *Islamic Law and Constitution* (Lahore: Islamic Publications, Ltd., 4th ed., 1969), p. 88.

[2]*Raf' al-Malām 'An al-A'immah al-A'lām*, M. H. al-Faqqī, ed. (Cairo: Matba'at al-Sunnah al-Muḥammadiyyah, 1958), p. 9.

[3]*Ibid.*, p. 11.

[4]Abū Zahrah, *Ibn Taymiyyah, Ḥayātuh Wa 'Usūruh*, p. 358.

[5]See *ibid.*, p. 445, where reference is made to Abū 'Amr, Ibn al-Ṣalāh, Ibn Ḥamdān, as well as to the work known as *Muswaddat al-Uṣūl*, written by Taqiyy al-Dīn's grandfather and completed by him.

[6]Abū Zahrah, *loc. cit.*

[7]*Ibid.*, n. 1.

[8]See Ibn al-Ṣalaḥ's *Al-Madkhal*, p. 185, as cited by Abū Zahrah in *ibid.*, p. 447.

[9]*Ibid.*, p. 450.

[10]See *Fatwā Fi al-Ijtihād* [in the appendix of *Raf' al-Malām 'An al-A'immah al-A'lām* (Beirut: Al-Maktab al-Islamī, 3rd ed., 1970)] , pp. 4-5.

[11]*Al-Fatawā al-Kubrā* (Cairo: Dār al-Kutub al-Ḥadīthah, 1966), Vol. II, p. 240; see also, IV, pp. 481-482.

[12]*Ibid.; Sūrah* IV (*Al-Nisā'*): 65, "But no, by thy Lord, they can have no (real) Faith, until they made thee judge in all disputes between them, and find in their souls no resistance against thy decision, but accept them with the fullest conviction."

[13]*Sūrah* XXXIII (*Al-Aḥzāb*): 36, "It is not fitting for a Believer, man or woman, when a matter has been decided by God and His Apostle, to have any option about their decision."

[14]*Op. cit.*, p. 238.

[15]*Ibid.*, p. 240

[16]The *ḥadīth* reads: "انّما الأعمال بالنيات،وانما لكل امرىء مانوى. فمن كانت هجرته الى الله ورسوله، فهجرته الى الله ورسوله، ومن كانت هجرته الى دنيا يصيبها . . ." and means, "Deeds are [judged] by the intentions [behind them]; and every man acquired what he wills. For whosoever seeks refuge in God and His Apostle he finds refuge in them [but] whosoever seeks after a world to achieve or a woman to marry, he will find what he seeks." See the separate monograph, *Sharḥ Ḥadīth "Innama al-A'māl Bi al-Niyyāt*, Cairo: Al-Matba'ah al-Munīriyyah, 1935-36.

[17]*Al-Fatāwā al-Kubrā*, IV, p. 33.

[18]*Majmū'at al-Rasā'il Wa al-Masā'il* (Cairo: Matba'at al-Manār, 1922-1930), Vol. I, pp. 211-229.

[19]Mainly in *Al-Fatāwā al-Kubrā*, III, pp. 406-420; see also, I, p. 256; II, p. 206; III, pp. 7-9, 470; IV, pp. 415 and 573.

[20]In Ibn Rushd's *al-Muqaddimāt al-Mumahhidāt*, as cited by Abū Zahrah, *op. cit.*, p. 395.

[21]The *ḥadīth* reads: "أحقّ الشروط ماستحللتم به الفــــروج" It roughly means, "The most rightful among conditions is to fulfill the obligations of the conjugal relationship." The *ḥadīth*, understood properly, turns what may be considered a "right" into a duty, and, obviously, does not concern itself with binding contractual conditions.

[22]*Loc. cit.*

[23]*Al-Fatāwā al-Kubrā*, II, p. 236.

[24]*Ibid.*, p. 235.

[25]*Op. cit.*, p. 353.

[26]*Ibid.*

[27]According to Abū Zahrah, *ibid.*

[28]His legal opinions of that period are collected in a work known as *Mukhtaṣar al-Fatāwā al-Miṣriyyah*.

[29]*Al-Fatāwā al-Kubrā*, II, pp. 159-163.

[30]See Abū Zahrah, *loc. cit.*

[31]*Ibid.*

[32]For the history of the development of the classical legal theory, see J. Schacht, *The Origins of Muhammadan Jurisprudence* (Oxford: Clarendon Press, 1967), pp. 2-6ff.

[33]See A. al-Khaṭīb, *Al-Tafkīr al-Qānūnī 'Ind Ibn Taymiyyah*, in M. Abū Zahrah, ed., *Usbū' al-Fiqh al-Islāmī...* (Cairo: Al Majlis al-A'lā, 1961), p. 889.

[34]*Majmū'at al-Masā'il Wa al-Rasā'il*, V, p. 20.

[35]*Sūrah* LIX (*Al-Hashr*): 7, "...So take what the Apostle assigns to you and deny yourselves that which he withholds from you..."

[36]*Loc. cit.*

[37]The *hadīth* reads, "أيؤمنني من في السماء ولا تؤمنوني؟" the inseparableness of the Qur'ān and the *Sunnah* in Ibn Taymiyyah's view is Ḥanbalī, no doubt; and is verified by his disciple Ibn al-Qayyim.

[38]See, for example, his "questions regarding the sources of religious law," and "the meaning of *ijmā'*" in *al-Fatāwā al-Kubrā*, I, pp. 444-465 and pp. 483-494, respectively. Cf. *Ma'ārij al-Wuṣūl* (Cairo: Al-Matba'ah al-Salafiyyah, 1967-68), pp. 25ff.

[39]*Al-Fatāwā al-Kubrā*, I, p. 484.

[40]*Ma'ārij al-Wuṣūl*, pp. 29-30.

[41]*Ibid.*, p. 27.

[42]*Ibid.*; the *ḥadīth* reads, "واقتدوا بالذين من بعدي، أبي بكر وعمر"

[43]*Ibid.*, p. 30.

[44]*Ibid.*

[45]On the basis of the assertion by al-Shāfi'ī, who is credited with the development of the theory of the Sources of Islamic law (See Schacht, *op. cit.*, p. 1), Ibn Taymiyyah adopts *ijmā'* as a legitimate source of jurisprudence. Although there is a debate (see synopsis in Abū Zahrah, *op. cit.*, p. 462) that al-Shāfi'ī had in fact utilized the Qur'ānic verse, "من يشاقق الرسول من بعد ما تبين له الهدى..." (IV: 115), Ibn Taymiyyah accepts the thesis that he had. Whether al-Shāfi'ī used this verse or a *ḥadīth*, and whether his text directly or indirectly relates to *ijmā'*, it was of little consequence to Ibn Taymiyyah.

[46]See Abū Zahrah, *op. cit.*, p. 469.

[47]*Risālat al-Qiyās* was previously published in the margin of *Minhāj al-Sunnah* (Cairo: edition of 1904), under the title *Muwāfaqat Ṣarīḥ al-Ma'qūl Li Ṣaḥīḥ al-Manqūl*.

[48]*Sūrah* LXV (*Al-Ṭalāq*): 6, "...and if they suckle your your (offspring), give them their recompense..."

[49]*Al-Qiyās Fī al-Shar' al-Islāmī* (Cairo: Al-Matba'ah al-Salafiyyah, 1955), p. 23.

[50]*Ibid.*, p. 25.

[51]*Ibid.*, p. 26ff.

[52] *Ibid.*, p. 29.

[53] Abū Zahrah, *op. cit.*, p. 474.

[54] *Al-Qiyās*, p. 32.

[55] *Majmū'at al-Rasā'il Wa al-Masā'il*, V, p. 21.

[56] *Ibid.*, p. 22.

[57] *Ibid.*

[58] *Ibid.*

[59] I.e., in legal contracts. See *Al-Fatāwā al-Kubrā*, III, p. 139.

[60] *Kitāb Iqāmat al-Dalīl Fī Ibṭāl al-Taḥlīl* in *ibid.*, III, pp. 269-271.

[61] *Ibid.*, p. 270.

[62] *Sūrah* IV (*Al-Nisā'*): 59, "O ye who believe! Obey God, and obey the Apostle, and those charged with authority among you..."

[63] *Ibid.*, "...If ye differ in anything among yourselves, refer it to God and His Apostle..."

[64] *Al-Fatāwā al-Kubrā*, II, p. 461.

[65] "من يرد الله بــه خــيرا يفقهــه فى الدين" ; *dīn*, of course, is the term used to signify "religion" as well as "judgment." In Islam, it is understood as one related concept, i.e., "religion/law." It is often rendered as "religious law," which is legitimate only when it is clear that the adjective is not intended to distinguish "religious" law from another kind of law. Islam does not make a distinction between religion and "secular" life.

[66] I. e., *tayammum wājib*, the ablution by sand (usually in the absence of water) of those with a major ritual impurity. In this case, the obligation to use this method is not necessitated by the absence of water, but as a preventative measure against contaminating it.

[67] See *Al-Fatāwā al-Kubrā*, II, p. 460.

[68] *Ibid.*, p. 458.

[69] *Ibid.*

[70] There are other issues related to divorce on which Ibn Taymiyyah took differing stands from those of the traditional schools. The issue of the oath has been selected because it was against this practice, so widely prevalent in his day, that Ibn Taymiyyah addressed his *fatwā*. See *Ibid.*, III, pp. 95 and 96.

[71]See Al-Khaṭīb, *op. cit.*, p. 895; Abū Zahrah, *op. cit.*, p. 419, etc.

[72]According to Abū Zahrah, *op. cit.*, p. 433, Ibn Taymiyyah favored the position of al-Ithnā ʿAshariyyah which dismisses any contingent clauses and insists that divorce is valid only when a man confronts his wife and tells her, "you are divorced."

[73]Elsewhere (*Al-Fatāwā Al-Kubrā*, III, p. 79), he discussed divorce under the conditions of drunkenness, and frivolous jest [*hazl*] (*ibid.*, p. 149), and has largely taken the Ḥanbalī position.

[74]The *ḥadīth* reads, "من حلف على يمين فرأى غيرها خيرا منها فليأت الذى هو خير وليكفّر عن يمينه"

[75]*Sūrah* V (*Al-Māʾidah*): 92, "God will not call you to account for what is futile in your oaths, but He will call you to account for your deliberate oaths: for expiation, feed ten indigent persons, on a scale of the average for the food of your families, or give a slave his freedom. If that is beyond your means, fast for three days. That is the expiation for the oaths you have sworn. But keep to your oaths..."

[76]*Sūrah* LXVI (*Al-Taḥrīm*): 2, "God has already ordained for you (O men), the dissolution of your oaths (In some cases)..."

[77]*Sūrah* LXV (*Al-Ṭalāq*): 1, "O Prophet! When ye do divorce women, divorce them at their prescribed periods, and count (accurately) their prescribed periods: And fear God your Lord: And turn them not out of their houses, nor shall they (themselves) leave, except in case they are guilty of some lewdness; those are limits set by God, and any who transgresses the limits of God, does verily wrong his (own) soul: Thou knowest not if perchance God will bring about thereafter some new situation."

[78]This is the summary of Ibn Taymiyyah's detailed discourse in *Al-Fatāwā al-Kubrā*, III, pp. 5ff.

[79]See *Al-Subkī*, *Risālat al-Durrah al-Muḍīʾah* (Damascus: 1929), p. 50.

[80]The *ḥadīth* reads, "من كان حالفا فليحلف بالله أو ليصمت."

[81]*Loc. cit.*

[82]Abū Zahrah, *op. cit.*, p. 435.

[83]Al-Khaṭīb, *op. cit.*, p. 895.

CHAPTER VII

NOTES

[1]See *Al-Siyāsah Al-Shar'iyyah* (Beirut: Dār al-Kutub al-'Arabiyyah, 1966), Appendix.

[2]*Ibid.*, p. 3.

[3]Henri Laoust, *Essai Sur Les Doctrines Sociales et Politique De Taki-d-Dīn b. Taimiya* (Le Caire: Institut Francais D'Archaeologie Orientale, 1939), p. 253.

[4]*Ibid.*

[5]*Ibid.*

[6]*Iqtiḍā' al-Ṣirāṭ al-Mustaqīm* (Cairo: Matba'at al-Sunnah al-Muḥammadiyyah, 1950), pp. 144ff.

[7]*Ibid.*

[8]*Sūrah* XLIII (*Al-Zukhruf*): 43-44, "So hold thou fast to the Revelation sent down to thee: verily thou art on a Straight Way. The Qur'ān is indeed the Message, for Thee and for thy people; and soon shall ye (all) be brought to account."

[9]*Sūrah* III (*Al-'Imrān*): 100, "Ye are the best of peoples, evolved for mankind, enjoining what is right, forbidding what is wrong, and believing in God."

[10]*Sūrah* VI (*Al-An'ām*): 124, ".. God knoweth best where (and how) to carry out His mission..."

[11]The *hadīth* reads: "إن الله حين خلقني جعلنى من خير خلقه، ثم حين خلق القبائل جعلنى من خير قبيلة، وحين خلق الانفس جعلنى من خير أنفسهم، ثم حين خلق البيوت جعلنى من خير بيوتهم"

[12]I.e., فقه العربية هو الطريق الى فقه أقواله، وفقه السنّة هو الطريق الى فقه اعماله
op. cit., p. 155.

[13]Al-Imām Al-Shāfi'ī, *Al-Risālah*. Aḥmad Shākir, ed. (Cairo: Muṣṭafā al-Bābi al-Ḥalabī, 1940), pp. 46-50.

[14]*Op. cit.*, pp. 148-205.

[15]The *hadīth* reads: "ياأيها الناس إن الرب واحد، والأب واحد والدين واحد إن العربية ليست لأحدكم بأبٍ ولا أم، إنما هى لسان، فمن تكلم العربية فهو عربى"
Although there is insufficient evidence for the accuracy of this *ḥadīth* according to Ibn Taymiyyah, it still holds the same intended meaning of the Prophet. See *op. cit.*, p. 169.

[16] *Sūrah* IX (*Al-Tawbah*): 97-98, "The Arabs of the desert are the worst in unbelief and hypocrisy, and most look upon their payments as a fine, and watch for disasters for you: on them be the disaster of Evil: For God is He that heareth and knoweth (all things)."

[17] *Sūrah* XLVIII (*Al-Fatḥ*): 11-12, "The desert Arabs who lagged behind will say to thee: 'We are engaged in (looking after) our flocks and herds, and our families: Do thou then ask forgiveness for us.' They say with their tongues what is not in their hearts. Say: 'Who then has any power at all (to intervene) on your behalf with God, if His will is to give you some loss or to give you some profit? But God is well acquainted with all that ye do..."

[18] *Sūrah* IX (*Al-Tawbah*): 98 and 101, "But some of the desert Arabs believe in God and the Last Day....(But Certain of the desert Arabs round about you are hypocrites as well as (desert Arabs) among the Medina folk: they are obstinate in hypocrisy; thou knowest them not: We know them. Twice shall we punish them...."

[19] *Sūrah* LXII (*Al-Jumu'ah*): 2 and 3, "It is He Who has sent among the Unlettered an apostle from among themselves, to rehearse to them His signs, to sanctify them, and to instruct them in Scripture and wisdom--although they had been before in manifest error;--As well as (to confer all these benefits upon) others of them, who have not already joined them: And He is Exalted in Might, Wise."

[20] *Sūrah* XLIX (*Al-Ḥujurāt*): 13, "O mankind! We created you from a single (pair) of a male and a female, and made you into nations and tribes, that ye may know each other (Not that ye may despise each other). The most honoured of you in the sight of God is (he who is) the most righteous of you. And God has full knowledge and is well acquainted (with all things)."

[21] The *ḥadīth* reads: "يأيها الناس، ألا أن ربكم عزّ وجلّ واحد، ألا ان أباكم واحد. ألا لا فضل لعربي على عجمي، ألا لا فضل لأسود على لأحمر الا بالتقوى. ألا قد بلّغت؟ قالوا نعم. قال ليبلغ الشاهد الغائب."

[22] The *ḥadīth* reads: "ان بنى فلان ليسوا لى بأولياء. انما وليّى الله...."

[23] The *ḥadīth* reads: "لو كان الايمان عند الثريّا لناله رجل من ابناء فارس"

[24] *Sūrah* XLVII (*Muḥammad*): 38, "...If ye turn back (from the Path), He will substitute in your stead another people."

[25] *Sūrah* III (*Al-'Imrān*): 103, "And hold fast, all together, by the Rope which God (stretches out for you), and be not divided among yourselves...."

[26] The *ḥadīth* reads: "مثل المؤمنين فى توادّهم وتراحمهم وتعاطفهم كمثل الجسد الواحد، اذا اشتكى عضو تداعى له سائر الجسد بالحمى والسهر"

[27] The *ḥadīth* reads: "لا تقاطعوا ولا تدابروا ولا تحاسدوا، وكونوا عباد الله كما أمركم الله"

[28]*Majmū'at al-Rasā'il al-Kubrā*, I, pp. 241-257.

[29]*Majmū'at al-Rasā'il Wa Al-Masā'il*, I, p. 154.

[30]*Majmū'at al-Rasā'il al-Kubrā*, I, p. 312.

[31]The *ḥadīth* reads: "والمؤمن للمؤمن كالبنيان يشدّ بعضه بعضا وشبك بين اصابعه"
also, "خمس تجب للمسلم على المسلم، يسلم عليه اذا لقيه، ويعوده اذا مرض، ويشمته اذا عطس، ويجيبه اذا دعاه، ويشيّعه اذا مات"

[32]The *ḥadīth* reads: "والذى نفسى بيده، لا يؤمن أحدكم حتى ما يحب لأخيه ما يحب لنفسه"

[33]The *ḥadīth* "المسلم أخو المسلم، لا يظلمه" is the basis of the "Pact of Fraternity" (*mu'akhāh*) which the Prophet constituted, when he came to Madīnah, between certain individuals for the sake of trade or of common inheritance. Cf. *Majmū'at al-Rasā'il Wa Al-Masā'il*, I, p. 158. Here, however, the reference is general, and presupposes the fraternity of all Muslims, and, therefore, does not require the formal agreement of a pact.

[34]*Sūrah* III: 103; see n. 25, above.

[35]*Sūrah* VI (*Al-An'ām*): 159, "As for those who divide their religion and break up into sects, thou hast no part in them in the least: Their affair is with God."

[36]*Majmū'at al-Rasā'il al-Kubrā*, I, p. 314.

[37]*Tawhid* is used here in this sense.

[38]See Laoust, *op. cit.*, p. 258, for this discussion; note particularly n. 1, for reference to his source.

[39]*Ibid.*

[40]*Ibid.*, p. 259.

[41]See *Minhāj al-Sunnah*, I, p. 28 and II, p. 86. See also *ibid.*

[42]*Ibid.*, p. 260.

[43]*Majmū'at al-Rasā'il Wa al-Masā'il*, I, pp. 156-157.

[44]See *Majmū'at al-Rasā'il al-Kubrā*, I, pp. 26-28; and *Minhāj al-Sunnah*, II, p. 103.

[45]See Laoust, *loc. cit.*

[46]*Ibid.*

[47]See *Majmū'at al-Rasā'il al-Kubrā*, I, pp. 31-32.

[48]*Al-Masa'il al-Mārdīniyyah* (Cairo: Matba'at Anṣār al-Sunnah, 1949), pp. 70-74.

[49]See *Majmūʻat al-Fatāwā al-Kubrā* (Cairo: Dār al-Kutub al-Ḥadīthah, 1966), Vol. II, pp. 28-30.

[50]*Al-Ikhtiyārāt al-ʻIlmiyyah*, in *Ibid.*, IV, pp. 602-606.

[51]*Al-Ṣārim al-Maslūl ʻAlā Shātim al-Rasūl* (Ṭanṭa [Egypt]: Maktabat al-Tāj, 1960), pp. 3ff.

[52]*Al-Ikhtiyārāt*, pp. 607-608.

[53]See *Majmūʻat al-Rasāʼil Wa al-Masāʼil*, pp. 105ff.

[54]*Majmūʻat al-Fatāwā al-Kubrā*, IV, pp. 83f.

[55]For the full details of the conditions, see *Majmūʻat al-Rasāʼil Wa al-Masāʼil*, p. 226.

[56]*Ibid.*, p. 229.

[57]See Laoust, *op. cit.*, p. 266.

[58]See *loc. cit.*

[59]Laoust, *op. cit.*, p. 267, calls attention to Ibn Taymiyyah's reference to their foolish practices as he calls them "the jackals of the Jews" (*ḥamīr al-Yahūd*); See note.

[60]*Op. cit.*, p. 232.

[61]*Al-Ṣārim al-Maslūl*, p. 209.

[62]The *ḥadīth* reads: " من آذى ذمّياً فقد آذانى "

[63]*Majmūʻat al-Rasāʼil Wa al-Masāʼil*, pp. 227-228. The *ḥadīths* are: " إن الله لم يأذن لكم أن تدخلوا بيوت أهل الكتاب إلّا بإذن ، ولا بضرب أبشارهم ، ولا بأكل ثمارهم إذا أعطوكم الذى عليهم " and, " ألا من ظلم معاهدا أو انتقصه حقه أو كلفه فوق طاقته أو أخذ منه شيئاً بغير طِيب نفسٍ فأنا حَجِيجَه يوم القيامة "

[64]*Ibid.*

[65]*Op. cit.*, p. 268.

[66]*Majmūʻat al-Fatāwā al-Kubrā*, IV, p. 219.

[67]*Ibid.*, p. 269.

[68]*Ibid.*, pp. 90f.

[69]*Majmūʻat al-Rasāʼil Wa al-Masāʼil*, I, p. 46.

[70]*Majmūʻat al-Rasāʼil Wa al-Masāʼil*, p. 232.

CHAPTER VIII

NOTES

[1]No doubt, Ibn Taymiyyah had thorough familiarity with the body of doctrine and law as formulated theretofore through the intellectual activity of Al-Māwardī, al-Ghazālī, Fakhr al-Dīn al-Rāzī, al-Nasafī, and the many other scholars whose thought contributed immensely to the understanding of Sunnī doctrine and practice.

[2]Henri Laoust translated this monograph into French under the title *Le Traité De Droit Publique D'Ibn Taimiya*, published in 1948.

[3]This last work, written in response to the *Shī'ī* interpretation of *imāmah* as expressed by al-Ḥilli in *Kitāb al-Karāmah* was condensed into a *Compendium* by al-Dhahabī, titled *Al-Muntaqā Min Minhāj al-I'tidāl*.

[4]In both *Al-Hisbah Fī al-Islām* (Damascus: Dār al-Bayān, 1967), pp. 3-5 and *Al-Siyāsah al-Shar'iyyah*, ed. M. al-Mubārak (Beirut: Dār al-Kutub al-'Arabiyyah, 1966), p. 77.

[5]*Al-Ḥisbah*, p. 4.

[6]*Sūrah* IV (*Al-Nisā'*): 58, "God doth command you to render back your trusts to those to whom they are due; and when ye judge between man and man, that ye judge with justice....For God is He Who heareth and seeth all things. O ye who believe! Obey God, and obey the Apostle, and those charged with authority among you. If ye differ in anything among yourselves, refer it to God and His Apostles, if ye do believe in God and the Last Day: That is best, and most suitable for final determination."

[7]The *ḥadīth* reads, " كلكم كراع، وكل راع مسئول عن رعيته " See *al-Siyāsah al-Shar'iyyah*, p. 7.

[8]See *ibid.*

[9]*Ibid.*, p. 17.

[10]*Sūrah* LVII (*Al-Ḥadīd*): 25, "We sent aforetime Our apostles with clear signs and sent down with them the Book and the Balance (of Right and Wrong), that men may stand forth in justice...."

[11]*Ibid.*, "...And We sent down Iron, in which is (material for) mighty war, as well as many benefits for mankind, that God may test who it is that will help, unseen, Him and His apostles."

[12]*Al-Ḥisbah*, p. 6.

[13]*Al-Siyāsah al-Shar'iyyah*, pp. 40-60.

[14]See *ibid.*, pp. 73-80.

[15] *Ibid.*, p. 85.

[16] *Ibid.*, pp. 89-90.

[17] *Al-Ḥisbah*, pp. 13, 14.

[18] *Al-Siyāsah al-Shar'iyyah*, pp. 19-25.

[19] *Ibid.*, p. 28.

[20] *Ibid.*, p. 29.

[21] *Ibid.*, p. 68.

[22] *Sūrah* II (*Al-Baqarah*): 190, "Fight in the cause of God those who fight you, but do not transgress limits; For God loveth not transgressors."

[23] *Sūrah* II (*Al-Baqarah*): 217, "Tumult and oppression are worse than slaughter."

[24] *Ibid.*, pp. 69, 70.

[25] *Ibid.*

[26] *Al-Ikhtiyārāt al-'Ilmiyyah*, p. 610.

[27] *Ibid.*

[28] *Sūrah* II: 190; see n. 22, above.

[29] The *ḥadīth* reads, "ان الخطيئة ان أخفيت لم تضر صاحبها ، ولكن اذا ظهرت فلم تنكر اضرت العامة"

[30] An added stipulation which safeguards potential suspects against exacting extreme punishment indiscriminately is given by Ibn Taymiyyah. He reminds that the *Sharī'ah* requires that *Qital* may not be a necessary means against those of the *kuffār* who may be brought under control. See *ibid.*, p. 68.

[31] *Ibid.*, pp. 79, 80.

[32] *Minhāj al-Sunnah* (Cairo: Maktabat al-'Urūbah, 1962), Vol. I, 112-115.

[33] *Ibid.*, p. 137.

[34] In view of this principle, Laoust criticizes Ibn Taymiyyah for admitting the Khārijī view with regard to *imāmah* (namely, that the *imām* need not arise from Quraysh), as compatible with the Sunnī political theory (See *Essai*, pp. 282, 283). Al-Mubārak (in *Ārā' Ibn Taymiyyah Fī al-Dawlah* [Beirut: Dār al-Fikr, 3rd ed., 1970], p. 41) contends, however, that Laoust's criticism is not entirely valid, if indeed it stresses at all the Quraysh requirement, since it was not Ibn Taymiyyah's intention at this point to discuss the chief political authority, i.e., *al-imāmah al-kubrā*. At any rate, it appears that Ibn Taymiyyah, in the *Minhāj* was more concerned generally with *al-imāmah al-kubrā* than

he was in *al-Siyāsah al-Shar'iyyah*, on the basis of the commandment to "obey God, the Apostle and them who rule," which dictum was as well received by the Khārijīs as by the rest of the Muslims.

[35]See al-Hillī's *Minhāj al-Yaqīn*, pp. 61ff., as referred to by Laoust, *op. cit.*, pp. 283-284.

[36]Ibn Taymiyyah attacks al-Hillī's argument on the basis of the latter's use of Qur'ānic texts and of *ḥadīths*. See *Minhāj al-Sunnah*, IV, pp. 80-129.

[37]Laoust, *loc. cit.*

[38]Commentators such as Rashīd Riḍā and al-Saqqā have reflected this thought in their works. See *ibid.*, p. 285.

[39]*Ibid.*

[40]*Ibid.*, p. 287.

[41]*Al-Fatāwā al-Kubrā*, IV, p. 500ff.

[42]Laoust, *loc. cit.*

[43]*Al-Siyāsah al-Shar'iyyah*, p. 88.

[44]*Minhāj al-Sunnah*, I, p. 126.

[45]*Ibid.*, p. 85.

[46]*Ibid.*

[47]*Ibid.*, II, pp. 84-85.

[48]*Ibid.*, III, pp. 116-117. Reference is made to this mutual cooperation between Mu'āwiyah and his subjects in *ibid.*, IV, p. 117.

[49]*Ibid.*

[50]The connection is made by Laoust between this idealization of the *imām* by the Shī'īs and the major influence of Islamic philosophy beginning with al-Farābī. Similarly in the Platonic conception of the ideal state, the function of the head of state is the noblest and most significant function in society. Thus, the *imām* "is to the Community what the heart is to an organism: he is the key to its viability, the principal model of order and of organization." Therefore, the post demanded the perfect man, physically, intellectually and morally. See *op. cit.*, p. 293.

[51]*Minhāj al-Sunnah*, II, p. 135.

[52]*Al-Ikhtiyārāt*, p. 620. Likewise, "the *imām* of government should not be expected to exceed, in his personal qualities, the *imām* of prayer."

[53]*Al-Ḥisbah*, p. 8.

[54]*Ibid.*, p. 9.

[55]*Ibid.*

[56]*Al-Siyāsah al-Shar'iyyah*, pp. 9-11, and *al-Ikhtiyārāt*, pp. 624-636.

[57]*Al-Ḥisbah*, p. 14.

[58]*Ibid.*, pp. 9-11.

[59]*Al-Siyāsah al-Shar'iyyah*, pp. 7-12.

[60]*Al-Fatāwā al-Kubrā*, IV, p. 170.

[61]*Al-Siyāsah al-Shar'iyyah*, p. 2.

[62]*Al-Fatāwā al-Kubrā*, IV, p. 19.

[63]*Sūrah* IV (*Al-Nisā'*): p. 59.

[64]*Minhāj al-Sunnah*, II, pp. 146-148.

[65]*Ibid.*; and p. 201.

[66]The *ḥadīth* reads, "الدين نصيحة، الدين نصيحة". See *Al-Sayāsah al-Shar'iyyah*, p. 91.

[67]*Op. cit.*, p. 313.

[68]*Ibid.*

[69]The Khārijīs, Zaydīs and Mu'tazilah; see *al-Ḥisbah*, p. 64.

[70]*Minhāj al-Sunnah*, II, p. 87.

CHAPTER IX

NOTES

[1]*Sūrah* IX (*Al-Tawbah*): 71, "The Believers, men and women, are protectors, one of another: they enjoin what is just and forbid what is evil...."

[2]See, for example, ʿAbd al-Raḥmān al-Shīrazī, *Nihāyat al-Rutbah Fī Ṭalab al-Ḥisbah* (Cairo: 1946), pp. 8-18.

[3]*Al-Ḥisbah Fī al-Islām* (Damascus: Dār al-Bayān, 1967), p. 9.

[4]*Ibid.*

[5]Such as Ibn Ḥanbal, Abu Yaʿlā, al-Māwardī, al-Shāfiʿī. al-Nuwayrī, al-Qalqashandī, etc.

[6]Such as al-Shīrazī, Ibn al-Ukhwah, Ibn Bassām, etc.

[7]As quoted by Muḥammad al-Mubārak, *Ārā Ibn Taymiyyah Fī al-Dawlah Wa Madā Tadakhkhuliha Fī al-Majāl al-Iqtiṣādī* (Beirut, Dār al-Fikr, 3rd ed., 1970), pp. 80-82.

[8]See Ibn Taymiyyah's "Introduction" in *op. cit.*, p. 2.

[9]*Ibid.*, p. 30.

[10]*Ibid.*, p. 16.

[11]*Ibid.*, p. 33.

[12]*Ibid.*, pp. 31-33.

[13]*Ibid.*, p. 42.

[14]*Ibid.*, p. 25.

[15]*Ibid.*, pp. 21, 22.

[16]*Sūrah* LXII (*Al-Ḥadīd*): 25, "We sent aforetime our apostles with Clear Signs and sent down with them the Book and the Balance (of Right and Wrong), that men may stand forth in justice...." See *ibid.*, p. 5.

[17]*Ibid.*

[18]*Ibid.*, p. 81.

[19]*Ibid.*, pp. 78, 79.

[20]Other issues to which Ibn Taymiyyah addresses himself include the collection and expenditure of public funds, monetary obligations of marriage, divorce, child support and/or custody,

and the like. Also subjects such as rentals, investments, interests, dissolution and disposition of estates, and other similar economic concerns are scattered throughout his collected works. See, for example, *Al-Qawā'id al-Nūrāniyyah al-Fiqhiyyah* (Cairo: Matba'at al-Sunnah al-Muḥammadiyyah, 1951), pp. 87-91; *Majmū'at al-Fatāwā al-Kubrā*, I, pp. 362, 365; II, 194, 197-205; III, pp. 154-156; IV, pp. 4-39, 188-194, 195-213, etc.

[21] *Al-Ḥisbah Fī al-Islām*, p. 21.

[22] *Ibid.*, p. 22.

[23] *Ibid.*, p. 25.

[24] *Ibid.*, pp. 13, 14.

[25] *Ibid.*

[26] *Ibid.*, p. 15.

[27] *Ibid.*, p. 39.

[28] *Ibid.*

[29] See *Ibid.*, p. 38.

[30] As reported by Musallam in his *Saḥīḥ*, and cited in *ibid.*

[31] Ibn Taymiyyah, *op. cit.*, p. 39.

[32] *Ibid.*, p. 17. The wording of Ibn Taymiyyah's paragraph delineating this point is ambiguous at times; but the paraphrase offered here would seem to convey his intention in accordance with the context.

[33] *Ibid.*

[34] *Ibid.*, p. 14.

[35] After Nāfi', as reported by Ibn 'Umar, "Let men alone, God benefits some through others." "دعوا الناس يرزق الله بعضهم من بعض" *Ibid.*, p. 15. See also p. 40.

[36] *Ibid.*, p. 30.

[37] *Ibid.*, p. 33.

[38] *Ibid.*

[39] *Ibid.*, p. 34; The *hadīth* reads:
"ان الله هو المسعّر القابض الباسط، وانى لأرجوان القى الله وليس أحد منكم يطلبنى بمظلمة فى دم ومال"

[40] *Ibid.*, p. 35.

[41] See p. 269, above.

[42]*Op. cit.*, p. 15.

[43]*Ibid.*, p. 42.

[44]*Ibid.*

[45]*Ibid.*, p. 36; *Sūrah* CVII (*Al-Mā'ūn*): 4-7, "So woe to the worshippers who are neglectful of their prayers, those who (want but) to be seen (of men) but refuse (to supply even) neighbourly needs."

CHAPTER X

NOTES

[1]For a summary review of the effect of these *Ṣūfī* concepts, see I. R. al-Farūqī, "The Social Order in the Arab World," *A Journal of Church & State*. (Vol. XI, No. 2, Spring 1969), pp. 239-251.

[2]See A. Hourani, *Arabic Thought in the Liberal Age, 1798-1939* (Oxford: The University Press, 1970), pp. 20-21.

[3]Ibn Taymiyyah, *Al-Siyāsah al-Shar'iyyah*, pp. 6-7.

[4]*Ibid.*, p. 174.

[5]Besides the known published works of Ibn Taymiyyah listed in the Bibliography, titles of other works as yet not traced anywhere are quoted by Ibn Shākir al-Kutubī in his *Fuwāt al-Wafiyyāt*, and by Isma'īl Pasha al-Baghdādi in his *Ḥadīth al-'Ārifīn: Asmā' al-Mu'allifīn wa Āthār al-Muṣannifīn* (Istanbul, 1901).

[6]The various manifestations of Arab Nationalism which produced certain attempts at political unions, such as between Syria and Egypt, and Libya and Egypt are but examples of this.

[7]Fazlur Rahman, "Revival and Reform in Islam," in *The Cambridge History of Islam*; ed. P. M. Holt, and K. S. Lambton, and Bernard Lewis. Cambridge: The University Press, 1970; Vol. 2, p. 635.

[8]*Majmū'at al-Tawḥīd*, p. 47.

[9]Cf. Hourani, *op. cit.*, p. 38.

[10]*Ibid.*

A SELECTED BIBLIOGRAPHY

I. Primary Sources

A. Works by Ibn Taymiyyah

Ibn Taymiyyah, Taqiyy al-Dīn Aḥmad. *'Aqīdat Ahl al-Sunnah Wa al-Firqah al-Nājiyyah.* Cairo: Maṭba'at Anṣār al-Sunnah, 1939.

__________. *'Arsh al-Raḥmān Wa Mā Warad Fīh Min al-Āyāt Wa al-Aḥādīth, Wa Yalīh Majmū'at al-Rasā'il Wa al-Masā'il.* Cairo: Maṭba'at al-Manār, 1927-28.

__________. *Falsafat Ibn Rushd: Faṣl al-Maqāl Fī Mā Bayn al-Ḥikmah Wa al-Sharī'ah Min al-Ittiṣāl; Al-Kashf 'An Minhāj al-Adillah; Al-Radd 'Alā Falsafat Ibn Rushd.* Cairo: [Publisher not listed], n.d.

__________. *Dar' Ta'āruḍ al-'Aql Wa al-Naql.* Edited by Muḥammad Rashād Sālim. Cairo: Dār al-Kutub, 1971.

__________. *[Risālat] Al-Fatwā al-Ḥamawiyyah al-Kubrā.* Cairo: Al-Maṭba'ah al-Salafiyyah, 1967-68.

__________. *Al-Fatāwā al-Kubrā.* Introduction by Ḥasanayn Muḥammad Makhlūf. 5 Volumes. Cairo: Dār al-Kutub al-Ḥadīthah, 1966.

__________. *Fatwā Fī Qawl al-Nabiyy "Unzil al-Qur'ān 'Alā Sab'at Aḥruf".* Cairo: [Publisher not listed], n.d.

__________. *Rasā'il Wa Nuṣūṣ Wa Fīh Fatwā Fī al-Qiyās Wa al-Alqāb.* Edited by Ṣalāḥ al-Dīn al-Munajjid. Beirut: Dār al-Kitāb al-Jadīd, 1960.

__________. *Al-Furqān Bayn Awliyā' al-Raḥmān Wa Awliyā' al-Shayṭān.* Cairo: Al-Maṭba'ah al-Salafiyyah, 1967-68.

__________. *Al-Furqān Bayn al-Ḥaqq Wa al-Bāṭil.* Edited by Muḥammad Abū al-Wafā. Cairo: Zakariyyā 'Alī Yūsuf, 1966.

__________. *Al-Ḥisbah Fī al-Islām.* Cairo: Maṭba'at al-Mu'ayyid, 1900. [Also, Damascus: Dār al-Bayān, 1967]

__________. *Ḥukm Ziyārat al-Qubūr Wa al-Istinjād Bi al-Maqbūr.* Tunis: Al-Maṭba'ah al-Mahdiyyah, 1947.

__________. *Īḍāḥ al-Dalālah Fī 'Umūm al-Risālah.* Cairo: al-Maṭba'ah al-Munīrīyyah, 1949-50.

__________. *Majmū'at al-Rasā'il al-Munīriyyah.* 3 Volumes in 2. Cairo: Idārat al-Ṭibā'ah al-Munīriyyah, 1924-25 to 1927-28.

__________. *Al-Ijtimā' Wa al-Furqah Fī al-Ḥālif Bi al-Ṭalāq.* Cairo: Maktabat al-Anṣār, 1923.

__________. *Al-Iklīl Fī al-Mutashābih Wa al-Ta'wīl.* Cairo: Maktabat Anṣār al-Sunnah al-Muḥammadiyyah, 1947.

__________. [*Kitāb*] *al-Īmān.* Cairo: Matba'at al-Sa'ādah, 1970. [Also, Damascus: Al-Maktab al-Islāmī, 1961.]

__________. *Iqtiḍā' al-Ṣirāṭ al-Mustaqīm.* Cairo: Matba'at al-Sunnah al-Muḥammadiyyah, 1950.

__________. *Jāmi' al-Rasā'il.* Vol. I. Edited by Muḥammad Rashād Sālim. Cairo: Matba'at al-Madanī, 1969.

__________. *Jawāb Ahl al-'Ilm Wa al-Īmān Bi Taḥqīq Mā Ukhbir Bih Rasūl al-Raḥmān.* Cairo: Al-Matba'ah al-Salafiyyah, 1956-57. [Also, Damascus: Dār al-Bayān, 1967.]

__________. *Al-Jawāb al-Bāhir Fī Zuwwār al-Maqābir.* Edited by Sulaymān Ibn 'Abd al-Raḥmān al-Ṣanī'. Cairo: Al-Matba'ah al-Salafiyyah, 1957.

__________. *Al-Jawāb al-Saḥīḥ Li Man Baddal Dīn al-Masīḥ.* 2 Volumes. Cairo: Matba'at al-Madanī, 1959-60.

__________. *Jawāb Shaykh al-Islām Ibn Taymiyyah Fī al-Kīmyā' Wa Bayān Daḥḍ al-Mumawwihīn Min Arbābihā.* Baghdad: Matba'at al-Zuhūr, 1914.

__________. *Al-Kalim al-Ṭayyib.* Cairo: Al-Matba'ah al-Munīriyyah, 1933-34. [Also, Beirut: Al-Maktab al-Islāmī, 1965.]

__________. *Kitāb al-Nubuwwāt.* Cairo: Al-Matba'ah al-Salafiyyah, 1966-67.

__________. [*Kitāb*] *Ma'ārij al-Wuṣūl Ilā Anna Uṣūl al-Dīn Wa Furū'uh Qad Bayyanahā al-Rasūl.* Cairo: Al-Matba'ah al-Salafiyyah, 1967-68.

__________. *Majmū'at al-Rasā'il al-Mufīdah al-Muhimmah Fī Uṣūl al-Dīn Wa Furū'uh.* Cairo: Matba'at al-Madanī, 1961.

__________. *Majmū'ah Raqm Wāḥid.* And *Majmū'ah Raqm Ithnayn.* Cairo: Matba'at Kurdistān al-'Ilmiyyah, 1911.

__________. *Majmū'at al-Rasā'il al-Kubrā.* 4 Volumes. Cairo: Muḥammad 'Alī Ṣubayḥ, 1966.

__________. *Majmū'at al-Rasā'il Wa al-Masā'il.* 5 Volumes in 1. Cairo: Matba'at al-Manār, 1922-1930.

__________. *Majmū'at Tafsīr Ibn Taymiyyah Min Sitt Suwar: al-Shams, al-Layl, al-'Alaq, al-Bayyinah, al-Kāfirūn.* Edited with Introduction and Notes by 'Abd al-Ṣamad Sharaf al-Dīn. Bombay: [The Editor], 1954.

__________. *Al-Masā'il al-Mārdīniyyah.* Cairo: Matba'at Anṣār al-Sunnah al-Muḥammadiyyah, 1949.

__________. *Minhāj al-Sunnah al-Nabawiyyah Fī Naqḍ Kalām al-Shī'ah Wa al-Qadariyyah.* Edited by Muḥammad Rashād Sālim. Cairo: Maktabat Dār al- 'Urūbah, 1962.

__________. *Al-Muntaqā Min Minhāj al-I'tdāl Fī Naqḍ Kalām Ahl al-Rafḍ Wa al-I'tizāl.* Edited by Muḥammad Ibn 'Uthmān al-Dhahabī. Cairo: Al-Matba'ah al-Salafiyyah, 1955.

__________. *Muqaddimah Fī Uṣūl al-Tafsīr.* Edited by Jamāl al-Dīn al-Shaṭṭī. Damascus: Matba'at al-Āthār al-Waṭaniyyah, 1936. [Also, Edited by Qusayy Muḥibb al-Dīn al-Khaṭīb. Cairo: Al-Matba'ah al-Salafiyyah, 1965-66.]

__________. *Naqḍ al-Manṭiq.* Edited by Muhammad Ḥāmid al-Faqqī. Cairo: Matba'at al-Sunnah al-Muḥammadiyyah, 1951.

__________. *Qā'idah Fī Anwā' al-Istiftāḥ Fī al-Ṣalāh Wa Anwā' al-Istidhkār Muṭlaqan.* Edited with a Preface [in English] by 'Abd al-Ṣamad Sharaf al-Dīn. Bombay: Al-Qayyimah Press, 1962. [Appendix includes *Māṭalib Surat al-Baqarah Ijmālan.*]

__________. *Qā'idah Jalīlah Fī al-Tawassul Wa al-Wasīlah.* Beirut: Al-Maktab al-Islāmī, 1970.

__________. *Al-Qawā'id al-Nūrāniyyah al-Fiqhiyyah.* Cairo: Matba'at al-Sunnah al-Muḥammadiyyah, 1951.

__________. and Al-Jawzī, Ibn al-Qayyim. *Al-Qiyās Fī al-Shar' al-Islāmī.* Cairo: Al-Matba'ah al-Salafiyyah, Second Impression, 1955.

__________. *Al-Radd 'Alā al-Manṭiqiyyīn.* Edited by 'Abd al-Ṣamad Sharaf al-Dīn, with a Preface by Sayyid Sulaymān Nadwī. Bombay: Al-Qayyimah Press (?), 1949.

__________. *Raf' al-Malām 'An al-A'immah al-A'lām.* Edited by Muḥammad Ḥāmid al-Faqqī. Cairo: Matba'at al-Sunnah al-Muḥammadiyyah, 1958. [Also, Damascus: Al-Maktab al-Islāmī, Second Impression, 1964.]

__________. *Al-Risālah al-'Arshiyyah.* Cairo: Al-Matba'ah al-Munīriyyah, 19--?

__________. *Al-Risālah al-Madaniyyah Fī Taḥqīq al-Majāz Wa al-Ḥaqīqah Fī Ṣifāt Allāh Ta'ālā.* Cairo: Maktabat Anṣār al-Sunnah al-Muḥammadiyyah, 1946.

__________. *Al-Risālah al-Qurashiyyah.* Cairo: Matba'at al-Muayyid, 1901.

__________. *Al-Risālah al-Tadmurriyyah.* Edited by Muḥammad Zuhrī al-Najjār. Cairo: [Publisher not listed], 1949. [Also, Beirut: Al-Maktab al-Islāmī, 1971.]

__________. *Risālah Fī Ḥaqīqat al-Ṣiyām*. Edited by Muḥammad Nāṣir al-Dīn al-Albānī. Damascus: Al-Maktab al-Islāmī, 1961. [Also, Beirut: 1969-70.]

__________. *Al-Ṣārim al-Maslūl ʿAlā Shātim al-Rasūl*. Edited by Muḥammad Muḥyī al-Dīn ʿAbd al-Ḥamīd. Ṭanṭa (Egypt): Maktabat al-Tāj, 1960.

__________. *Sharḥ al-ʿAqīdah al-Iṣfahāniyyah*. Edited with an Introduction by Ḥasanayn Makhlūf. Cairo: Dār al-Kutub al-Ḥadīthah, 1966.

__________. *Sharḥ Ḥadīth al-Nuzūl*. Damascus: Al-Maktab al-Islāmī, 1961.

__________. *Sharḥ Ḥadīth Innamā al-Aʿmāl Bi al-Niyyāt*. Cairo: Al-Maṭbaʿah al-Munīriyyah, 1935-36.

__________. *Ṣiḥḥat Uṣūl Madhhab Ahl al-Madīnah*. Edited by Zakī ʿAlī Yūsuf. Cairo: Maṭbaʿat al-Imām, 1964.

__________. *Al-Siyāsah al-Sharʿiyyah Fī Iṣlāḥ al-Rāʿī Wa al-Raʿiyyah*. Edited by Muḥammad al-Mubārak. Beirut: Dār al Kutub al-ʿArabiyyah, 1966.

__________. *Al-Ṣūfiyyah Wa al-Fuqarāʾ, Fatwā*. Cairo: Maṭbaʿat al-Manār, 1909. [Also, edited by Muḥammad ʿAbd Allah al-Sammān. Cairo: Al-Maktab al-Fannī, 1961.]

__________. *Tafsīr Sūrat al-Ikhlāṣ*. Cairo: Maktabat al-Khanjī, 1905. [Also, Al-Maṭbaʿah al-Munīriyyah, 1934; and, edited by Ṭāha Yūsuf Shāhīn. Cairo: Maktabat Anṣār al-Sunnah al-Muḥammadiyyah, 1969.]

__________. *Tafsīr Sūrat al-Nūr*. Cairo: Al-Maṭbaʿah al Munīriyyah, 1939.

__________. *Talkhīs Kitāb al-Istighāthah al-Maʿrūf Bi al-Radd ʿAlā al-Bakrī*. Cairo: Al-Maṭbaʿah al-Salafiyyah, 1927.

__________. *Ṭarīq al-Wuṣūl Ilā ʿIlm al-Maʿmūl: Mukhtār Min Kutub Ibn Taymiyyah*. Compiled by ʿAbd al-Raḥmān al-Nāṣir al-Saʿdī. Cairo: Maṭbaʿat al-Imām, 1952.

__________. *Al-Tuḥaf al-ʿIrāqiyyah Fī al- Aʿmāl al-Qalbiyyah*. Cairo: Al-Maṭbaʿah al-Munīriyyah, 19--?

__________. *Al-ʿUbudiyyah Fī al-Islām*. Cairo: Al-Maṭbaʿah al-Salafiyyah, 1967. [Also, Damascus: Al-Maktab al-Islāmī, 1962; and Beirut: Second Impression, 1969.]

__________. *Al-Wāsiṭah Bayn al-Ḥaqq Wa al-Khalq*. Damascus: Al-Maktab al-Islāmī, 1962.

__________. *Al-Wāsiṭah al-Jāmiʿah Li Khayr al-Dunyā Wa al-Ākhirah*. Cairo: Maktabat Anṣār al-Sunnah, 1949.

B. Translations of, and Commentaries on, Works by Ibn Taymiyyah

Farrukh, ʻUmar. *Ibn Taymiyyah on Public and Private Law in Islam, Or, Public Policy in Islamic Jurisprudence.* Beirut: Khayats, 1966. [Translation of *Al-Siyāsah al-Sharʻiyyah.*]

Al-Ghurābī, ʻAlī Muṣṭafā. *Al-Minḥah Fī Sharḥ al-ʻAqīdah Al-Wāsiṭiyyah.* Cairo: Matbaʻat Muḥammad ʻAlī Ṣubayḥ, 1963.

Ibn Fayyāḍ, Zayd ʻAbd al- Azīz. *Al-Rawḍah al-Nadiyyah: Sharḥ al-ʻAqīdah al-Wāsiṭiyyah.* Al-Riyaḍ (Saudi Arabia): Matbaʻat al-Riyaḍ, 1958.

Laoust, Henri. *Le Traitê De Droit Publique D'Ibn Taimiya.* Beyrouth (Beirut: Institut Francais De Damas, 1948).

__________. *Contribution, Une Etude de La Methodologie Canonique De Taki-d-Dīn Aḥmad b. Taimiya.* Le Caire: L'Institut Francais D'Archaeologie Orientale, 1939.

Al-Rashīd, ʻAbd al-ʻAzīz. *Al-Tanbīhāt al-Saniyyah ʻAlā Sharḥ Al-ʻAqīdah al-Wāsiṭiyyah.* Cairo: Matbaʻat al-Imām, 1958.

C. Reference Works

ʻAbd al-Baqī, Muḥammad Fuʻād. *Al-Muʻjam al-Mufahras Li Alfāẓ al-Qurʼān al-Karīm.* With an Introduction by Manṣūr Fahmī. Cairo: Maṭābiʻ al-Shaʻb, 1959.

The Holy Qurʼān: Text, Translation and Commentary. Translation and Commentary by ʻA. Yūsuf ʻAlī. Lahore: Third Edition, 1938.

Wehr, Hans. *A Dictionary of Modern Written Arabic.* Edited by J. Milton Cowan. Ithaca (New York): Cornell University Press, 1960; Second Printing, 1966.

D. Studies and Collaborated Works

Abū Zahrah, Muḥammad, ed. *Usbūʻ al-Fiqh al-Islāmī Wa Mahrajān al-Imām Ibn Taymiyyah [16-21 Shawwāl, 1380 (1961)] Fī Dimashq.* Cairo: Al-Majlis al-Aʻlā Li Riʻāyat al-Funūn Wa al-Ādāb Wa al-ʻUlūm al-Ijtimāʻiyyah, 1961.

Al-Bahiyy, Muḥammad. *Muḥāḍarāt Fī al-Fikr al-Islāmī Fī Marḥlat-ihi al-Thāniyah.* Cairo: Dār al-Zaynī Li al-Ṭibāʻah Wa al-Nashr, 1962.

Al-Istanbūlī, Muḥammad Mahdī. *Ibn Taymiyyah Baṭal al-Iṣlāḥ al-Dīnī.* Damascus: Dār al-Ḥayāh, 194-?

Laoust, Henri. *Essai Sur Les Doctrines Sociales et Politiques de Taki-d-Dīn Ahmad B. Taimiya.* Le Caire: Institut Francais d'Archaeologie Orientale, 1939.

Al-Mubārak, Muḥammad. *Ārā' Ibn Taymiyyah Fī al-Dawlah Wa Madā Tadakhkhulihā Fī al-Majāl al-Iqtiṣādī.* Beirut: Dār al-Fikr, Third Edition, 1970.

__________. *Al-Dawlah Wa Niẓām al-Ḥisbah 'Ind Ibn Taymiyyah.* Damascus: Dār al-Fikr, 1967.

E. Biographies

Abū Zahrah, Muḥammad. *Ibn Taymiyyah: Ḥayātuh Wa 'Uṣūruh.* Cairo: Dār al-Fikr al-'Arabī, 1952.

'Alī, Muḥammad Kurd. *Tarjamat Shaykh al-Islām Ibn Taymiyyah.* Damascus: Al Maktab al-Islāmī, Second Impression, 1969.

Al-Bayṭār, Muḥammad Bahjat. *Ḥayāt Shaykh al-Islām Ibn Taymiyyah, Muhadarāt Wa Maqalāt Wa Dirasāt.* Damascus: Al Maktab al-Islāmī, 1961.

Hāfiẓ, 'Abd al-Salām Hāshim. *Al-Imām Ibn Taymiyyah.* Cairo: Muṣṭafā al-Bābī al-Halabī, n.d.

Al-Kurdī, Faraj Allah Zakī. *Al Majmū' al-Shāmil....* Cairo: Matba'at Kurdistan al-'Ilmiyyah, 1911.

Ibn 'Abd al-Hādī, Muḥammad Ibn Aḥmad. *Al-'Uqūd al-Durriyyah Fī Manāqib Shaykh al-Islām Ibn Taymiyyah.* Edited by Muḥammad Ḥāmid al-Faqqī and Maḥmūd Tawfīq. Cairo: Matba'at al-Hijāzī, 1938.

Ibn al-'Imād. *Shadharāt al-Dhahab.*

Ibn Khallīkān. *Tarjamāt Wafiyāt al-A'yān.*

Ibn al-Nadīm, Muḥammad Ibn Isḥāq. *Fihrist.* Translated and edited by Bayard Dodge. New York: Columbia University Press, 1970.

Ibn Shākir, Muḥammad (al-Kutbī). *Fawāt al-Wafiyyāt.* Volume I. Cairo: Matb'at Būlaq, 1863.

Al-Maqrīzī. *Al-Muqaffā.* Volume III. Ms. Leyde (Leiden). Copy in the Egyptian Library (History Section) #5372.

Mūsā, Muḥammad Yūsuf. *Ibn Taymiyyah.* Cairo: Al-Mu'assasah al-Miṣriyyah al-'Āmmah Li al-Ta'līf Wa al-Ṭibā'ah Wa al-Nashr, 1962.

F. Critiques of Ibn Taymiyyah's Doctrines and Method

Harrās, Muḥammad Khalīl. *Ibn Taymiyyah al-Salafī, Naqduh Li Masālik al-Mutakallimīn Wa al-Falāsifah Fī al-Ilāhiyyāt.* Ṭanṭa (Egypt): Al-Matba'ah al-Yūsufiyyah, 1952.

Khān, Qamaruddīn. *The Political Thought of Ibn Taymiyyah.* Islamabad: Islamic Research Institute, 1973.

Khayr al-Dīn, Nu'mān Ibn al-Alūsī al-Baghdādī. *Jalā' al-'Aynayn Fī Muḥākamat al-Aḥmadayn.* Cairo: Al-Mu'assasah al-Sa'ūdiyyah, 1961.

Al-Subkī, Taqiyy al-Dīn 'Alī 'Abd al-Kāfī. *Al-Durrah al-Muḍī'ah Fī al-Radd 'Alā Ibn Taymiyyah.* Damascus [Publisher not listed], 1929.

'Uways, Manṣūr Muḥammad Muḥammad. *Ibn Taymiyyah Laysa Salafiyyan.* Cairo: Dār al-Nahḍah al-'Arabiyyah, 1970.

G. Bibliographies

Brockelmann, B. C. *Geschichte der Arabischen Litteratur.* Berlin: [Publisher not listed], 1902, and supplements.

Al-Jawziyyah, Ibn al-Qayyim. *Asmā' Mu'allafāt Ibn Taymiyyah.* Edited by Ṣalāḥ al-Dīn al-Munajjid. Damascus [Publisher not listed], 1953.

Laoust, Henri. *Essai Sur Les Doctrines Sociales et Politiques de Taki-d-Dīn b. Taimiya.* Le Caire: Institut Francais D'Archaeologie Orientale, 1939; pp. 633-644.

II. Secondary Sources

A. Historical Works

Abū Zahrah, Muḥammad. *Tarīkh al-Madhāhib al-Islāmiyyah.* Cairo: Dār al-Fikr al-'Arabī, n.d.

Gibb, H. A. R. *Mohammadanism: An Historical Survey.* London: 1949.

Goitein, S. D. *Studies in Islamic History and Institutions.* Leiden: 1966.

Holt, P. M. et al., eds. *The Cambridge History of Islam.* 2 Volumes. Cambridge (England): 1970.

Huart, Cl. *Histoire Des Arabes.* Paris: 1912.

Ibn al-Athīr. *Al-Kāmil Fī al-Tārīkh.* Beirut: 1965 [Also, Leiden, 1867.]

Irvine, W. *The Army of the Indian Mongols.* London: 1903 [Also, New Delhi: 1962.]

Lapidus, I. M. *Muslim Cities in the Later Middle Ages.* Cambridge (Massachusetts): 1967.

Mājid, ʻAbd al-Munʻim. *Al-ʻIlāqāt Bayn al-Sharq Wa al-Gharb Fī al-ʻUsūr al-Wusṭā.* Beirut; 1966.

Pradwin, Michael. *The Mongol Empire: Its Rise and Legacy.* London: 1961.

Saunders, J. J. *A History of Medieval Islam.* New York: 1965.

__________. *Aspects of the Crusades.* Christchurch (New Zealand): 1962.

__________. *The History of the Mongul Conquests.* London: 1971.

__________, ed. *The Muslim World on the Eve of Europe's Expansion.* Englewood Cliffs (New Jersey): 1966.

Sauvaget, J. *Introduction a L'Histoire de L'Orient Musulman.* Second Edition revised by Cl. Cahen. Paris: 1961. [English version revised and expanded: *Introduction to the Muslim East.* Berkeley and Los Angeles: 1965.]

Von Grunebaum, Gustave E. *Medieval Islam: A Study in Cultural Orientation.* Chicago: Second Edition, 1969.

Zaydān, Jurjī. *Tārikh al-Tamaddun al-Islāmī.* 5 Volumes. Beirut: 1967.

B. Atlases

Hazard, H. W. *Atlas of Islamic History.* Princeton: Third Edition, 1954.

Roovelink, R. *Atlas of the Arab World and the Middle East.* London: 1960.

__________. *Historical Atlas of the Muslim Peoples.* Amsterdam: 1957.

C. Historiographical Works

Lewis, Bernard and Holt, P.M. *Historians of the Middle East.* London: 1962.

D. History of the Development of Islamic Jurisprudence and Theology

Arberry, A. J. *Introduction to the History of Sufism.* London: 1942.

Coulson, N. J. *A History of Islamic Law.* Edinburgh: 1964.

Evans-Pritchard, E. E. *The Sanusi of Cyrenaica.* Oxford: 1949.

Kedourie, E. *Afghanī and ʿAbduh.* London: 1966.

Macdonald, B. D. *Development of Muslim Theology, Jurisprudence and Constitutional Theory.* New York: 1903. [Also, Beirut: 1964.]

Nader, A. N. *La Systeme Philosophique des Muʿtazilah.* Beirut: 1956.

Rosenthal, A. I. J. *Islam in the Modern National State.* Cambridge (England): 1965.

__________. *Political Thought in Medieval Islam: An Introductory Outline.* Cambridge (England): 1958.

Schacht, J. *The Origins of Muhammadan Jurisprudence.* Oxford: 1950.

Tyan, E. *Histoire de L'Organisation Judiciare en Pays d'Islam.* Leiden: Second Edition, 1960.

Watt, W. Montgomery. *Islamic Political Thought.* [*Islamic Surveys* No. 6.] Edinburgh: 1966.

__________. *The Formative Period of Islamic Thought.* Chicago: 1973.

Ziadah, N. A. *Sanūsiyyah.* Leiden: 1958.

E. Other Sources

ʿAbduh, Muḥammad. *A Theology of Unity.* Translated by Isḥāq Musʿad and Kenneth Cragg. London: George Allen and Unwin, 1966.

Amīn, Ahmad. *Zuʿamāʾ al-Iṣlāḥ Fī al-ʿAṣr al-Ḥadīth.* Beirut: Dār al-Kitāb al-ʿArabī, n.d.

Abū Zahrah, Muhammad. *Abū Ḥanīfah: Ḥayātuh Wa ʿAṣruh.* Cairo: Dār al-Fikr al-ʿArabī, 1947.

__________. *Ibn Ḥanbal: Ḥayātuh Wa ʿAṣruh.* Cairo: Dār al-Fikr al-ʿArabī, n.d.

__________. *Mālik: Ḥayātuh Wa 'Aṣruh.* Cairo: Dār al-Fikr, al-'Arabī, 1952.

al-Jaṭīlī, 'Abd al-Rahmān. *Shaykh al-Islām Muḥammad Ibn 'Abd al-Wahhāb.* Kuwait: [Privately published] , 1972.

Hourani, Albert. *Arabic Thought in the Liberal Age 1798-1939.* Oxford: Oxford University Press, 1970.